INCO Q&A

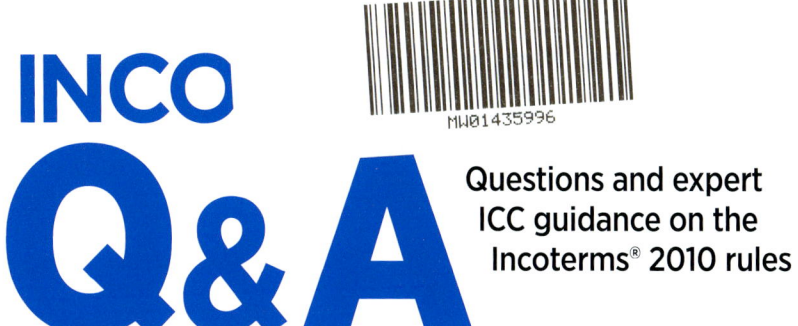

Questions and expert ICC guidance on the Incoterms® 2010 rules

Edited by
Emily O'Connor

INCOTERMS® 2010 Q&A

Copyright © 2013

International Chamber of Commerce (ICC)
All rights reserved.

ICC holds all copyright and other intellectual property rights in this work. No part of this work may be reproduced, distributed, transmitted, translated or adapted in any form or by any means, except as permitted by law, without the written permission of ICC.

Permission can be requested from ICC through pub@iccwbo.org.

ICC Services
Publications Department
38 Cours Albert 1er
75008 Paris
France

ICC Publication No. 744E
ISBN: 978-92-842-0183-9

PREFACE AND ACKNOWLEDGEMENTS

The constituency of the International Chamber of Commerce (ICC) consists of business enterprises and associations from every corner of the globe. ICC would like to express its gratitude to the many international trade experts who have contributed to the ICC's Incoterms® rules for the use of domestic and international trade terms becoming one of the world's most well-known global trading standards. The Incoterms® rules are used in countless international sale transactions every year, helping exporters and importers all over the world conclude precise, trouble-free agreements.

In particular, ICC would like to express its gratitude to the Co-Chairs of the Incoterms® 2010 Drafting Group – Charles Debattista (United Kingdom), and Christoph Martin Radtke (France) – as well as the other members of the Drafting Group and ICC Incoterms® rules experts who have contributed to the preparation of the questions and answers on the Incoterms® 2010 rules and additional new materials: Jens Bredow (Germany); Ercüment Erdem (Turkey); Johnny Herre (Sweden); David Lowe (United Kingdom); Emily O'Connor (France); Lauri Railas (Finland); Frank Reynolds (United States); Miroslav Subert (Czech Republic); and Koen Vanheusden (Belgium).

In addition, thanks are due to the experts who developed the wealth of historical materials herein, which were edited by Guillermo C. Jiménez (United States): Ray Battersby (UK); Mauro Ferrante (Italy); Carine Gelens (Belgium); Jean Guédon (France); Emmanuel Jolivet (France); Jan Ramberg (Sweden); Asko Räty (Finland); Bart Van der Veire (Belgium); and Alexander Von Ziegler (Switzerland).

Finally, we would like to thank the ICC National Committees around the world, and the thousands of businesses working with them, which contributed so valuably to the development and dissemination of Incoterms® 2010. Through this broad consultative approach, we hope to carry forward the lessons and knowledge of our history, as well as the insight and innovativeness of our business members, so that the Incoterms® rules will continue to serve the world trade community in the 21st century and beyond.

TABLE OF CONTENTS AND QUESTION LIST

CHAPTER ONE – INTRODUCTION TO THE INCOTERMS® RULES

Background 1

The 5 Basic Questions:
What, How, Where, Who, and Why? 4
- What are the Incoterms® rules? 4
- How are the Incoterms® rules properly used? 8
- Where do you find the Incoterms® rules? 9
- Who is bound by the Incoterms® rules? 10
- Why should importers and exporters use and understand the Incoterms® rules in detail? 12

Documents for reference
- Incoterms® 2010 Guidance Notes 15
- Specimen form of ICC Model International Sale Contract 26

How does one choose the right Incoterms® rule? –
A decision-making checklist 35

The Incoterms® 2010 rules and documents –
documents commonly needed in sale transactions
under the Incoterms® rules 38

A note on 'delivery' under the Incoterms® rules 39

Other common questions 40

The Golden Rules of the Incoterms® rules 42

CHAPTER TWO – GUIDANCE ON SELECTED INCOTERMS® RULES QUESTIONS BY ICC EXPERTS

Real-life questions received by ICC with responses giving interpretive guidance, prepared by a group of the world's foremost experts on the Incoterms® rules

Incoterms® 2010 – General questions 47

1. Use of ® trademark symbol and letters of credit 47
2. 'Terminal handling charges' 47
3. Costs of security charges 47
4. Export clearance 'applicable' in F-family of rules? 49
5. Non-freight costs during transit in C-family of rules 50
6. Stowage of full container loads 51
7. Incoterms® rules not designed to resolve accounting issues such as revenue recognition 51
8. Buyer faced with multiple charges from carrier under C-family of rules 52
9. Incoterms® 2010 rules do not address pipeline transactions 54
10. Containers going by sea under C-family of rules 54
11. Goods damaged prior to arrival at departure terminal under C-family of rules 55
12. Global insurance policy 56
13. Mandatory local law overriding Incoterms® 2010 rules 56
14. 'Transport documents' in the Incoterms® 2010 rules 57
15. 'Usual proof of delivery' v. 'usual transport document' in FCA, FAS and FOB 58
16. Obligation v. custom for transport documents in C-family of rules 59

Incoterms 1990 – General questions 61
   1. Customs not recognizing the Incoterms® rules............. 61
   2. Should industry standard terms refer
      to the Incoterms® rules?... 62
   3. The Incoterms® rules as 'payment terms' –
      COD/CAD.. 66
   4. The Incoterms® rules and the European
      Single Market... 67
   5. Bonded goods and bail cover costs............................... 69
   6. Letters of credit and the Incoterms® rules 71
   7. 'C + I' – Interpretation 76
   8. 'C'-family of Incoterms® rules v. 'D'-family
      of Incoterms® rules 77

Incoterms® 2010 – Multimodal questions............................. 78
   17. 'Seller's premises' in FCA.. 78
   18. 'Seller's means of transport' in FCA 78
   19. 'First carrier' in CPT and CIP 78
   20. Seller using own means of transportation
       under DAT, DAP and DDP 78
   21. 'Terminal' in DAT 79
   22. Where to unload in DAT?... 79
   23. Buyer does not arrive to collect goods under DAP 79
   24. Documents under DAP and DDP.................................. 80
   25. VAT and DDP.. 81
   26. Does need for on board transport document
       rule out FCA for containers?.. 81
   27. Can seller refuse to load buyer's arriving truck
       under FCA?... 83
   28. Who is 'shipper' on transport document
       under FCA?... 84
   29. Destination contract with seller unloading,
       but not at a terminal... 84
   30. Domestic arrival contracts for pre-imported
       foreign goods – DAP or DDP?.. 85
   31. Seller doubts safety of buyer's arriving truck
       under EXW... 85
   32. Who pays 'container cleaning charges'
       under DAP?.. 86

- **33.** Relation of risk passage and export formalities under FCA, CPT and CIP... 86
- **34.** Delivery date under CIP?.. 87

Incoterms® 1990 – Multimodal questions 88
- **9.** FCA – Forwarder's handling fees................................... 88
- **10.** FCA – Manner of delivery.. 89
- **11.** FCA – Import duties levied by seller's customs authorities.. 90
- **12.** FCA – Port/airport handling charges not 'official' charges 91
- **13.** DDU – Wharfage fee 92
- **14.** DDU – Customs clearance... 93
- **15.** DDU/DDP – Offloading and discharging 94
- **16.** DDU – Customs clearance within reasonable time 95

Incoterms® 2010 – Maritime questions.. 98
- **35.** Ship and goods on different quays under FAS............. 98
- **36.** Containerized shipments and FOB, CFR and CIF... 99
- **37.** What does 'on board' mean in FOB, CFR and CIF?.. 100
- **38.** Risk transfer in 'free in stowed and secured' under FOB, CFR and CIF.. 100
- **39.** Goods destroyed mid-loading under FOB.................. 101
- **40.** Packaging, containers and break bulk under FOB...... 101
- **41.** Proof of delivery, bill of lading, under FOB 102
- **42.** Loading a ship under FOB, CFR and CIF..................... 103
- **43.** Formalities in intra-EU sale under FOB....................... 104
- **44.** Risk and port charges under FOB................................ 105

Incoterms 1990 – Maritime questions 107

17. FAS – Delivery period 107
18. FAS – Who should be listed as shipper? 108
19. FAS/FOB – Differences between the two rules 109
20. FOB – Berthing and demurrage charges 110
21. FOB – Terminal handling charges 112
22. FOB – Transhipment 113
23. 'FOB Airport' – Payment of dangerous goods fee 114
24. FOB – 'Deadfreight' claim 115
25. FOB – What does it mean to 'effectively' pass ship's rail? 116
26. CFR – Transfer of risk point 119
27. CFR – Unloading 'liner out' 121
28. CFR – Unloading charges – Tramp vessels 122
29. CFR – Importer refusing to timely receive goods 122
30. CIF – Unloading costs 123
31. 'CIF landed' 124
32. CIF – Date of shipment 124
33. CIF – Customs costs 125
34. CIF – Additional 10% insurance cover 126
35. CIF – 'Destination delivery charges' (DDC) 127
36. CIF – Quay dues at destination 128
37. CFR/CIF – Transfer of risk point/insurance 132
38. DES – Legal obligation to insure v. Commercial need to insure 133
39. DES – Quay dues 134

ANNEXES

- ANNEX 1 - Glossary – International trade and transport terms 135
- ANNEX 2 – Sample Incoterms® 2010 decision flowcharts 170
- ANNEX 3 – Documents commonly used in Incoterms® 2010 sales 178
- ANNEX 4 – Incoterms® 2010 rules 209
- ICC at a Glance 334
- Selected ICC Publications 335

Chapter One
INTRODUCTION TO THE INCOTERMS®¹ RULES

BACKGROUND

The basic nature of the Incoterms® rules – are they purely contractual terms, standard trade usages and customs, and/or the 'international law of merchants' (lex mercatoria)?

The International Chamber of Commerce (ICC)'s Incoterms® rules are probably the world's best-known import/export tool. They are a common, basic element in every import or export contract for goods. That means that the Incoterms® rules are used in countless commercial transactions every day, in every country. But what exactly are these indispensable tools called the 'Incoterms® rules'?

First, we must understand that the set of rules today known as the 'Incoterms® rules' has a long history. The Incoterms® rules are in fact based on venerable precedents in international trade customs, as evidenced by an 1812 British court decision involving FOB.

In the 19th century, as international trade expanded rapidly, usage of terms such as FOB and CIF became a common international trade practice that arose from the need to clearly specify, in international transactions, the respective risks and responsibilities of seller-exporter and buyer-importer. International traders in those early times were not compelled by any laws to use terms such as FOB or CIF – rather, these terms were voluntarily adopted as a convenient shortcut for negotiating international contracts. Thus, custom of usage of international trade terms (of which the Incoterms® rules are today the world's leading example) arose because they filled a practical business need.

The courts and legal systems of the world, in turn, eventually ratified and supported these long-standing practices of international merchants. In countless court decisions it was

---

1   "Incoterms" is a registered trademark of the International Chamber of Commerce.

gradually established that these long-standing practices of international merchants were susceptible to a more or less uniform interpretation. Thus, ever since the first publication of the Incoterms® rules in 1936, the courts have virtually always enforced the Incoterms® rules whenever they are applicable to a particular contractual dispute.

In the early part of the twentieth century, prior even to the founding of ICC in 1919, it had become clear to exporters that trade 'customs' could be subject to widely varying interpretations in different national courts. One could distinguish a 'German CIF' from an English one, or an 'American FOB' from a French one. These differences were inevitably the source of misunderstandings, which led to unnecessary costs and uncertainties. Thus, the Incoterms® rules were created in 1936 to harmonize and standardize the meanings of trade terms at an international level. Trade terms were already widely accepted before 'Incoterms 1936', but their meaning had never been so fully and completely standardized.

The purpose of the Incoterms® rules was to create a global standard rule of interpretation, which pre-supposed that national courts around the world would enforce the provisions of the Incoterms® rules, even if these were at variance with national jurisprudence. In fact, the courts and legislatures of the world have generally deferred to the Incoterms® rules as a definitive statement of international trade customs. The United Nations Commission on International Trade Law (UNCITRAL) and the Working Party on Facilitation of International Trade Procedures of the Economic Commission for Europe of the United Nations (UNECE) have formally endorsed the Incoterms® rules, citing their usefulness to international trade.

However, ICC recognized that the practice of international trade is not static, but rather evolves with developments in technology and other global changes. So, for example, when in the 1960s and 1970s the rapid expansion of containerized and multimodal transport substantially changed the conduct of international trade, ICC updated the Incoterms® rules to meet these new transport practices. In particular, the older rules that had grown out of traditional maritime practice – FOB, CFR and CIF – generated new Incoterms® rule counterparts with a view to accommodating multimodal and containerized traffic: FCA, CPT, CIP and, in the current version of the rules – *Incoterms® 2010* – DAT (Delivered at Terminal) and DAP (Delivered at Place).

These 'newer' Incoterms® rules, borne from the need to keep pace with developments in containerization and multimodality, must derive their authority from principles other than trade customs and long-standing usage. Thus, for example, the express contractual incorporation of the newer terms, which is strongly recommended by ICC, can virtually ensure that the newer terms

BACKGROUND

will survive any legal challenge. In this light, it is also important to emphasize that the Incoterms® rules are a product of a world business organization, a neutral body set up solely to further the interests of international trade. If a party hesitates to incorporate the Incoterms® rules in a particular contract, the counterparty can reassure them that Incoterms are a reliable, neutral, and universally accepted standard.

Over the seven-and-a-half decades that the Incoterms® rules have existed, ICC has periodically sought to improve them wherever possible. Certain questions sent to ICC by export trade professionals over the decades have revealed areas of unnecessary ambiguity. These questions have proved extremely useful in helping ICC's drafting experts update the Incoterms® rules so as to produce more effective versions that reflect evolving trade conditions.

The questions explored in the second part of this book represent the effort of top ICC Incoterms® rules experts to grapple with challenging questions of how to interpret the Incoterms® rules. The reader should always keep in mind that in order to be widely applicable and easily understood, the Incoterms® rules need to rely on general expressions and clear wording. This is the only way to develop a standard that can be used by every different kind of company in every country in the world.

INTRODUCTION TO THE INCOTERMS® RULES

THE 5 BASIC QUESTIONS: WHAT, HOW, WHERE, WHO, AND WHY?

- What are the Incoterms® rules?
- How are the Incoterms® rules properly used?
- Where do you find the Incoterms® rules?
- Who is bound by the Incoterms® rules?
- Why should importers and exporters use the Incoterms® rules?

What are the Incoterms® rules?

The Incoterms® rules are standard 'trade terms' used in international and domestic sale contracts to allocate certain costs and risks between the seller and the buyer.

The best-known and most widely used of the 11 Incoterms® rules are FOB and CIF (sometimes also spelled f.o.b. or c.i.f.), but several other rules are very common as well.

By referring to an Incoterms® rule in the sale contract or export quote, the exporter and importer have a short-hand way of choosing from among a set of 11 different alternatives as to: 1) who must pay for transport, 2) who must bear the risks of loss of or damage to the goods during transport, and 3) who is responsible for customs formalities and duties upon export and import. Two particular Incoterms® rules (CIF and CIP) in addition place a specific requirement on the seller to obtain at least minimum insurance coverage for the goods.

In essence, the Incoterms® rules are a way of letting the buyer know what is 'included' in the sales price. By choosing an Incoterms® rule, the parties allocate transport costs and risks, as well as the responsibility for insurance and customs formalities, between seller and buyer.

THE 5 BASIC QUESTIONS: WHAT, HOW, WHERE, WHO, AND WHY?

Grouping of obligations under 10 headings

The obligations of the parties for each rule are grouped under the same main headings: SELLER'S OBLIGATIONS (A1-A10) and BUYER'S OBLIGATIONS (B1-B10). These are the 10 obligations that may fall upon the parties, numbered as follows:

	SELLER'S OBLIGATIONS		BUYER'S OBLIGATIONS
A1	Provision of goods in conformity with the contract	B1	Payment of the price
A2	Licences, authorizations, security clearances and other formalities	B2	Licences, authorizations, security clearances and other formalities
A3	Contracts of carriage and insurance	B3	Contracts of carriage and insurance
A4	Delivery	B4	Taking delivery
A5	Transfer of risks	B5	Transfer of risks
A6	Allocation of costs	B6	Allocation of costs
A7	Notices to the buyer	B7	Notices to the seller
A8	Delivery document	B8	Proof of delivery
A9	Checking-packaging-marking	B9	Inspection of goods
A10	Assistance with information and related costs	B10	Assistance with information and related costs

There are 11 Incoterms® rules in the current version of the rules known as 'Incoterms® 2010' (ICC Publication No. 715) – 7 rules that may be used for any mode or a combination of different modes of transport (frequently known as 'multimodal' transport), and 4 rules that may be used only for sea and inland waterway transport (frequently known as 'maritime' transport). Within each of these two categories, the Incoterms® 2010 rules can be thought of as representing a stepladder of increasing responsibility from seller's premises to buyer's premises. Thus, in the rules for use with any mode or modes of transport, the Incoterms® rule that represents the minimum responsibility for the seller is EXW (Ex Works), which is generally used in cases involving delivery at the seller's factory or warehouse. At the other extreme, the Incoterms® rule DDP (Delivered Duty Paid) represents maximum responsibility on the part of the seller, with delivery generally at the buyer's premises.

INTRODUCTION TO THE INCOTERMS® RULES

A buyer on EXW terms knows that nothing 'extra' (in terms of transport, customs clearance or insurance) is included in the sales price – the buyer must handle the entire transport operation itself. A buyer on DDP terms ('Delivered Duty Paid') knows that the quoted price includes all transport costs, risks and formalities up to the final destination. Between these two extremes, there are nine other Incoterms® rules, representing a range of options for the division of costs/risks between the parties. Please note, though, that there are potentially insurmountable practical difficulties involved in using either EXW or DDP – parties should proceed with open eyes when using these, and are well advised to read the Guidance Notes to both EXW and DDP at pages 15 and 20, respectively.

Where does the word 'Incoterms' come from?

ICC derived the word 'Incoterms' from '**In**ternational **Co**mmercial **Terms**'. ICC prefers to refer to the Incoterms® rules as 'rules' or 'trade terms', in recognition of the fact that they have multiple functions. People sometimes refer to Incoterms® rules such as FOB or CIF as 'shipping terms', 'delivery terms' or 'payment terms', all of which are much less satisfactory than 'trade terms' because they do not communicate the range of obligations covered by the Incoterms® rules: the Incoterms® rules cover not only transport, but also risk, minimum insurance coverage, packaging, customs obligations, etc. Note also that even though the first part of the word 'Incoterms' comes from a reference to the word 'international', the rules are equally applicable to domestic or intra-bloc trading, or customs union contracts.

Why is a particular year mentioned, such as 'Incoterms® 2010'?

The Incoterms® rules are periodically revised by ICC in order to take into account changes and developments in prevailing international trade and transport practices. ICC published the first version of the Incoterms® rules in 1936. Subsequent revisions were published in 1953, 1967, 1976, 1980, 1990, and 2000. The current valid version is Incoterms® 2010.

Parties to a contract of sale are well advised to make reference to a particular version of the Incoterms® rules in their contracts, to avoid confusion if a dispute arises. If, for example, a contract were signed in 2009 mentioning simply 'Incoterms' and a dispute regarding the contract arose in 2011, a judge or arbitrator would have to decide whether the version of the rules applicable at the time of signing the contract – Incoterms 2000 – or the version in force when the dispute arose – Incoterms® 2010 – should be applied. Parties may choose any version of the Incoterms® rules they like (though they are advised to use the current version, which best reflects the current trading environment); the most important thing is that they specify clearly in the contract which version they intend to apply.

INTRODUCTION TO THE INCOTERMS® RULES

How are the Incoterms® rules properly used?

The Incoterms® rules can be incorporated into contracts by simple reference, e.g. 'FCA 38 cours Albert 1er, Paris, France, Incoterms® 2010'.

TRADERS SHOULD EXPLICITLY REFER TO 'INCOTERMS® 2010'. To be certain to benefit from the Incoterms® rules, traders should link their contracts to the Incoterms® rules by explicitly referring to a particular Incoterms® rule in the quoted price. The common practice of quoting a price as follows, '$100/ton FCA New York' (i.e. without an explicit reference to 'Incoterms® 2010') can be DANGEROUS. In the absence of a specific reference to the Incoterms® rules, the trader may lose the right to apply the Incoterms® rules to the contract. The contract may consequently be subjected to a national legal definition of a particular trade term, with surprising results. A more correct formulation of the above contract would be '$100/ton FCA New York Incoterms® 2010'.

In practice, it would appear that one of the most common ways of incorporating an Incoterms® rule into a contract is to include it in the General Terms and Conditions of the exporter or importer. This allows both the exporter and importer to 'forget' about specifying the application of the Incoterms® rules while they negotiate the other terms of the contract. Although this can be a helpful backstop, one wonders if it does not also lead some exporters and importers to conclude erroneously that the Incoterms® rules are mere 'technicalities' or details for the 'fine print'. Such an attitude might lead traders to downgrade the importance of the choice of a particular Incoterms® rule, which could prove unfortunate, as we will see. Another common tactic is to place a reference to the chosen Incoterms® rule somewhere in the pro forma invoice. Whichever technique is chosen, reference to the Incoterms® rules should be clear and unequivocal and refer to the year of the current valid version of the Incoterms® rules (e.g., 'Incoterms® 2010').

THE 5 BASIC QUESTIONS: WHAT, HOW, WHERE, WHO, AND WHY?

Where do you find the Incoterms® rules?

The Incoterms® rules are found in international sale contracts and any of the common documents that may evidence such contracts, such as a pro forma invoice or purchase order.

The legal nature of the Incoterms® rules is frequently misunderstood. The Incoterms® rules are creatures of contract, not legislation. The Incoterms® rules apply to a contract whenever the parties can demonstrate that they both intended the Incoterms® rules to apply. That is why it is important to explicitly incorporate the Incoterms® rules.

There are, however, important exceptions. If trade customs, general sales conditions, commercial usages or previous contractual dealings indicate that the parties intended to use the Incoterms® rules, then the Incoterms® rules may apply even in the absence of a specific mention in the sales contract. Under some legal systems, great weight is given to customs of trade and there may be a presumption that the Incoterms® rules constitute a custom of trade. In such countries, courts or arbitrators might take judicial notice of an Incoterms® rule to resolve a case, although no Incoterms® rule had been incorporated into the contract.

In which parts of the world are the Incoterms® rules most commonly used? Are there any regions or countries where the Incoterms® rules are not allowed by law, or not found in practice?

The Incoterms® rules have been longest known and understood in Europe. This may be due historically to the large number of exporting countries in Europe and the fact there is a high amount of intra-European trade. ICC is encouraged to see that understanding and use of the Incoterms® rules has been growing exponentially around the world, with newly opened countries, such as Myanmar, requesting training to bring their traders up to speed on this essential feature of commercial commerce. There is hardly a country in the world whose traders are unfamiliar with the idea of the Incoterms® rules – the challenge for ICC now is to educate users around the globe about how to use them most effectively.

INTRODUCTION TO THE INCOTERMS® RULES

Who is bound by the Incoterms® rules?

The Incoterms® rules govern certain responsibilities between the *seller* and the *buyer* under the *contract of sale*; they should not be confused with the allocation of responsibilities between the *shipper*, *carrier* and consignee under the *contract of carriage*.

One of the most common misunderstandings related to the Incoterms® rules involves confusing the *contract of sale* with the *contract of carriage*.

Note carefully the distinction:

- Contract of *sale* – The Incoterms® rules are embedded in this contract, an agreement between the *seller* and the *buyer*.

- Contract of *carriage* – This contract is between the *shipper* and the *carrier* (or the carrier's agent). Depending on the contract of sale and the chosen Incoterms® rule, the shipper may be either the seller or the buyer. This means that the contract of carriage is necessarily linked to the contract of sale, because whoever is obligated under the contract of sale to take care of transport will then become the *shipper*, and will have to enter into a carriage contract with a *carrier* (a company offering transport services, like a marine shipping line, and airline, or a freight consolidator).

The key lesson to keep in mind to avoid misunderstandings is this: The Incoterms® rules are not part of the contract of carriage. There is indeed a relationship between the Incoterms® rules and carriage contracts, because the choice of a specific Incoterms® rule may oblige the shipper to obtain a certain type of contract of carriage (such as a clean 'on board' bill of lading) with particular conditions. One reason for confusion is that terms in the contract of carriage may resemble the Incoterms® rules (for example, in their usage of the word 'free') – but traders should remember that these are separate contracts with separate sets of responsibilities.

THE 5 BASIC QUESTIONS: WHAT, HOW, WHERE, WHO, AND WHY?

Many traders also appear to expect that the transport contract will *automatically* accord with the Incoterms® rule in the sales contract. It is indeed important that the transport responsibilities required by the Incoterms® rule in the contract of sale accord with the terms of the contract of carriage, but there is nothing automatic about it. It is up to the shipper to make the effort to give precise instructions to the carrier or freight forwarder so that the proper transport arrangements are made and so that the invoices for transport services are prepared accordingly. In some cases, inexperienced traders do not even inform the carrier as to the Incoterms® rule in the contract of sale, then profess surprise later when the billing for transport services does not accord with the Incoterms® rule.

Two Incoterms® rules, CIF and CIP, impose an obligation on the seller to pay for insurance coverage. They do not regulate the insurance contract itself, but merely the relations between the seller and buyer as regards insurance. The party responsible for the payment of the insurance coverage, i.e. the seller, will have to enter into a specific insurance contract. The mention of an Incoterms® rule in this latter contract does not allocate particular obligations to the parties to the insurance contract.

INTRODUCTION TO THE INCOTERMS® RULES

Why should importers and exporters use and understand the Incoterms® rules in detail?

In order to understand the value of the Incoterms® rules, we might ask ourselves: what would happen if a trader forgot to use the Incoterms® rules, or failed to understand the allocation of risks/obligations thereunder?

Let us consider the example of a transaction where the sale contract (or at least the pro forma invoice, if there is no sale contract) mentions 'FCA' but does not specifically mention 'Incoterms® 2010' or even 'Incoterms® rules'. In such a case, if a dispute or uncertainty should arise, the traders would first have to ask themselves the preliminary question – where will we look for a definitive interpretation of FCA? Who decides what FCA means? The courts? ICC? In the absence of a specific reference to the Incoterms® rules in the contract of sale, it is possible that the only way to arrive at a definitive interpretation is to look to the national law. Unfortunately, this is a potentially complicated undertaking, as it requires one to ascertain which national law is applicable to the contract, which in turn requires an analysis of the conflict of laws rules of any national law that might be applied to the contract. Such a procedure sounds complicated, and it is. If there is litigation over the dispute, lawyers' time may have to be spent studying all pertinent jurisprudence on trade terms, and this analysis can be very expensive. All of this is unnecessary if the parties simply remember to take the precaution of specifically incorporating the Incoterms® rules into the contract of sale.

Many international traders, unfortunately, have only a general idea of the differences between such Incoterms® rules as EXW, FCA, FOB, CIF or DDP. As a result, they are unprepared for certain common contingencies with respect to transfer of risk, loading/unloading, customs clearance and insurance. Thus, for example one of the most common questions asked the ICC about the Incoterms® rules is: Who is responsible for loading (or unloading) the goods? As a matter of fact, the rule on loading varies from one Incoterms® rule to another, and this is an important area in which international trade professionals should develop their understanding.

THE 5 BASIC QUESTIONS: WHAT, HOW, WHERE, WHO, AND WHY?

In light of the above, traders clearly need to understand the nature, extent and limitations of the Incoterms® rules' coverage. The Incoterms® rules do not cover all possible legal or practical issues arising out of an international sale. The Incoterms® rules are merely a sort of contractual shorthand that allows the parties to easily specify their understanding as to: 1) the transport costs that the seller will cover; 2) the point at which risk of loss will be transferred from seller to buyer; 3) who must handle customs formalities and pay duties; and, 4) in the case of CIF and CIP, what are the responsibilities of the seller to provide insurance cover. All other important details should be dealt with specifically in the contract of sale.

For example, there is nothing in the Incoterms® rules on how the seller should transport the goods to the named delivery point. Thus, if a sale is 'FCA Terminal 4, Buenos Aires Airport, Incoterms® 2010' the buyer has no control – under the Incoterms® rules – over how the seller gets the goods to Buenos Aires; that is up to the seller, and is considered outside the remit of the FCA rule. However, in some cases it may be very important to the buyer that the goods be transported in a certain way, for example, in refrigerated containers. If this is the case, the buyer must specify in the contract how the goods should be transported up to the delivery point.

The Incoterms® rules cannot be expected to make up for a contract that is not sufficiently precise. In many cases it is advisable to include in the sales contract precise details on exact place and method of delivery, allocation of loading and/or unloading charges, extent of insurance, and mode of transport.

The Incoterms® rules cover only those cases where one party has an *obligation* to the other party to do something. The Incoterms® rules do not indicate when a trader should do something because it is *prudent* or advisable. This is frequently misunderstood. Thus, traders will ask why the seller is not obliged to insure the merchandise under a DDP sale, since it would seem obvious that the seller has to be responsible for the goods all the way to destination. Yet this approach confuses a business need with a legal obligation – the Incoterms® rules refer only to the legal obligations, and are silent on matters of common business needs and usages.

Thus, similarly, a buyer of merchandise in an FCA contract has no obligation to take out insurance, and the Incoterms® rule FCA is silent on this matter. But since the risk of loss is on the buyer once the goods have been loaded, the buyer would be very foolish not to take out insurance.

The Incoterms® rules and transfer of title: what relation?

One of the key areas *not* governed by the Incoterms® rules is that of the transfer of property or title to goods. In fact, there is no international legal harmonization as regards the transfer or title or property in international transactions. Thus, the matter is not resolved by the 1980 Vienna Convention on the International Sale of Goods (CISG).

Since the law on transfer of property rights differs from country to country, the parties to a contract of sale may wish to specifically provide for this matter in the contract, but only after determining what is permissible under the applicable law. Under many jurisdictions it is possible for the seller to retain title and ownership of the property until the purchase price is paid in full, even if this takes years. This '*retention of title*' by the seller is usually set out in a clause in the contract of sale (see discussion above in the section on Contract of Sale). Thus, one typical question raised by newcomers to the Incoterms® rules is: Where are the provisions on transfer of property in the Incoterms® rules? Such a question may arise, for example, because the goods have been damaged or lost during transit, and the seller may be eager to find out if the damage occurred when the goods were still his or her property, or if the damage took place only after the goods had become the property of the buyer; this question is primarily of interest for insurance purposes.

However, these questions remain largely governed by national law alone. It is possible for the parties to add to their contracts, in addition to the Incoterms® rule, a clause that clearly establishes the place and manner of transfer of ownership/title in the goods. Drafting such clauses requires knowledge of the transfer of property laws of both countries involved, as well as their respective conflict of law rules with regard to such property laws. Seeking specialist advice is advisable.

DOCUMENTS FOR REFERENCE

Incoterms® 2010 Guidance Notes

The Guidance Notes for each of the 11 Incoterms® 2010 rules give a snapshot of the general characteristics of each rule, and may be useful to provide readers with a quick overview of the various categories of rules. The Guidance Notes, however, do not give the full picture, and relying on them alone is dangerous. It is therefore essential that readers consult the text of *Incoterms® 2010*, including the concise and useful Introduction, which is reproduced in full at Annex 4.

The 7 Incoterms® 2010 rules for use with any mode or modes of transport ('multimodal' rules)

This rule may be used irrespective of the mode of transport selected and may also be used where more than one mode of transport is employed. It is suitable for domestic trade, while FCA is usually more appropriate for international trade.

'**Ex Works**' means that the seller delivers when it places the goods at the disposal of the buyer at the seller's premises or at another named place (i.e., works, factory, warehouse, etc.). The seller does not need to load the goods on any collecting vehicle, nor does it need to clear the goods for export, where such clearance is applicable.

The parties are well advised to specify as clearly as possible the point within the named place of delivery, as the costs and risks to that point are for the account of the seller. The buyer bears all costs and risks involved in taking the goods from the agreed point, if any, at the named place of delivery.

EXW represents the minimum obligation for the seller. The rule should be used with care as:

a. The seller has no obligation to the buyer to load the goods, even though in practice the seller may be in a better position to do so. If the seller does load the goods, it does so at the buyer's risk and expense. In cases where the seller is in a better position to load the goods, FCA, which obliges the seller to do so at its own risk and expense, is usually more appropriate.

INTRODUCTION TO THE INCOTERMS® RULES

    b. A buyer who buys from a seller on an EXW basis for export needs to be aware that the seller has an obligation to provide only such assistance as the buyer may require to effect that export: the seller is not bound to organize the export clearance. Buyers are therefore well advised not to use EXW if they cannot directly or indirectly obtain export clearance.

    c. The buyer has limited obligations to provide to the seller any information regarding the export of the goods. However, the seller may need this information for, e.g., taxation or reporting purposes.

FCA

This rule may be used irrespective of the mode of transport selected and may also be used where more than one mode of transport is employed.

"**Free Carrier**" means that the seller delivers the goods to the carrier or another person nominated by the buyer at the seller's premises or another named place. The parties are well advised to specify as clearly as possible the point within the named place of delivery, as the risk passes to the buyer at that point.

If the parties intend to deliver the goods at the seller's premises, they should identify the address of those premises as the named place of delivery. If, on the other hand, the parties intend the goods to be delivered at another place, they must identify a different specific place of delivery.

FCA requires the seller to clear the goods for export, where applicable. However, the seller has no obligation to clear the goods for import, pay any import duty or carry out any import customs formalities.

"Carrier": For the purposes of the Incoterms® 2010 rules, the carrier is the party with whom carriage is contracted.

16 | INCOTERMS® 2010 Q&A

CPT

This rule may be used irrespective of the mode of transport selected and may also be used where more than one mode of transport is employed.

"**Carriage Paid To**" means that the seller delivers the goods to the carrier or another person nominated by the seller at an agreed place (if any such place is agreed between the parties) and that the seller must contract for and pay the costs of carriage necessary to bring the goods to the named place of destination.

When CPT, CIP, CFR or CIF are used, the seller fulfils its obligation to deliver when it hands the goods over to the carrier and not when the goods reach the place of destination.

This rule has two critical points, because risk passes and costs are transferred at different places. The parties are well advised to identify as precisely as possible in the contract both the place of delivery, where the risk passes to the buyer, and the named place of destination to which the seller must contract for the carriage. If several carriers are used for the carriage to the agreed destination and the parties do not agree on a specific point of delivery, the default position is that risk passes when the goods have been delivered to the first carrier at a point entirely of the seller's choosing and over which the buyer has no control. Should the parties wish the risk to pass at a later stage (e.g., at an ocean port or airport), they need to specify this in their contract of sale.

The parties are also well advised to identify as precisely as possible the point within the agreed place of destination, as the costs to that point are for the account of the seller. The seller is advised to procure contracts of carriage that match this choice precisely. If the seller incurs costs under its contract of carriage related to unloading at the named place of destination, the seller is not entitled to recover such costs from the buyer unless otherwise agreed between the parties.

CPT requires the seller to clear the goods for export, where applicable. However, the seller has no obligation to clear the goods for import, pay any import duty or carry out any import customs formalities.

INTRODUCTION TO THE INCOTERMS® RULES

CIP

This rule may be used irrespective of the mode of transport selected and may also be used where more than one mode of transport is employed.

"**Carriage and Insurance Paid to**" means that the seller delivers the goods to the carrier or another person nominated by the seller at an agreed place (if any such place is agreed between the parties) and that the seller must contract for and pay the costs of carriage necessary to bring the goods to the named place of destination.

The seller also contracts for insurance cover against the buyer's risk of loss of or damage to the goods during the carriage. The buyer should note that under CIP the seller is required to obtain insurance only on minimum cover. Should the buyer wish to have more insurance protection, it will need either to agree as much expressly with the seller or to make its own extra insurance arrangements.

When CPT, CIP, CFR or CIF are used, the seller fulfils its obligation to deliver when it hands the goods over to the carrier and not when the goods reach the place of destination.

This rule has two critical points, because risk passes and costs are transferred at different places. The parties are well advised to identify as precisely as possible in the contract both the place of delivery, where the risk passes to the buyer, and the named place of destination to which the seller must contract for carriage. If several carriers are used for the carriage to the agreed destination and the parties do not agree on a specific point of delivery, the default position is that risk passes when the goods have been delivered to the first carrier at a point entirely of the seller's choosing and over which the buyer has no control. Should the parties wish the risk to pass at a later stage (e.g., at an ocean port or an airport), they need to specify this in their contract of sale.

The parties are also well advised to identify as precisely as possible the point within the agreed place of destination, as the costs to that point are for the account of the seller. The seller is advised to procure contracts of carriage that match this choice precisely. If the seller incurs costs under its contract of carriage related to unloading at the named place of destination, the seller is not entitled to recover such costs from the buyer unless otherwise agreed between the parties.

CIP requires the seller to clear the goods for export, where applicable. However, the seller has no obligation to clear the goods for import, pay any import duty or carry out any import customs formalities.

This rule may be used irrespective of the mode of transport selected and may also be used where more than one mode of transport is employed.

"**Delivered at Terminal**" means that the seller delivers when the goods, once unloaded from the arriving means of transport, are placed at the disposal of the buyer at a named terminal at the named port or place of destination. "Terminal" includes any place, whether covered or not, such as a quay, warehouse, container yard or road, rail or air cargo terminal. The seller bears all risks involved in bringing the goods to and unloading them at the terminal at the named port or place of destination.

The parties are well advised to specify as clearly as possible the terminal and, if possible, a specific point within the terminal at the agreed port or place of destination, as the risks to that point are for the account of the seller. The seller is advised to procure a contract of carriage that matches this choice precisely.

Moreover, if the parties intend the seller to bear the risks and costs involved in transporting and handling the goods from the terminal to another place, then the DAP or DDP rules should be used.

DAT requires the seller to clear the goods for export, where applicable. However, the seller has no obligation to clear the goods for import, pay any import duty or carry out any import customs formalities.

INTRODUCTION TO THE INCOTERMS® RULES

DAP

This rule may be used irrespective of the mode of transport selected and may also be used where more than one mode of transport is employed.

"**Delivered at Place**" means that the seller delivers when the goods are placed at the disposal of the buyer on the arriving means of transport ready for unloading at the named place of destination. The seller bears all risks involved in bringing the goods to the named place.

The parties are well advised to specify as clearly as possible the point within the agreed place of destination, as the risks to that point are for the account of the seller. The seller is advised to procure contracts of carriage that match this choice precisely. If the seller incurs costs under its contract of carriage related to unloading at the place of destination, the seller is not entitled to recover such costs from the buyer unless otherwise agreed between the parties.

DAP requires the seller to clear the goods for export, where applicable. However, the seller has no obligation to clear the goods for import, pay any import duty or carry out any import customs formalities. If the parties wish the seller to clear the goods for import, pay any import duty and carry out any import customs formalities, the DDP term should be used.

DDP

This rule may be used irrespective of the mode of transport selected and may also be used where more than one mode of transport is employed.

"**Delivered Duty Paid**" means that the seller delivers the goods when the goods are placed at the disposal of the buyer, cleared for import on the arriving means of transport ready for unloading at the named place of destination. The seller bears all the costs and risks involved in bringing the goods to the place of destination and has an obligation to clear the goods not only for export but also for import, to pay any duty for both export and import and to carry out all customs formalities.

DDP represents the maximum obligation for the seller.

INCOTERMS® 2010 GUIDANCE NOTES

The parties are well advised to specify as clearly as possible the point within the agreed place of destination, as the costs and risks to that point are for the account of the seller. The seller is advised to procure contracts of carriage that match this choice precisely. If the seller incurs costs under its contract of carriage related to unloading at the place of destination, the seller is not entitled to recover such costs from the buyer unless otherwise agreed between the parties.

The parties are well advised not to use DDP if the seller is unable directly or indirectly to obtain import clearance.

If the parties wish the buyer to bear all risks and costs of import clearance, the DAP rule should be used.

Any VAT or other taxes payable upon import are for the seller's account unless expressly agreed otherwise in the sales contract.

The 4 Incoterms® 2010 rules for use with sea or inland waterway transport ('maritime' rules)

FAS

This rule is to be used only for sea or inland waterway transport.

"**Free Alongside Ship**" means that the seller delivers when the goods are placed alongside the vessel (e.g., on a quay or a barge) nominated by the buyer at the named port of shipment. The risk of loss of or damage to the goods passes when the goods are alongside the ship, and the buyer bears all costs from that moment onwards.

The parties are well advised to specify as clearly as possible the loading point at the named port of shipment, as the costs and risks to that point are for the account of the seller and these costs and associated handling charges may vary according to the practice of the port.

The seller is required either to deliver the goods alongside the ship or to procure goods already so delivered for shipment. The reference to "procure" here caters for multiple sales down a chain ('string sales'), particularly common in the commodity trades.

INTRODUCTION TO THE INCOTERMS® RULES

Where the goods are in containers, it is typical for the seller to hand the goods over to the carrier at a terminal and not alongside the vessel. In such situations, the FAS rule would be inappropriate, and the FCA rule should be used.

FAS requires the seller to clear the goods for export, where applicable. However, the seller has no obligation to clear the goods for import, pay any import duty or carry out any import customs formalities.

FOB

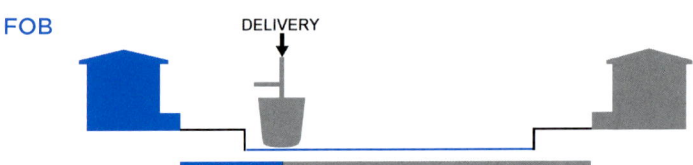

This rule is to be used only for sea or inland waterway transport.

"**Free on Board**" means that the seller delivers the goods on board the vessel nominated by the buyer at the named port of shipment or procures the goods already so delivered. The risk of loss of or damage to the goods passes when the goods are on board the vessel, and the buyer bears all costs from that moment onwards.

The seller is required either to deliver the goods on board the vessel or to procure goods already so delivered for shipment. The reference to "procure" here caters for multiple sales down a chain ('string sales'), particularly common in the commodity trades.

FOB may not be appropriate where goods are handed over to the carrier before they are on board the vessel, for example goods in containers, which are typically delivered at a terminal. In such situations, the FCA rule should be used.

FOB requires the seller to clear the goods for export, where applicable. However, the seller has no obligation to clear the goods for import, pay any import duty or carry out any import customs formalities.

CFR

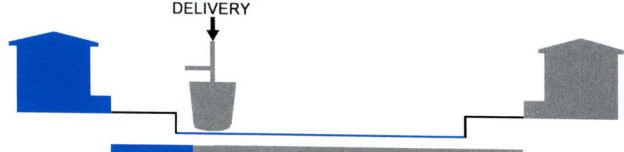

This rule is to be used only for sea or inland waterway transport.

"**Cost and Freight**" means that the seller delivers the goods on board the vessel or procures the goods already so delivered. The risk of loss of or damage to the goods passes when the goods are on board the vessel. The seller must contract for and pay the costs and freight necessary to bring the goods to the named port of destination.

When CPT, CIP, CFR or CIF are used, the seller fulfils its obligation to deliver when it hands the goods over to the carrier in the manner specified in the chosen rule and not when the goods reach the place of destination.

This rule has two critical points, because risk passes and costs are transferred at different places. While the contract will always specify a destination port, it might not specify the port of shipment, which is where risk passes to the buyer. If the shipment port is of particular interest to the buyer, the parties are well advised to identify it as precisely as possible in the contract.

The parties are well advised to identify as precisely as possible the point at the agreed port of destination, as the costs to that point are for the account of the seller. The seller is advised to procure contracts of carriage that match this choice precisely. If the seller incurs costs under its contract of carriage related to unloading at the specified point at the port of destination, the seller is not entitled to recover such costs from the buyer unless otherwise agreed between the parties.

The seller is required either to deliver the goods on board the vessel or to procure goods already so delivered for shipment to the destination. In addition, the seller is required either to make a contract of carriage or to procure such a contract. The reference to "procure" here caters for multiple sales down a chain ('string sales'), particularly common in the commodity trades.

CFR may not be appropriate where goods are handed over to the carrier before they are on board the vessel, for example goods in containers, which are typically delivered at a terminal. In such circumstances, the CPT rule should be used.

INTRODUCTION TO THE INCOTERMS® RULES

CFR requires the seller to clear the goods for export, where applicable. However, the seller has no obligation to clear the goods for import, pay any import duty, or carry out any import customs formalities.

CIF

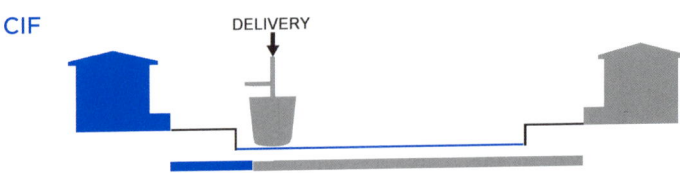

This rule is to be used only for sea or inland waterway transport.

"**Cost, Insurance and Freight**" means that the seller delivers the goods on board the vessel or procures the goods already so delivered. The risk of loss of or damage to the goods passes when the goods are on board the vessel. The seller must contract for and pay the costs and freight necessary to bring the goods to the named port of destination.

The seller also contracts for insurance cover against the buyer's risk of loss of or damage to the goods during the carriage. The buyer should note that under CIF the seller is required to obtain insurance only on minimum cover. Should the buyer wish to have more insurance protection, it will need either to agree as much expressly with the seller or to make its own extra insurance arrangements.

When CPT, CIP, CFR, or CIF are used, the seller fulfils its obligation to deliver when it hands the goods over to the carrier in the manner specified in the chosen rule and not when the goods reach the place of destination.

This rule has two critical points, because risk passes and costs are transferred at different places. While the contract will always specify a destination port, it might not specify the port of shipment, which is where risk passes to the buyer. If the shipment port is of particular interest to the buyer, the parties are well advised to identify it as precisely as possible in the contract.

The parties are well advised to identify as precisely as possible the point at the agreed port of destination, as the costs to that point are for the account of the seller. The seller is advised to procure contracts of carriage that match this choice precisely. If the seller incurs costs under its contract of carriage related to unloading at the specified point at the port of destination, the seller is not entitled to recover such costs from the buyer unless otherwise agreed between the parties.

The seller is required either to deliver the goods on board the vessel or to procure goods already so delivered for shipment to the destination. In addition the seller is required either to make a contract of carriage or to procure such a contract. The reference to "procure" here caters for multiple sales down a chain ('string sales'), particularly common in the commodity trades.

CIF may not be appropriate where goods are handed over to the carrier before they are on board the vessel, for example goods in containers, which are typically delivered at a terminal. In such circumstances, the CIP rule should be used.

CIF requires the seller to clear the goods for export, where applicable. However, the seller has no obligation to clear the goods for import, pay any import duty or carry out any import customs formalities.

INTRODUCTION TO THE INCOTERMS® RULES

Specimen form of ICC Model International Sale Contract

Model Form
International Sale Contract
ICC International Sale Contract
(Manufactured Goods)

CONTRACT

Seller's reference N° 2013-001
Buyer's reference N° 090309117

A.
SPECIFIC CONDITIONS

These Specific Conditions have been prepared in order to permit the parties to agree the particular terms of their sale contract by completing the spaces left open or choosing (as the case may be) between the alternatives provided in this document. Obviously this does not prevent the parties from agreeing other terms or further details in Box A-17 or in one or more annexes. Any reference to "Articles" means "Articles of the General Conditions of the ICC Model International Sale Contract (Manufactured Goods)".

SELLER	
Name, corporate form and address VERONESE spa Via Masaccio 24 Milano Italy Tax identification code/Other registration code: TN IT012345678901	CONTACT PERSON Name Stefano Romani Telephone +39 800 123 456 E-mail sromani@veronese.it

BUYER	
Name, corporate form and address Zhongxin Import.co No 65 Pujian Road Shanghai China Tax identification code/Other registration code: CR 123456789	CONTACT PERSON Name Debra Hsu Telephone +86 21 1234 56 78 E-mail dhsu@xyz.com

SPECIMEN FORM OF ICC MODEL INTERNATIONAL SALE CONTRACT

A-1	GOODS SOLD
Item/packages – item description – product code – origin – commodity code[6] – quantity		
1 SPECTRA ENG.220 V SO HZ, CE MARK type 80090795		
Made in Italy		
HS 901890		
If there is insufficient space parties may use an annex		

A-2	CONTRACT PRICE (ART. 4)
Indicate the currency referring to the ISO -3 currency code (e.g. USD, EUR etc.)[7]		

Currency: USD

Amount: 1,570,000   Amount in words: one million five hundred and seventy thousand

A-3	DELIVERY TERMS (ART. 8)
Recommended terms *(according to the Incoterms® 2010 rules): see Introduction, §5*		

☐ **FCA** Free Carrier   Named place: _____
                            Shipped by (when different from buyer) _____

☐ **CPT** Carriage Paid To   Named place of destination: _____
                                Shipped from: _____

☒ **CIP** Carriage and Insurance Paid To
   Named place of destination: Shanghai Airport
   Shipped from: Milano Malpensa
   Insurance cover: ☒ max. cover   ☒ War Risk / SRCC[8]

☐ **DAT** Delivered at Terminal   Named terminal or quay of destination: _____

☐ **DAP** Delivered at Place   Named place of destination: _____

---

6. The commodity code or customs code is the 6-digit code of the product under the Harmonised System of the World Customs Organisation (http://www.wcoomd.org/home_hsoverviewboxes.htm) or any more specific (extended) code under national customs legislation. In the latter situations it might be wise to indicate the nature of the code (TARIC, MERCOSUR, TVNED, etc.)
7. UNECE ECE/Trade/203 Recommendation n°9 – Alphabetic Code for the Representation for Currencies; available at http://www.unece.org/cefact/recommendations/rec_index.html.
8. Strikes, Riots and Civil Commotion

INTRODUCTION TO THE INCOTERMS® RULES

Other terms *(according to the Incoterms® 2010 rules): see Introduction, §5*

☐ **EXW** Ex Works Named place: _____

☐ **DDP** Delivered Duty Paid Named place of destination: _____

☐ **FAS** Free Alongside Ship Named port of shipment: _____
Shipped by (when different from buyer) _____

☐ **FOB** Free On Board Named port of shipment: _____
Shipped by (when different from buyer) _____

☐ **CFR** Cost and Freight Named port of destination: _____
Shipped from: _____

☐ **CIF** Cost Insurance and Freight Named port of destination: _____
Shipped from: _____
Insurance cover: ☐ max. cover ☐ War Risk /SRCC

CARRIER OR FORWARDER (where applicable)

NAME AND ADDRESS	CONTACT PERSON
TRANSWORLD spa	Fabrizio Linetta
Terminal X	+39 800 654 321
Milano Malpensa Airport	Flinetta@transworld.org

A-4	**TIME OF DELIVERY**
	FOURTH WEEK OF MARCH 2013

*Indicate here the date or period (e.g. week or month) at which or within which the Seller must perform its delivery obligations of the respective Incoterms® rule according to Box A-3 ('Delivery Terms') (see Introduction, § 6) **and, when applicable, a date of shipment (see Introduction, §7)***

SPECIMEN FORM OF ICC MODEL INTERNATIONAL SALE CONTRACT

A-5	INSPECTION OF THE GOODS (ART. 3)

☐ Upon shipment   Surveyor _____

☒ Before shipment Surveyor BIVAC   Place of inspection: Carrier's Terminal-Milan

☐ Other: _____

☐ Inspection fee on Seller's account

☒ Inspection fee on Buyer's account

A-6	RETENTION OF TITLE (ART. 7)

☒ YES   ☐ NO

A-7	PAYMENT CONDITIONS (ART. 5)

☐ **Payment on open account (art. 5.1)**
Time for payment (if different from art. 5.1) ____ days from date of invoice. Other: ____
  ☐ Open account backed by demand guarantee or standby letter of credit (art. 5.6)

☐ **Payment in advance (art. 5.2)**
Date (if different from art. 5.2): _____
  ☐ Total price
  ☐ ____% of the price; remaining amount ____% to be paid at _____
  ☐ Payment in advance backed by advance payment bond

☐ **Documentary collection (art. 5.4)**
  ☐ D/P Documents against payment
  ☐ D/A Documents against acceptance

☒ **Irrevocable documentary credit (art. 5.3)**
  ☐ Confirmed
  ☒ Unconfirmed

Place of issue (if applicable): Shanghai, China   Place of confirmation (if applicable): Milan

INTRODUCTION TO THE INCOTERMS® RULES

Credit available: *Partial shipments:*   *Transhipment:*

☒ At sight   __ Allowed   **x** Allowed

☐ By deferred payment at: ___ days   **x** Not allowed   __ Not allowed

☐ By acceptance of drafts at : ___ days

☐ By negotiation

Date on which the documentary credit must be notified to seller (if different from art. 5.3)

_____ days before date of shipment   other: _____

☐ **Irrevocable Bank Payment Obligation (art. 5.5)**

    ☐ Settlement by Payment

    ☐ Settlement by Deferred Payment Undertaking and payment at maturity. Deferred payment terms____ days after sight or after date of ____

Date on which the Bank Payment Obligation must be notified to seller (if different from art. 5.5)

_____ days before date of shipment   other: _____

☐ **Other:** _____

(e.g. cheque, bank draft, electronic funds transfer to designated bank account of seller)

Seller's Bank Details

IBAN[9]/bank account number   IT60 X054 2811 1010 0000 0123 456

BIC/Swift code[10]   BITAITR1318

---

[9]. http://www.ecbs.org/iban.htm
[10]. https://www2.swift.com/directories/

A-8	DOCUMENTS (ART.9)

Indicate here documents to be provided by Seller. Parties are advised to check the Incoterms® 2010 rule they have selected under A-3 of these Specific Conditions. As concerns transport documents, see also Introduction, § 8

[X] **Commercial Invoice**   number of originals/copies 1/2

specific requirements _____ (language, legalization, etc.)

[X] **Packing list**   number of originals/copies   1/0

[X] **Certificate of origin**   ___ preferential (indicate type)
  X economic
  number of originals/copies   1/0
  specific requirements _____ (language, legalization, etc.)

[X] **Transport documents**: Airway bill   *(indicate type of transport document required)*
  ___ full set   number _____
  specific requirements _____ (e.g. consignee, notify, etc.)

[ ] **Insurance document:**

[ ] **Other:** _____

A-9	CANCELLATION DATE

To be completed only if the parties wish to modify Art. 10

If the goods are not delivered for any reason whatsoever (including force majeure) by _____ (date), the Buyer will be entitled to declare the contract avoided immediately by notification to the Seller.

INTRODUCTION TO THE INCOTERMS® RULES

A-10	LIABILITY FOR DELAY (ART. 10.2)	A-11	LIMITATION OF LIABILITY FOR DELAY (ART. 10.4)
To be completed only if the parties wish to modify Art.10.2		*To be completed only if the parties wish to modify Art.10.4*	
Liquidated damages for delay in delivery shall be: ____ % (of price of delayed goods) per week, with a maximum of ____ % (of price of delayed goods)		In case of avoidance for delay, Seller's liability for damages for delay is limited to ___% of the price of the non-delivered goods.	

A-12	PLACE OF EXAMINATION AT ARRIVAL (ART. 11.1)

To be completed only if the parties wish to modify Art.11.1

The goods delivered will have to be examined after their arrival at the following place :

☐ Place of business of the consignee to which the goods are sent or redirected

☐ Other: ....

A-13	MAXIMUM DELAY FOR NOTIFICATION OF NON-CONFORMITY (ART 11.1)

To be completed only if the parties wish to modify Art.11.1

Defects must be notified to the Seller immediately upon discovery or as soon as they ought to have been discovered, but not later than _____ after arrival of the goods. This shall not affect the periods of limitation (art. 11.6).

SPECIMEN FORM OF ICC MODEL INTERNATIONAL SALE CONTRACT

A-14	LIMITATION OF LIABILITY FOR NON-CONFORMITY (ART. 11.4)

To be completed only if the parties wish to modify Art.11.4

Seller's liability for damages arising from lack of conformity of the goods shall be:

limited to proven loss (including consequential loss, loss of profit, etc.) not exceeding _____ % of the contract price

OR

_____ (specify amount)

A-15	APPLICABLE LAW (ART. 1.2)

To be completed only if the parties wish to choose a law other than the Seller's law for questions not covered by the CISG

Any questions not covered by CISG will be governed by the law of Italy (country).

A-16	RESOLUTION OF DISPUTES (ART. 14)

The two solutions hereunder (arbitration or litigation before ordinary courts) are alternatives: parties cannot choose both of them. If no choice is made, ICC arbitration will apply, according to art.1

[X] ARBITRATION

    [X] ICC (according to art.14.2)

    [ ] Other _____ (specify)

Place of arbitration Singapore

Language of the arbitration English

Number of arbitrators 1

[ ] LITIGATION (ordinary courts)

In case of dispute the courts of _____ (place), shall have exclusive jurisdiction.

A-17	OTHER

The present contract of sale will be governed by these Specific Conditions (to the extent that the relevant boxes have been completed) and by the General Conditions of the ICC Model International Sale Contract (Manufactured Goods) which constitute Part B of this document.

Shanghai (place), January 9, 2013 (date)

The Seller *[signature]*

Name Stefano Romoni

Title Director, ASEAN

The Buyer *[signature]*

Name Debra Hsu

Title Purchase Manager

HOW DOES ONE CHOOSE THE RIGHT INCOTERMS® RULE?
A DECISION-MAKING CHECKLIST

Perhaps the most important question concerning the Incoterms® rules is, which Incoterms® rule should my company choose in a given case?

What is the commercial reality – are there any restrictions?

The commercial reality is that many companies just continue to use the same trade terms they have always used, e.g.: 'My grandfather shipped FOB, my father shipped FOB, so I ship FOB.' Moreover, in some cases, government restrictions require companies to limit themselves to certain terms. For example, in certain countries there are foreign exchange restrictions under which domestic buyers are required to buy on the cheapest terms allowed by national laws concerning international transactions, (which often means FCA or FOB), and to sell on the most expensive terms allowed by these laws (often CIP or CIF). These kinds of laws and regulations are less common than in the past as economies around the world have opened up and governments have begun to realize the enormous economic returns to be made from trade facilitation.

The continued existence of these kinds of regulations in some countries is lamentable and unfortunate. By restricting parties in their choice of Incoterms® rules, governments reduce the options available to traders, and raise transaction costs. Economic growth in the export sector is thereby restrained. One can only hope that governments worldwide will make trade facilitation, and the elimination of these kinds of regulations, one of their highest priorities.

How do I choose an Incoterms® rule? How do I know if my counterparty's choice is good for me?

These are the crucial questions that face not only the beginning exporter or importer, but also the experienced trader. Whenever the trader has to deal with a new type of sale, an unfamiliar party, an unknown transport provider, or some other source of uncertainty, it is important to consider wisely the choice of Incoterms® rule.

In all international sales negotiations, the overall commercial context and the relative bargaining power of the parties will determine many of the issues covered by the Incoterms® rules. Some of the following basic principles, 'rules of thumb', and common notions are worth noting (they are by no means the only possible cost considerations):

INTRODUCTION TO THE INCOTERMS® RULES

1. Many disputes arise concerning payment of loading or unloading charges, charges arising from handling the goods in terminals, container rental charges, and/or customs processing charges. This happens even when the parties have clearly chosen a particular Incoterms® rule, because in some cases the Incoterms® rule is quite general. Why not just make a checklist of such potentially troublesome issues and clarify them systematically with your counterparties? If necessary, include language in your contract in addition to the chosen Incoterms® rule so that it is clear that you have a particular allocation in mind that is more detailed than the basic rule set out in the chosen Incoterms® rule (e.g., 'FOB Baltimore Port, stowed and trimmed').

2. Many small or beginning exporters like to quote EXW (Ex Works) because they perceive that it requires the least amount of knowledge of export procedures, and the least work. This is basically accurate, but there are a number of concerns about using EXW in international transactions (see the Guidance Note for EXW at page 15) and exporters are well advised to consider using EXW, if at all, only for domestic sales. Moreover, if an exporter limits itself to agreeing to sales using only one Incoterms® rule, he or she may miss opportunities for sales in those cases where the buyer insists on other Incoterms® rules, such as FCA, CIP or DAP. So it is important for even small exporters to understand the full range of Incoterms® rules, because someday they may be called for. Moreover, even small exporters usually have access to the services of a freight forwarder or a transport carrier. These transport service providers can often counsel the small trader on how to choose amongst the different Incoterms® rules, and they may then also offer the services associated with fulfilling the trader's transport obligations under the given Incoterms® rule. However, to delegate such responsibilities to the freight forwarder intentionally, it is preferable for the trader to have a good general understanding of the Incoterms® rules. The same kind of thinking applies to small importers who believe that they should only buy DDP, since it requires the fewest obligations on their part; they may be right, but there are many opportunities for complications in transactions using DDP (see the Guidance Note for DDP at page 20), so a thorough knowledge of all Incoterms® rules is still necessary.

HOW DOES ONE CHOOSE THE RIGHT INCOTERMS® RULE?

3. The Incoterms® rule chosen will vary primarily according to whether it is the seller or the buyer who has to effect the main transport. The first practical issue is therefore: Who wants or proposes to take care of transport? Who can obtain the cheapest transport rates? There is a strong economic argument in favour of allocating the larger portion of transport duties to whichever of the parties can obtain the cheapest or most efficient transport services.

4. The next practical issue is to consider at what point risk will transfer from the seller to the buyer. If you are the seller, you would like to transfer this risk as soon as possible; you can do this to some extent with EXW, FCA, FOB, CFR, CIF, CPT and CIP, depending on which point you choose as the named delivery point. If you are the buyer, conversely, you might wish to accept no risk at all for the goods until they are safely in your possession; then your preference would be for the D family of Incoterms® rules, DAT, DAP, and DDP. The actual choice, again, will depend on the entire commercial context, as well as on the relative interests and bargaining power of the parties.

5. Does the choice of an Incoterms® rule require you to effect customs formalities or pay duties in a foreign country? If so, better check to make sure you know what will be required of you. It might be advisable to ask for a clause allowing you time-extensions and force majeure termination if there are customs problems.

6. As an exporter, would you like to earn money by charging a commission for arranging transport services? If so, you may wish to choose an Incoterms® rule that places a lot of transport responsibilities on the seller (such as the C and D families of rules), so that you can then earn revenues on the provision of these services. Even if you do not want to earn money on transport, if you are able to find or organize cheaper transport than your buyer or your competitors, it may be to your advantage to quote C or D rules, because your total offer will then be cheaper and more competitively priced.

To see sample decision-making flowcharts regarding the choice of an Incoterms® 2010 rule, see Annex 2. Note, though, that any flowchart is necessarily very general and should be considered only as a starting point for thinking about which Incoterms® rule to choose. As noted in point 4 of the checklist, above, in any given real-life transaction, there are a number of considerations particular to that deal that parties must factor in to their final decision on which Incoterms® 2010 rule to choose. A flowchart alone cannot provide the answer.

THE INCOTERMS® 2010 RULES AND DOCUMENTS – DOCUMENTS COMMONLY NEEDED IN SALE TRANSACTIONS UNDER THE INCOTERMS® RULES

Annex 3 sets out the most common documents users may need to provide, respond to, or accommodate in connection with sales of goods that incorporate one of the Incoterms® 2010 rules. While the Incoterms® 2010 rules do not set out detailed rules for many of the documents that may be needed in connection with a sale of goods, nonetheless some general guidance in this area may be helpful. Users are of course well advised to read this guidance in the context of the specific needs of their particular sale transaction.

The information is divided into 11 sections, one for each of the Incoterms® 2010 rules. In each section, there is an explanation of what documents may be required in various areas: proof of delivery, customs, transport, financing, and insurance, and what issues users should consider regarding the interaction of these various kinds of documents.

Mismatches between documents and the requirements under the Incoterms® rules are common and can lead to costly complications for traders – readers are therefore well advised to study Annex 3 carefully before entering into a sale transaction, to avoid problems before they arise.

A NOTE ON 'DELIVERY' UNDER THE INCOTERMS® RULES

1. ICC has been asked to comment on the definition of 'delivery' in the introduction to the Incoterms® 2010 rules. The following note is issued by way of guidance to users of the Incoterms® 2010 rules.

2. One of the main advantages of the Incoterms® rules has been to give a precise definition of the contractual place of delivery based on the physical location of the goods in the supply chain. Under the Incoterms® rules (unlike many sales laws) the place of delivery is also the place where the risk for the consequences of loss of or damage to the goods transfers from the seller to the buyer under the contract of sale.

3. Both notions – delivery and risk - are crucial since the physical delivery and transfer of risk mark the point at which the seller performs what is usually its most significant obligation under the contract of sale, i.e. to pass the goods to the buyer.

4. Since delivery and transfer of risk can be defined differently under the law applicable to the sales contract, it may often be complicated to determine under a particular sales contract when exactly the seller performs its delivery obligation and when risk passes to the buyer. This may cause misunderstandings and conflicts between the parties to the contract of sale. Delivery could take place at the seller's premises, at the buyer's premises or at a point in between. Thus, for example, Article 31 of CISG fixes delivery at the place where the goods are handed over to the first carrier.

5. Article A4 in each Incoterms® rule specifies the place of delivery. Therefore, by incorporating one of the Incoterms® rules into a sales contract, the parties can clarify precisely where the seller performs its obligation to deliver under the sales contract.

6. In order for article A4 in each Incoterms® rule to work to its best advantage, however, it is important for the parties to clearly define in the contract the precise point within the agreed place of delivery.

7. It should be noted that under most Incoterms® rules contractual delivery takes place when the goods are handed over not directly to the buyer but to a third party – often a carrier – at a pre-determined place. Moreover, customs for handing over goods to carriers may vary depending on the place.

8. It is at the point of delivery that the risk passes from the seller to the buyer (subject to some narrow exceptions). This is clarified in article A5 of each Incoterms® rule and explained in the Introduction to *Incoterms® 2010*. The clear identification of the place of delivery therefore avoids the confusion that could arise because different applicable laws might fix the passage of risk to diverging places.

9. In conclusion, the Incoterms® 2010 rules, as do all prior versions, respond to the practical need for a clear definition of the contractual place of delivery.

OTHER COMMON QUESTIONS

Why is it important to put the year 2010?

The Incoterms® rules are revised periodically (approximately every 10 years), so it is important to make sure you are working with the most recent valid version. The last Incoterms® rules revision was published in autumn 2010, became effective on 1 January 2011, and is referred to as Incoterms® 2010.

Are Incoterms® rules the law?

In most countries, the Incoterms® rules are NOT explicitly referred to in laws or statutes, so the Incoterms® rules are not 'laws' in the sense of rules that are developed by a government and are obligatory for all market participants.

Am I legally obliged to follow the Incoterms® rules?

Generally speaking, parties are not obliged to follow the Incoterms® rules, but rather the other way round: parties choose voluntarily to have the Incoterms® rules apply to their contracts (that is, parties voluntarily submit themselves to the Incoterms® rules, which are then binding as part of the contract of sale).

Does FOB include stowing and trimming? What are 'stowing' and 'trimming'?

Stowing and trimming are operations that must be performed upon bulk commodities after they are loaded into a ship's hold. The FOB seller is generally not responsible for stowing or trimming, which is why some buyers in some cases seek to explicitly bind the seller by adding the following formulation to the Incoterms® rule: 'FOB stowed and trimmed' See Q&A No. 38 on page 100 for more on stowing and trimming .

OTHER COMMON QUESTIONS

Who pays for unloading costs under CIF?

If the unloading costs are for the seller's account under the contract of carriage, then the costs are for the seller; if the costs are not included for seller's account under the contract of carriage, then the costs are for the buyer.

What is the difference between FOB in a sale contract and FOB in a bill of lading?

The Incoterms® rules can be used only in contracts of sale, not in contracts of carriage or bills of lading. ICC strongly discourages the use of terms resembling the Incoterms® rules in contracts of carriage. When a term like 'FOB' is used in the context of a transport contract, it is meant to refer to the transport responsibilities of the carrier, and as a result the Incoterms® rules have no application (remember, the Incoterms® rules govern only the rights and responsibilities of sellers and buyers, and they do not at all govern the duties of carriers).

What is the difference between the Incoterms® rules, Liner terms and Charter party terms?

As stated in the Introduction, perhaps the single most common misunderstanding related to the Incoterms® rules involves confusing the contract of sale with the contract of carriage. Note the distinction:

- Contract of *sale* – The Incoterms® rules are embedded in this contract, an agreement between the seller and the buyer. The contract terms deal with price, quality and delivery terms of the contract merchandise.

- Contract of *carriage* – This contract is between the *shipper* and the *carrier* (or its agent). Depending on the contract of sale and the chosen Incoterms® rule, the shipper may be either the seller or the buyer. The carriage contract terms relate to the price of the carrier's transport services (i.e. freight rates) and the extent of the carrier's liability for goods delivered. It is in this context that we encounter 'liner terms', 'charter parties' and 'charter party terms'.

The Incoterms® rules are not part of the contract of carriage, though the choice of Incoterms® rule may oblige the shipper to obtain a contract of carriage with particular conditions.

'Liner terms' – With 'liner' transport the shipper entrusts its goods to a 'shipping line' .

Certain costs may be included in the freight (such as loading or unloading charges) charged by regular shipping lines – hence, 'liner terms'. With liner terms, for example, discharging expenses are frequently included in the freight. Shippers should take care to ensure that the charges included in the liner terms accord with the shipper's transport responsibilities under the given Incoterms® rule.

'Charter parties' – Another basic form of maritime transport is via charter party, under which the shipper hires a ship or part of a ship. In this context, 'free in' and 'free out' mean that the loading and unloading obligations are not included in the charter party hire.

Thus, when a seller under one of the 'C' group of Incoterms® rules has chartered a vessel on 'free out terms', he or she will have assumed the costs of loading and discharge vis-à-vis the ship owner. It will be in the seller's interest to require the buyer to discharge the goods within a certain number of days (referred to as the 'laytime'). Conversely, a ship owner may provide for a bonus (known as 'dispatch money') to the seller (when the seller is the charterer) for timely discharging, which the seller may pass on as an incentive to the buyer. The relationship between the charter party arrangement and the agreement between seller and buyer should be clarified in the contract of sale.

THE GOLDEN RULES OF THE INCOTERMS® RULES

1. Explicitly incorporate the Incoterms® rules into your sales contracts, as by the specific mention 'FCA, 38 cours Albert 1er, Paris, France, Incoterms® 2010'. Always include the words 'Incoterms® 2010' in your contracts until an updated version of the rules is released, at which point you should begin to incorporate the newer version of the Incoterms® rules into your contracts.

2. Have access to a copy of the full set of definitions of the Incoterms® 2010 rules, contained in the ICC publication 'Incoterms® 2010', included here at Annex 4.

3. Recognize the 11 current Incoterms® 2010 rules, and refer to them by their 3-letter abbreviations:

   - EXW – Ex Works (… named place of delivery)
   - FCA – Free Carrier (… named place of delivery)
   - CPT – Carriage Paid To (… named place of destination)
   - CIP – Carriage and Insurance Paid To (… named place of destination)
   - DAT – Delivered At Terminal (… named terminal at port or place of destination)
   - DAP – Delivered at Place (… named place of destination)
   - DDP – Delivered Duty Paid (… named place of destination)
   - FAS – Free Alongside Ship (… named port of shipment)
   - FOB – Free On Board (… named port of shipment)
   - CFR – Cost and Freight (… named port of destination)
   - CIF – Cost, Insurance and Freight (… named port of destination)

   Note that the Incoterms 2000 rules 'DAF', 'DES', 'DEQ' and 'DDU' have been removed and replaced by the more general Incoterms® 2010 rules 'DAT' and 'DAP'. 'DAP' may be used instead of 'DAF', 'DES' and 'DDU', and 'DAT' may be used to replace 'DEQ', since in both DAT and the deleted DEQ, the seller unloads goods from the arriving vehicle at destination.

4. Be very careful to distinguish between those Incoterms® 2010 rules that should be used exclusively for traditional maritime transport (for example, bulk goods and commodities loaded directly on board the ship), and the more general Incoterms® 2010 rules appropriate for all modes of transport, particularly containerized and multimodal transport:

INTRODUCTION TO THE INCOTERMS® RULES

- *Containerized/multimodal/general* – Use EXW, FCA, CPT, CIP, DAT, DAP and DDP for all modes of transport or a combination of modes of transport (this combination may include marine transport).

- *Maritime* – Use FAS, FOB, CFR, and CIF, for traditional maritime transport (goods lifted directly on board the ship).

5. Understand that the Incoterms® rules are meant for use in the contract of *sale* between buyer and seller, which should not be confused with the related contract of *carriage* between the shipper and carrier/transporter. Traders should give precise directions to their transporters as to the Incoterms® rule they have chosen in a particular contract of sale; this will ensure that the contract of carriage is consistent with the contract of sale.

6. Understand that the Incoterms® 2010 rules basically cover the transfer of risks and costs between seller and buyer and certain customs and insurance responsibilities. However, several other important conditions of a sales contract may need to be specified in addition to the Incoterms® rule. You may be well-advised to:

    a. Specify how delivery will take place.

    b. Specify how much insurance coverage you want, and the geographical and time extent of the insurance coverage (where and when coverage begins and ends).

    c. Specify any necessary limitations on what kind of transport is appropriate (i.e., refrigerated containers, not carried on deck, etc.).

    d. Make sure that your contract contains force majeure, exoneration, or time-extension clauses if you are responsible for customs clearance or foreign delivery at an inland point.

7. Understand that CIF, CFR, CIP and CPT are NOT 'arrival contracts', they are 'shipment contracts'. This means that the point of transfer of risk with these C rules is the same as with F rules: in the country of departure.

Chapter Two

QUESTIONS AND ANSWERS ON THE INCOTERMS® RULES

Guidance on selected Incoterms® rules questions by ICC experts

As the publisher of the Incoterms® 2010 rules, ICC is committed to serving its members and the broader international trading community by offering expert interpretive guidance on selected questions that have arisen regarding the Incoterms® 2010 rules. The guidance is intended to help users gain a deeper and more nuanced understanding of the Incoterms® rules, so that they can prepare clear and precise sale and purchase contracts, and avoid many of the common costly missteps that we see arising from the uninformed use of the rules.

ICC recognizes that each case involving the Incoterms® rules is different depending on place, parties, industry, applicable laws and relevant customs and usages, so we do not call this general guidance 'official' and readers should not expect it to be determinative in case of a dispute.

The Incoterms® rules Q&As are organized into three categories, starting with questions on the Incoterms® 2010 rules within each category, followed by historical questions on the Incoterms 1990 rules:

1. General, which includes questions relating to more than one Incoterms® rule where at least one of the asked-about rules is from the multimodal category and at least one from the maritime category;

2. Multimodal, dealing exclusively with the Incoterms® rules for use with any mode or modes of transport; and

3. Maritime, dealing exclusively with the Incoterms® rules for use with sea or inland waterway transport.

Readers are encouraged to supplement their learning on the rules by consulting the full text of *Incoterms® 2010*, at Annex 4, and the *ICC Guide to Incoterms® 2010*, available at the ICC Business Bookstore at: http://www.iccbooks.com/Product/ProductInfo.aspx?id=657

Why has ICC included old questions and answers relating to the Incoterms 1990 rules?

In 1998, ICC published a volume of questions and expert ICC answers relating to the then-current version of the Incoterms® rules, *Incoterms 1990*. We have decided to retain these older questions and answers here for several reasons:

- Much of the thinking behind the Incoterms® rules remains pertinent from one revision to the next; and
- Many readers will find it interesting to have a view onto the evolution of the rules themselves and, in some cases, their interpretation.

We recommend that you read through the Q&As for both *Incoterms® 2010* and *Incoterms 1990*, as there is valuable general information included in the older answers that will doubtless enrich your understanding of the landscape in which the Incoterms® rules operate. Be careful, though, to remember when reading the older materials that (i) some of the rules that existed in earlier versions of the Incoterms® rules no longer exist, and (ii) other conditions in the international trading arena may have evolved in the years since the older materials were written.

Who provided the guidance on the Incoterms® 2010 rules questions on behalf of ICC?

The Incoterms® rules are supervised by an international committee of trade professionals and lawyers, known as the ICC Commission on Commercial Law and Practice. This Commission designated an international Drafting Group to prepare the Incoterms® 2010 rules, which agreed – along with an Incoterms® rules expert who serves as one of the Commission Co-Chairs – to provide their expert thinking on questions received by ICC on the operation and interpretation of the Incoterms® 2010 rules.

The historical answers relating to *Incoterms 1990* were drafted by a dedicated Panel of Incoterms® Experts.

INCOTERMS® 2010 GENERAL QUESTIONS

2010 Question 1

Use of ® trademark symbol and letters of credit

Letters of credit citing *Incoterms® 2010* with the circled R trademark indicator may cause unintended discrepancies for beneficiaries unable to do likewise in their documents (as with typewriters).

Guidance from ICC experts

The absence of the ® trademark symbol in a citation to any version of the Incoterms rules, including *Incoterms® 2010*, should not render a document discrepant with a letter of credit that includes the ® trademark symbol in its citation to the Incoterms® rules.

2010 Question 2

'Terminal handling charges'

Who pays for THC (terminal handling charges) under the new Incoterms® 2010 rules?

Guidance from ICC experts

- Allocation of costs between the buyer and seller under the rules are set out in articles A6/B6, which in the new rules have been made clearer and in some cases clarify the relation between the contract of sale and the contract of carriage.

- 'Terminal handling charges' is a broad category and each charge being considered needs to be analyzed to see whether it occurred before or after delivery under article A4 of the relevant Incoterms® rule, and whether it relates to an obligation treated specifically in the rules, as, for example, an import or export clearance charge, obligations with respect to which are set out in articles A2/B2.

2010 Question 3

Costs of security charges

There are questions regarding who bears costs for 'security charges' (A2/B2 and A10/B10) under the Incoterms® 2010 rules. Since 1 January 2011, for example, all deliveries coming into the European Common Market are subject to an ENS-filing to be done 24 hours before loading the ship. We observe that carriers deal with this issue differently in terms of payment. Since there are a great number of legal reporting regulations (e.g. in the field of hazardous materials, veterinarian, port authorities), these costs are in some cases added to the usual sea freight and the fees are invoiced in accordance with sea freight (either prepaid or collect). Other carriers (mainly Asian) treat the ENS fees as purely prepaid costs to be covered by the shipper.

Independent of this example, different points of view to this question are represented in practice, such as how to account the current security fees and whether or not they should be treated as import or export formalities.

While the Incoterms® rules are clauses to be used in sales contracts, within shipping company and freight contracts, they are treated as 'francatur-clauses' with the result that the carrier making reference to Incoterms clauses in contracts for carriage charges the costs either to the seller (shipper) or the buyer (consignee). Therefore, in our opinion, it is very important that clear statements should be made.

We think it necessary that a common practice should be determined and would be grateful if you could answer some of our questions:

- Who should according to the Incoterms® 2010 rules bear the costs for safety precautions for the transport of goods? Should this always be the buyer?

- Have you heard of similar issues within other economic sectors?

Guidance from ICC experts

- At the time of preparing Incoterms® 2010 the drafting group reviewed the various cargo security arrangements around the world. It became evident that although cargo security is a much more important issue than it was in 2000, there was no consistent global practice. Given the lack of consistent global practice, the drafting group was reluctant to impose change. Therefore articles A2/B2 and A10/B10 were changed but only to a limited extent.

- The allocation of costs for security will vary between seller and buyer depending on the Incoterms rule chosen – for example DAT will be different to FCA.

- Note the Incoterms rules relate to the sale of goods contract between buyer and seller, and NOT to the relationship with the carrier.

- Under FCA then (assuming delivery point is not the seller's premises):

  ‣ The seller is responsible for clearing export, but not import, formalities. Therefore, a seller in Japan is not responsible for an ENS filing such as is required for import.

INCOTERMS® 2010 GENERAL QUESTIONS

▸ However, under A10/B10 the seller must provide the buyer with documents or information required by the buyer to complete the ENS filing at the buyer's risk and expense.

▸ Where safety precautions are required for transport after the delivery point, then they are the buyer's responsibility UNLESS it is a mandatory requirement to allow the goods to be exported (but note that the seller must in any event appropriately package the goods under article A9). Under A10, the seller is responsible for providing information and data.

■ For example, for DAP (buyer's premises Paris), where the seller is based outside the European Community (EC) and the first point of import into the EC is in France:

▸ The ENS filing is an import requirement for the EC. Under DAP the seller is not responsible for clearing import requirements. Therefore, if the seller is based outside of the EC, the seller is not responsible for ensuring the ENS filing is completed.

▸ However, the ENS filing is completed by the ocean carrier. In this example the seller will have contracted with the ocean carrier, as the seller is responsible for transportation to the Paris destination. Therefore, the carriage contract will require that the seller provide the information needed for the ENS filing and the carrier may charge the seller for supplying it.

▸ The buyer is obliged to provide the information needed for the seller to provide to the ocean carrier for the ENS filing. This is because the buyer is obliged to clear import requirements under B2.

▸ As ENS filing is an import obligation, the buyer is obliged to reimburse the seller for the cost of ENS filing.

2010 Question 4 Export clearance 'applicable' in F-family of rules?

A seller under one of the Incoterms® 2010 rules in the F-family (FCA, FAS or FOB) delivers goods in seller's own country, but the goods are destined post-delivery for another country. The buyer arranges and pays for carriage and risk for the goods has already passed to buyer at delivery in seller's country.

It is not clear from the language of the Incoterms® 2010 rules that in such a situation export clearance is 'applicable' for the seller under article A2. If it is 'applicable', why? If not, then isn't the requirement on the seller even lower than under article A2 in EXW, where seller is required at least to provide assistance to the buyer for export of the goods?

Guidance from ICC experts

If the goods are destined for another country, then export clearance is applicable and the seller needs to do it. The words 'where applicable' are used to denote that Incoterms® 2010 can be used in an entirely domestic setting as well. In EXW, the seller only needs to provide assistance for export clearance but is not responsible for it.

2010 Question 5 — Non-freight costs during transit in C-family of rules

Under Incoterms® 2010 rules CPT, CIP, CFR and CIF, the seller must contract on usual terms at its own expense for the carriage of the goods to the named place or port of destination. After delivery at the place or port of departure, the buyer bears all risks for the goods (article B5) and must pay all costs and charges relating to the goods while in transit until their arrival at the place or port of destination, unless such costs and charges were for the seller's account under the contract of carriage (article B6(b)).

What costs would realistically arise during transit not related to the freight being paid by seller? It seems these would arise only in extraordinary cases. Would the buyer have to pay for things like an increase in rates, charges connected with extra deviation, or a change of rotation?

Guidance from ICC experts

- Under article A6(b) of the C-terms, seller must pay for freight and other costs relating to obtaining a contract of carriage. In any case, if the freight-included pricing of the goods offered by the seller is accepted by the buyer and the sale contract is enacted between the parties on such terms, then the seller should bear any subsequent increases in the freight tariffs.

- In the sense of article B6 under C-terms, the transfer of risk also determines the division of costs. If something occurs as a result of contingencies after shipment, such as stranding, collision, strikes, governmental commands, or bad weather conditions, or any other unanticipated costs charged by the carrier as a result of these contingencies, the unanticipated costs mentioned will be for the account of the buyer (unless specified as for the seller's account in the contract of carriage).

2010 Question 6 — Stowage of full container loads

Why are full-container-load sellers not responsible for container stowage as part of their obligation to load the collecting vehicle?

Guidance from ICC experts:

- When establishing the interpretation of the word 'packaging' as it is used in article A9 of each of the Incoterms® 2010 rules, the Drafting Group decided to limit its meaning to (i) the packaging of the goods to comply with any requirements under the contract of sale, and (ii) the packaging of the goods so that they are fit for transportation.

- The Incoterms® 2010 rules are silent on the stowage of containers including the performance of the actual task as well as the costs connected therewith. Under transport law, containers may be treated differently based on whose containers they are and whether full container loads (FCL) or less than full container loads (LCL) are concerned and this may be reflected in the transport conditions to which some Incoterms® 2010 rules yield themselves when it comes to the delivery under the contract of sale. Parties wishing to make the seller unequivocally responsible for the stowage of containers specify this in the contract of sale.

- The Incoterms® 2010 rules are intended for use with all types of goods and forms of transport. There is no consistent market practice on or allocation of responsibility for stowage across all types of goods, all forms of transport and in all parts of the world.

2010 Question 7 — Incoterms® rules not designed to resolve accounting issues such as revenue recognition

We have a question on revenue recognition. For most sales of tangible goods, Generally Accepted Accounting Principles (GAAP) require at a minimum that ownership pass from the seller and that the seller's risk for the condition of the goods end. This is a major concern for companies in the United States, particularly for publicly traded corporations under pressure to recognize revenue at the earliest moment. While presently primarily a US issue, GAAP-like rules are starting to appear internationally as International Financial

Reporting Standards (IFRS), and users of the Incoterms® 2010 rules are also starting to raise questions on expense recognition. How are the Incoterms® 2010 rules related to revenue recognition?

Guidance from ICC experts:

- The Incoterms® rules are not designed to resolve accounting issues and do not speak to ownership transfer. Risk transfer occurs when goods are delivered, which is covered in article A4 of each of the Incoterms® 2010 rules. For contracts *silent* about when ownership transfer takes place, and covered by the law of a US common law state, UCC Part 2-401 makes delivery the default transfer mechanism. Other laws (e.g., the UN Convention on Contracts for the International Sale of Goods (CISG) or, under English law, the Sale of Goods Act 1979) may differ, as well as treatment of contracts that aren't silent on transfer of ownership.

- It is essential in the contract to make it clear when ownership passes from the seller to the buyer.

- Note that assessing the accounting treatment of ownership of goods will be influenced by who is legally in control of the goods, who takes legal risk and who has legal ownership, but may take account of other factors.

2010 Question 8: Buyer faced with multiple charges from carrier under C-family of rules

Two related questions:

1. Many buyers that import goods from Asian countries under Incoterms® 2010 rules CFR and CIF have discovered that as consignees they are frequently requested by the carriers to pay substantial additional charges (in some cases comparable to the total freight cost when buying under FCA). These numerous additional charges may include dues that some Asian ports levy on export shipments, but may also include more opaque charges such as 'China additional'. The question arises as to which charges carriers are entitled to claim from the consignee under the contract of sale when freight is indicated to be prepaid in line with the practice under CFR and CIF, and what is the buyer's position in relation to the carrier and the seller in situations where apparently superfluous charges are levied against the buyer by the carrier? The question does not concern Terminal Handling Charges (THC) at the port of destination.

INCOTERMS® 2010 GENERAL QUESTIONS

2. The C-family of rules allocates costs under article A6 as follows:

> The seller must pay [...] b) the freight and all other costs resulting from A3 a), including the costs of loading the goods [on board] and any charges for unloading at the [place of destination] [agreed port of discharge] that were for the seller's account under the contract of carriage; [...]

Demurrage, detention, congestion surcharges, peak season surcharge, winter surcharge, ... are these 'other costs' invoiced by the carrier under the contract of carriage and thus due by the contracting party to the contract of carriage (the shipper = the seller). Are these costs under the contract of sale for the account of the C-seller or the C-buyer?

Guidance from ICC experts:

- The main rule under CFR and CIF as well as under CPT and CIP is that the seller must contract on 'usual terms' at its own expense for the carriage of the goods to the named port (CFR and CIF) or place (CPT and CIP) of destination.

- Except for the change to state that unloading costs that were for the seller's account under the contract of carriage are for the seller, no other change has been made to the C-family in the Incoterms® 2010 rules on allocation of costs.

- What constitutes 'usual terms' will vary to reflect current market practice.

- However, it is currently well established under the C-family of rules that the buyer is expected to pay only costs that are unforeseen, such as those arising from stranding, collision, strikes, governmental commands, or bad weather conditions. Outside such clear cases, it is sometimes difficult to verify which costs are in accordance with usual transport terms. For instance, is the carrier entitled to charge the consignee for notification of arrival? When only unforeseen costs fall on the buyer, the question arises: By whom are such costs unforeseen, the seller or the carrier?

It can be generally stated that the freight prepaid by the seller should include all ordinary transport costs until the destination including the costs of handling, storage, and transhipment... The seller is obliged to contract for carriage by a usual route in a vessel of the type normally used for the type of goods sold. As much as it is evident that the vessel must be fit to carry the goods to the destination safely, the seller must contract with a carrier who is capable of anticipating ordinary cost items during the transportation and including them in the prepaid freight. Later currency adjustments in the freight are for the seller.

- Therefore, a buyer faced with port export levies and 'China additional' should consider challenging these costs.

- A buyer should also seek to specify in the contract of sale which specific costs will be borne by the seller and which costs by the buyer to avoid dispute.

- Buyers should be wary of using the C family of rules – they are complex and should be used only where the buyer has a full understanding of them.

2010 Question 9 Incoterms® 2010 rules do not address pipeline transactions

Do the Incoterms® 2010 rules cater for materials transported by pipeline, such as oil and gas?

Guidance from ICC experts:

While developing the Incoterms® 2010 rules, ICC considered addressing pipeline transactions but decided not to for several reasons.

1. Frequently, the product shipped is not the product actually received. Instead, a specified product is placed into the pipeline at the seller's end, and a fungible product is withdrawn at the buyer's end.

2. There are already numerous trade practices that address this situation.

2010 Question 10 Containers going by sea under C-family of rules

In containerized shipments going by sea, what is the difference between the maritime Incoterms® 2010 rules CFR/CIF and the corresponding multimodal rules CPT/CIP with respect to the:

- Article A4 delivery obligation, and
- Article A8 documentary obligation?

Guidance from ICC experts:

- While delivery under CFR and CIF must be made on board the vessel at the port of shipment, under CPT and CIP the goods must be handed over to the carrier. Therefore, the delivery obligation is no longer related to the vessel, but to the carrier. When parties intend to use several carriers and do not agree on a specific point of delivery in their sales contract, under CPT and CIP the seller fulfils its delivery obligation when the goods have been delivered to the first carrier. Under CIF and CFR, the delivery is not completed until the goods have been placed on board a vessel at the port of shipment. Therefore, the principle of delivery to the first carrier cannot be applied under CFR and CIF, unless the carriage to the port of shipment is also performed by sea or inland waterway transport. The important difference occurs between CPT/CIP and CFR/CIF in this respect.

- In general, 'usual transport document' in article A8 would refer to the receipt of the carrier to whom the goods are handed. In maritime carriage, negotiable bills of lading are traditionally used. However, other documents such as liner waybills and cargo quay receipts are also used. Parties seeking to avoid the legal uncertainty of maritime transport documents will not find not many uniform rules on this matter. They may refer to the Uniform Rules for Sea Waybills adopted by Comité Maritime International (CMI) in June 1990.

2010 Question 11 — Goods damaged prior to arrival at departure terminal under C-family of rules

A C-seller has used an independent carrier ('first carrier') to bring the goods to the terminal from which the ship/plane will leave to the agreed place of destination (CMR seller's premises → departure terminal). The goods are damaged prior to arrival at the departure terminal. There will be no shipment from the terminal to the agreed place of destination (no bill of lading or air waybill to the agreed place of departure). Is the C-seller in breach?

- For non-delivery (Article A4)? or
- For not providing a delivery document (Article A8)?

Guidance from ICC experts:

- If the CPT or CIP Incoterms® 2010 rule were chosen, then the delivery obligation would not be breached, since the delivery would be fulfilled by handing over the goods to the first carrier. However, if CFR or CIF were chosen, then the seller would breach its delivery obligation by not delivering the goods to the port of shipment and not placing the goods on board the vessel.

- In the first case (CPT/CIP), the receipt document obtained from the first carrier, to whom the goods are handed over, serves as the usual transport document under article A8. Therefore, the required delivery document would have been provided and there would be no breach in this respect. In the latter case (CFR/CIF), the seller would be in breach since it would not be in a position to provide the sufficient maritime delivery document.

2010 Question 12 Global insurance policy

When a seller has concluded a global transport insurance policy (police d'abonnement), is it selling under CIF/CIP or DAP/DDP?

Guidance from ICC experts:

CIF and CIP require the seller to obtain at its own expense cargo insurance complying at least with the minimum cover as provided by Clauses (C) of the Institute Cargo Clauses (LMA/IUA), contracted with underwriters or an insurance company of good repute. The insurance should entitle the buyer, or *any other person having an insurable interest in the goods, to claim directly from the insurer*. Moreover, the insurance shall cover, at a minimum, the price provided in the contract plus ten per cent (110%). Any other insurance concluded by the seller, which does not have these minimum qualifications, shall not fulfill the seller's insurance obligation under CIP/CIF article A3(b).

Therefore, if the seller concludes a global transport insurance policy, such policy would not fulfil the requirements of the CIF/CIP rules since it does not normally automatically allow the buyer to claim directly from the insurer – the seller would normally have to enter into special arrangements with the insurer. Otherwise, it would be preferential for the buyer to choose the DAP or DDP rules, since the seller must bear all risks of loss or damage to the goods until they are delivered at the place of destination.

2010 Question 13 Mandatory local law overriding Incoterms® 2010 rules

In the Introduction of the Incoterms® 2010 book, it is provided that, '…parties should be aware that mandatory local law may override any aspect of the sale contract, including the chosen Incoterms rule.' We understand that local law may override terms of the sale contract that are not covered by the Incoterms® 2010 rules (such as remedies for breach, payment terms, marking requirements, etc.), but how does local law override the agreed Incoterms® rule?

INCOTERMS® 2010 GENERAL QUESTIONS

Guidance from ICC experts:

- Incorporating an Incoterms® rule into a contract is tantamount to drafting the relevant clauses of the chosen Incoterms® rule in that contract – the language of the chosen Incoterms® rule becomes part of the contract. So mandatory local law may override (theoretically) any provisions of a contract, including any that happen to have been incorporated from the book, Incoterms® 2010, or other, earlier version of the rules.

- An example would be the way the United States addresses export clearance. Article A2 of each Incoterms® rule except EXW tasks this to the seller. United States Foreign Trade Regulations state that exports must be reported by the freight forwarder whenever it is appointed by the buyer, as is usual with F-group Incoterms® rules. (As an exception, the buyer may appoint another party to report, but again this would be done on behalf of the buyer.)

2010 Question 14 'Transport documents' in the Incoterms® 2010 rules:

What exactly do the words 'transport document[s]' refer to in the Incoterms® 2010 rules? Some sources on the subject of freight and forwarding define these words to mean all documents used in transport activity, but the meaning of 'transport document' in the Incoterms® rules seems to be somewhat more limited, perhaps related to the legal function or validity of certain types of documents.

Guidance from ICC experts:

- *Incoterms® 2010* does not contain a general definition of a transport document. The term 'transport document' is generally used in Articles A8 and B8 of the C-terms, which require the seller to provide the buyer with the usual transport document(s) for the transport that the seller has contracted. The obligations as to whether the seller has to provide a negotiable or non-negotiable transport document, or any transport document, depend on the Incoterms® rules used, on the practice in the trade and on the parties' agreement. Moreover, under the F-family of rules, the seller must assist the buyer in obtaining a transport document. Should the seller exceptionally contract for carriage on usual terms at the buyer's risk and expense, it is incumbent upon the seller to provide a transport document under equivalent principles, as in the C-family of rules. In all other situations, the more generic term 'delivery document' is used in Article A8. A ´delivery document´ must be a transport document under the C rules and, in other Incoterms® rules, it can be a transport document or other document such as a receipt, depending on the circumstances.

- A usual transport document follows usually from the relevant transport legislation and from the practice of the trade. Thus, bills of lading are used in maritime transport when goods are sold in transit. The characteristics of the bill of lading are defined by both legislation and practice. Similarly, for land, rail and air transport, both legislation and practice define what usual transport documents are in each case. Generally speaking, transport documents represent receipts and proof that the goods are taken in the charge of the carrier and they evidence the contract of carriage by containing or referring to the transport conditions. Moreover, negotiable transport documents (bills of lading) allow the goods to be sold in transit by the delivery and endorsement of the bill. For road, rail and air transport, usual transport documents have functions in respect of right of control. Documents other than those with the above functions may also be used in the context of carriage of goods, such as mate's receipts, but these are not the transport documents envisaged in the Incoterms® 2010 rules.

2010 Question 15: 'Usual proof of delivery' v. 'usual transport document' in FCA, FAS and FOB

In article A8 of the Incoterms® 2010 F category of rules (FCA, FAS and FOB), the seller must provide the buyer with 'usual proof that the goods have been delivered', but in the C rules they may have to provide the buyer with the 'usual transport document[s]'. Why is the 'usual proof that the goods have been delivered' not considered to be the same as the 'usual transport document[s]'? Why use different formulations?

Guidance from ICC experts:

- The reason for different formulations is that the seller and the buyer have different tasks under FCA, FAS and FOB as opposed to CPT, CIP, CFR and CIF when it comes to making contracts of carriage.

- Under FCA, FAS and FOB, the normal situation is that the buyer contracts for carriage, and the transport document is issued to the buyer. The seller has to render assistance for the buyer in obtaining a transport document, but the seller needs to prove

INCOTERMS® 2010 GENERAL QUESTIONS

only that goods are delivered to the carrier or (in FCA) to a person named by the buyer.

- When it comes to the C-family of rules, the seller must contract for transport and provide the buyer with (a) usual transport document(s) because the seller must, in addition to providing proof that the goods are delivered to the carrier, give the buyer the possibility to exercise rights on the basis of the contract of carriage against the carrier as evidenced by the transport document. In case of negotiable transport documents, the seller also transfers the indirect possession of the goods by the transfer of the bill of lading.

2010 Question 16 — Obligation v. custom for transport documents in C-family of rules

Why in article A8 of the Incoterms® 2010 rules CIP and CPT does the seller have to provide transport documents only if it is customary or if the buyer so requests, while in CFR and CIF the seller must in every case provide the buyer with transport documents? The functions of all the C-rules seem to be generally the same regardless of which means of transport are used, so why is this provision different for the rules used for any mode or modes of transport (CPT, CIP) and those used only for sea and inland waterway transport (CFR, CIF)?

Guidance from ICC experts:

- The difference between CPT and CIP on the one hand and CFR and CIF on the other lies in the nature of the transport documents used in traditional maritime transport, where CFR and CIF are used, and those in the other modes of transport including multimodal transport.

- Under CFR and CIF, the seller must deliver the goods on board a vessel, and the only document that traditionally evidences this is an on board bill of lading. Moreover, the document must enable the buyer to sell the goods in transit. Since selling goods in transit is possible only by either using a bill of lading or by notification to the carrier (this refers to electronic platforms replicating the use of bills of lading) one cannot normally dispense with a transport document. Therefore, both tradition and the required functions of a transport document require that the seller provide the buyer with one.

- However, when it comes to CPT and CIP, the presumption is a non-negotiable transport document. In some practices, transport documents are as a rule not issued at all. Transport laws require carriers to issue transport documents on request, and should the buyer be in need of a transport document, the buyer may ask the seller to provide one, and the seller may the convey the request to the carrier.

- The difference between the two approaches described above is largely semantic, since if the practice is not to issue transport documents, then there is no usual transport document either.

INCOTERMS® 1990 GENERAL QUESTIONS

1990 Question 1

Customs not recognizing the Incoterms® rules

Why do certain customs bodies still not accept the Incoterms® rules?

Answer of the Panel of Incoterms® Experts:

This is purely a matter of lack of knowledge by customs bodies and officers. ICC has contacted the World Customs Organization as well as individual customs bodies, but parties having difficulty in a particular case may either formulate a FOB or CIF price to satisfy the authorities, or simply direct the authorities to the ICC to verify the authenticity of the Incoterms® rules.

1990 Editor's notes and observations[2]:

Is it possible for customs to 'reject' certain Incoterms® rules?

It is common for customs authorities to require that the value of goods exported or imported be declared as having either an 'FOB' or 'CIF' value. The purpose of this is to standardize assessment of customs duties, which obviously must be assessed on some declared value or price. If customs authorities did not have a standard practice, this could leave open the question – should duty be assessed on the value of the goods including or excluding international transport?

However, the requirement by customs authorities that customs declarations be either in FOB or CIF does *NOT* mean that traders dealing with the country in question are obliged to enter only into contracts on these terms – rather, it means that customs authorities must be given an FOB or CIF value for the purposes of calculating duties and any other official purposes. Practically, this means that traders who have used in their contracts terms other than FOB or CIF will be forced to 'translate' their contract into the required FOB or CIF value. This should not be difficult.

---

2 The Editor's notes and observations on the 1990 Incoterms® Questions were drafted by Guillermo C. Jiménez, who edited the 1998 publication, 'Incoterms Q&A – Incoterms 1990 Questions and Answers'. While the answer of the Panel of Incoterms Experts was considered at the time to be an authoritative one issued on behalf of the ICC, the Editor's view here was a personal one intended primarily to provide background explanation and provocative commentary, and therefore did not necessarily reflect the views of the Working Party or the ICC.

1990 Question 2
Should industry standard terms refer to the Incoterms® rules?

Is it correct to inform members of a trade association to reject the Incoterms® rules and reject their incorporation into standard contracts on the grounds that Incoterms could 'conflict with the existing clauses of contracts and the applicable law under which these are governed'?

Facts:

At a conference of the Timber Trade Federation, a suggestion was put forward by the Finnish delegation that the Federation's standard contracts incorporate the Incoterms® rules. The Federation rejected the request on the grounds that such an incorporation would conflict with existing contracts and with applicable law. The Federation went on to state that 'it is important that members reject these terms whenever there is an attempt to include them in contracts'.

Answer of the Panel of Incoterms® Experts:

The following questions are raised by the question from the ICC Finnish Delegation (the questions are followed by our brief answers):

1. Are the Incoterms® rules to be recommended by the ICC to the Timber Trade Federation?

Answer: Yes

2. Is there any absolute legal impediment to the use of the Incoterms® rules in standard contracts of the Timber Trade Federation?

Answer: No

3. Can the use of an Incoterms® rule alter the parties' legal rights or responsibilities?

Answer: Yes

Analysis:

1. Are the Incoterms® rules to be recommended to the Timber Trade Federation? Yes.

In order to answer this question, one has to understand the benefits of the use of the Incoterms® rules. The Incoterms® rules are standardized international trade terms, providing benefits of speed, clarity and predictability in international contracting. Incoterms 1990 are used throughout the world and have been endorsed by the United Nations Commission on International Trade Law (UNCITRAL). In the drafting of the 1980 Vienna Convention on the International Sale of

Goods, UNCITRAL concluded that no attempt to provide a uniform legal interpretation of trade terms should be made, given the prevalence of trade custom as evidenced by the widespread international use of the Incoterms® rules.

The benefits of standards are not always easy to quantify, but the fact that the Incoterms® rules, which have been translated into more than 25 languages, are used by such a broad base of international traders is the perhaps the most concrete argument in their favour. The Incoterms® rules are the most widely-distributed of the International Chamber of Commerce (ICC) publications. Ultimately, the decision of a company or organization to deal on the basis of the Incoterms® rules is equivalent to a message to the international community in support of adherence to common, world-wide standards instead of insistence on national standards.

Weighing both the costs and potential benefits of adoption of the Incoterms® rules in their standard form contracts, the ICC can only encourage the Timber Trade Federation to give serious consideration to the important potential benefits offered by the Incoterms® rules.

2. Is there any absolute legal impediment to the use of the Incoterms® rules in standard contracts of the Timber Trade Federation? No.

The following points must be made here:

i) The Incoterms 1990 rules do not determine applicable law, nor do the Incoterms® rules have any impact on the parties' choice of applicable law. The Incoterms® rules are neutral as to the law that applies to a contract.

ii) Parties' contractual provisions will always prevail over the Incoterms® rules in the event of a conflict. This reduces the significance of any possible conflict between the Incoterms® rules and the rest of the contract. Moreover, parties can contractually stipulate that in the event of a conflict between national law and the Incoterms® rules, the applicable national law will prevail.

iii) The choice of the Incoterms® rules for standard contracts will not have a direct legal impact on those contracts already concluded.

3. Can the use of an Incoterms® rule alter the parties' legal rights or responsibilities? Yes.

Despite the analysis made above in 2., it is nonetheless true that choosing the Incoterms® rules can change things. Thus, for example, we may ask ourselves, what will happen if, having decided to incorporate one of the Incoterms 1990 rules into a contract, it then transpires that application of the substantive law will lead to a different result than that envisaged by the chosen Incoterms® rule? Generally, in cases of this type of conflict, the Incoterms® rule will prevail unless the particular national rule is judged mandatory. Thus, the choice of an Incoterms® rule can indeed alter the position of the parties. However, as stated above, it is clearly possible to stipulate that in the event of conflict between the Incoterms® rules and national law, that national law will prevail. Clearly, traders should be well-informed on any differences between their national law and the Incoterms® rules when considering adoption of the Incoterms® rules.

1990 Editor's notes and observations:

The Incoterms® rules – global standards for the common good?

The Incoterms® rules, like all other global standards, challenge individuals and firms to move beyond allegiance to national interests in the pursuit of a greater global good. Therefore, as a general principle, the ICC encourages sectoral, regional, national or proprietary groups to abandon their reliance on trade standards other than the Incoterms® rules.

This basic principle raises the question: is it not possible, since the Incoterms® rules are said by the ICC to represent a very *general* level of codification, that *specific* industries or particular transactions will call for more precise sets of definitions than those provided by the Incoterms® rules? What of the common practice, for example, of including in so-called 'General Terms and Conditions' or model forms a particular, industry-specific or company-specific definition of C.I.F.?

The ICC's is that parties should be encouraged to abandon any particular interests which cause them to deviate from the Incoterms® rules. Although minor modifications or additions do not do injury to the basic harmonization value of the Incoterms® rules, their value is lost when parties depart entirely from the Incoterms® rules, such as by specifying a purely tailor-made definition of a particular term.

Several arguments can be put forth in favour of moving to a single, global standard:

INCOTERMS® 1990 GENERAL QUESTIONS

1. The Incoterms® rules carefully balance the interests of buyer and seller according to time-tested practice and logic; definitions which vary the basic structure of the Incoterms® rules may not incorporate the same emphasis on balance and neutrality;

2. Standardization in international trade generates savings related to:

   a. reduced misunderstanding,
   b. more efficient education,
   c. more efficient communication,
   d. more effective dispute-resolution.

(These savings are not available when particular sectors or companies seek to gain a contractual advantage by departing from the Incoterms® rules principles);

3. In those countries in which certain industry sectors depart from the Incoterms® rules, a risk of misunderstanding will arise with trading partners, because of the inconsistency between industry standard terms and the Incoterms® rules.

Eloquent support for the ICC position is provided in the following text from Ray Battersby, the UK SITPRO delegate to the Incoterms® Working Party (excerpted from his article on the Incoterms® rules and the Single Market in *Incoterms in Practice*, ICC Publication No. 505):

❝ The inclusion of Incoterms as part of the mandatory information that has to be supplied to national administrations through Intrastat Supplementary Declarations has had the positive effect of increasing EU traders' general awareness of Incoterms' existence. In the long term, this can only be of benefit to the role that Incoterms can play in providing a level playing field for international trade. The more widely Incoterms are used, the easier it becomes for sellers and buyers to treat their international and national sales on the same basis, thus achieving the ultimate goal of transparency of delivery. The continuing growth of international trade and its importance to the wealth of individual nations provides an ideal opportunity for Incoterms to be used as an effective tool for encouraging best business practice between sellers and users. ❞

The elaboration of an international standard has proven to be a fundamental issue in modern trade. The UNECE, in the preamble of the Recommendation No. 5 (reproduced hereafter) has officially recognized the use of the Incoterms® rules as the appropriate standard tool responding to the need for harmonization, regardless of the trade sector concerned.

1990 Question 3: The Incoterms® rules as 'Payment terms' – COD/CAD

Do the Incoterms® rules also include definitions of payment terms, such as COD (cash on delivery), CAD (cash against documents), etc.?

Answer of the Panel of Incoterms® Experts:

It is incorrect to call the Incoterms® rules payment terms, and the Incoterms® rules do not define COD or CAD terms. The Incoterms® rules only specify under section B1 that the buyer must pay the price as provided in the contract of sale.

1990 Editor's notes and observations:

The Incoterms® rules and payment – what connection?

Although a terse export offer might specify a given monetary amount in association with an Incoterms® rule (e.g., '$100/ton FOB Liverpool Incoterms 1990'), this should not mislead traders into thinking that the Incoterms® rules are 'payment terms'.

There is an obvious and clear link between the contract price and the chosen Incoterms® rule. For example, an FOB price, which does not include the cost of international freight, will always be cheaper than the CIF price, simply because the FOB price does not include ocean freight. But when traders refer to 'payment terms' or 'payment conditions', they are generally referring to the various options or modes for performance of the buyer's payment obligation, i.e., payment by cheque, bank draft, electronic transfer or documentary credit, etc.

If not payment or shipping terms, what kind of 'terms' are the Incoterms® rules?

The Incoterms® rules deal principally with the costs and risks of transporting the goods from seller to buyer; how the price is paid is a distinct issue. It would nonetheless be an oversimplification to call the Incoterms® rules 'transport terms' or 'delivery terms', because they deal with more than just transport and delivery – they also deal with the allocation of risk, customs responsibilities, and insurance. Despite this, Incoterms are commonly referred to as 'delivery terms', 'consignment terms', or 'sales terms', which is regrettable because they focus exclusively on transport or pricing responsibilities.

INCOTERMS® 1990 GENERAL QUESTIONS

The ICC prefers to call the Incoterms® rules 'trade terms', because they govern an essential bundle of rights and obligations that are at the heart of the export trade transaction.

Since the Incoterms® rules are all represented by three-letter codes, many inexperienced traders leap to the assumption that any three-letter code used in international trade must be an Incoterms® rule. There are hundreds of abbreviations that could be confused with the Incoterms® rules in this fashion. Fortunately, there are only 13 currently valid Incoterms® rules, and for complete clarity it is preferable that the three-letter Incoterms® rule abbreviation be combined with a reference to *Incoterms 1990* (or date of current version).

1990 Question 4: The Incoterms® rules and the European Single Market

What changes in the Incoterms® rules use may be occasioned by the arrival of the European Single Market on 1 January 1993?

Answer of the Panel of Incoterms® Experts:

There does not yet appear to be a need for specific Incoterms® rules adapted for the Single Market. *Incoterms 1990* remain applicable. However, certain of the sections in the Incoterms® rules, notably those dealing with customs clearance, have become less useful or inapplicable within the European Single Market. In particular, the term DDU will no longer be of particular utility after 1997 because of the move to an origin-based VAT instead of the currently destination-based system. Then, the term DDP would have to be preferred. The word 'Duty' in DDU and DDP should be interpreted as including not only duties but also taxes, official charges and customs clearance, and in any event the term 'duty' here only applies if in fact there are any duties.

Analysis:

The Incoterms® rules deal with several other important issues aside from customs obligations, such as transfer of risk and allocation of costs, and therefore should remain useful even within customs-free trade areas such as the European Single Market.

1990 Editor's notes and observations:

The question is an important one, not only because Europe is one of the world's leading trading centers, but also because the European drive to customs-free union has been echoed in a similar trend in other parts of the

world, notably Mercosur (bringing together Brazil, Uruguay and Argentina).

The response of the Panel of Incoterms® Experts should be understood in the context of its timing: the answer was given *before* the extension of the delay for establishing an origin-based VAT system. Although the dates of the European transition period are no longer of interest, the principles stated in the response of the Panel remain correct and of particular interest.

Essentially, the Incoterms® rules are useful whenever one can ascribe an 'international' aspect to a particular transaction, and even in purely domestic cases, regardless of the abolition of customs-unions. The Incoterms® rules deal with the crucial issues of transfer of risk and division of transport costs between seller and buyer. These issues are standardized in international practice by the Incoterms® rules. Even if two countries were to completely fuse their legal systems, the Incoterms® rules might well remain useful as a standard so as not to put domestic traders at a disadvantage vis-à-vis foreign exporters adhering to the Incoterms® rules' global standard.

This is the view expressed by one of the Incoterms® Panel Experts, Ray Battersby of SITPRO, in his article, 'Incoterms and the Single Market', printed in the ICC's *Incoterms in Practice* (ICC Publication No. 505):

❝ [T]he abolition of customs formalities at internal frontiers does not exempt sellers and buyers from licensing or official authorization requirements for strategic goods (which still need to be accompanied by official documentation) or other official authorization requirements for strategic goods (which still need to be accompanied by official documentation) and other goods which are purchased from non-EU member states... [EU] sellers and buyers should thus be aware that there are a number of areas in which Single Market transactions should not be treated on entirely the same basis as domestic sales. Goods subject to excise controls also fall within the category of goods not in free circulation. ❞

This still leaves the following potentially awkward questions: in customs-free zones, which Incoterms® rule is preferable, DDU or DDP? And why do these terms retain the word 'duty', even for use in contexts where no duty could be assessed?

INCOTERMS® 1990 GENERAL QUESTIONS

1990 Question 5

Bonded goods and bail cover costs

Does the arrival of the European Single Market have any impact on the allocation of bail cover costs for goods subject to excise tax?

Answer of the Panel of Incoterms® Experts:

This in not precisely an Incoterms® rule question, but rather a tax question.

Analysis:

Bail cover has previously been included in the cost of the T2 transport document. After 1 January 1993, the carriage of goods subject to excise tax is ruled by EEC decision 92/12 which states that these goods can be stored and sent only by an authorized bonder or licensed operator who must be guaranteed by a bail cover. Application of the new regime will vary depending on national fiscal rules. Fiscal and taxation rules are not covered by Incoterms. However, in the case where a fiscal matter is connected with a document, Incoterms will determine who is responsible for and in charge of the said document according to sections A2 and B2 or A10 and B10. Consequently, when the bond is linked with a document, the payment for the cost of the bond will be dealt with by A2 and B2.

1990 Editor's note and observations:

What is bail cover? What is a 'T2'? 'SAD'? Bonded warehouse?

The above Panel Answer may require some explanation for readers from outside the European Union, or who are otherwise unfamiliar with the practice of bonded warehouses.

First, as regards European Union transport procedures, the abolition of the Single Administrative Document (SAD) in intra-EU transactions has theoretically liberated European exporters and importers from the obligation of completing customs declarations at any intra-EU borders. Nonetheless, the SAD system is being replaced by a system which specifies that certain minimum fiscal and statistical information is required by national EU-member state administrations. The necessary statistical information for intra-EU trade will be provided in supplementary statistical forms called INTRASTAT forms.

There are other official forms which are of particular interest as regards transit of goods in or through European Union countries, in particular the 'T2' form, used whenever goods from one EU country and destined for another EU country have to transit through a third, non-EU country.

The objective of harmonized European transit forms is to prevent goods being delayed at frontiers, and to ensure duty free admission in member states (via form T2) or to indicate that goods are subject to duty (via form TI).

EXW and FAS are the only Incoterms® rules that do not place any responsibility on the seller for export customs clearance, and therefore it may be argued that these are the only terms that would not put a requirement on the seller to provide even the minimum statistical forms. In practice, it is likely that even EXW and FAS sellers in the EU would perform the minimum duty of providing statistical information to the authorities, but this service would be performed at the cost and risk of the buyer.

Certain goods, such as tobacco and alcohol, are subject to highly-specific tax/fiscal regimes, and in particular to excise taxes. The transit of such goods through some countries must be guaranteed by a bond ('bail cover') which assures customs authorities that the required duties will be paid on the goods. Bart Van de Veire explains the impact of the bonding obligation on the Incoterms® rules as follows (***Incoterms in Practice*** (ICC Publication No. 505), chapter 2):

> [T]he cost of the bond will be borne by the so-called 'principal' on the document. The principal will invoice the one who gave him the order to issue the transit form, i.e., the seller or the buyer according to the chosen Incoterm; the invoice will cover both his own operations for issuance of the document as well as the price of the bond. In 'F' or 'C' – terms, the charge for the transit is to the buyer's account. In fact, for practical reasons, it will be often taken care of by the seller who is in the country of departure, but again, the seller will have given the buyer assistance in obtaining a necessary document, the cost for which will fall on the buyer according to article A10 of Incoterms.

Bonded warehouses are used to store and/or inspect dutiable goods prior to payment of the import duty (or in the alternative, prior to re-export to another country). Generally, the proprietor of the warehouse must provide a bond to the customs authorities in order to cover any potential liability for duties. The utility of these warehouses is that the importer can inspect the goods, or have her customers inspect them, before paying the duty. Moreover, in the case of goods assessed a high duty (such as tobacco or alcohol), payment of the duty can be delayed by storage in a bonded warehouse, which may enable the importer to utilize capital more efficiently.

1990 Question 6: Letters of credit and the Incoterms® rules

Under a contract concluded on FOB terms, is a seller bound to accept a letter of credit opened by the buyer which specifies that the trade term is the FCA Incoterms® rule?

Facts:

A French company concluded a contract on FOB terms for goods to be delivered to an Algerian buyer; 80% of the goods were to be shipped by sea on conventional pallets, and payment was to be by letter of credit. The Algerian bank opened a credit under FCA terms specifying to seller that according to the mode of shipment this was the correct term, given that the goods in question were not intended to be loaded over the ship's rail. Was seller bound to accept this credit?

Answer of the Panel of Incoterms® Experts:

1. The Incoterms® rules do not seek to regulate the mechanism agreed by the parties for the payment of the price; they simply impose on the buyer the duty to pay it: (FOB B1).

2. The mechanism for the payment of the price is a matter for the contract of sale to spell out, and the interpretation and effect of such contractual clauses will depend on the law governing the contract of sale. It would therefore be inappropriate for the Panel to give specific advice to the seller in this case as to this rights and remedies under the contract of sale.

3. However, given that both the Incoterms® rules and the UCP 500 originate with the ICC, this question does raise a number of practical points which are worth making in a general way:

i) When choosing an Incoterms® rule for incorporation into the contract of sale, it is essential to have proper regard to the method of transport to be used.

ii) When applying for the opening of a letter of credit, it is important for the buyer to give the bank clear documentary instructions, avoiding instructions which are not documentary. Thus, for example, an instruction that the commercial invoice must mention FCA *Incoterms 1990* is a documentary instruction, whereas a general instruction that the documentary credit should be issued 'under FCA terms' is not.

iii) From the issuing bank's point of view: when requested to open a letter of credit which contains a documentary requirement related to the chosen Incoterms® rule, the issuing bank should refrain from proposing any unilateral modification of this documentary requirement. The bank should understand that legal consequences may follow from issuance of a letter of credit specifying an Incoterms® rule different from the Incoterms® rule specified in the contract of sale. Thus, as a general rule a bank should avoid issuance of a credit which may be at variance with the requirements of the contract of sale. If the issuing bank believes that the Incoterms® rule chosen in the contract of sale is inappropriate, it may merely wish to draw the attention of the applicant to this fact, and suggest that the applicant contact the beneficiary to propose an appropriate revision of the contract of sale. Both issuing bank and applicant should be wary of taking any steps which may constitute an attempted unilateral modification of the contract of sale.

iv) When receiving a letter of credit, a seller should take care to read its terms and to ensure that it imposes on him the same documentary duties as are imposed upon him by the contract of sale and by the same Incoterms® rule incorporated into his contract of sale.

1990 Editor's notes and observations:

This cases raises a variety of interesting questions concerning the inter-relationship of two important sets of ICC uniform rules, the Incoterms® rules and the ICC's rules for letters of credit (documentary credits).

In practice, the use of documentary credits is most frequently associated with the classic maritime terms, CFR (also known as C&F) and CIF, and to a lesser extent, FOB. Historically, these were the first trade terms, and the international commercial practice of payment by letter of credit grew in parallel with the evolution of a common international understanding of FOB and CIF. For some traders and bankers, it has been difficult to adjust to the use of new transport modes and documentation, and to the newer Incoterms® rules (FCA/CPT/CIP) associated with them.

The role of the ocean bill of lading is crucial to understanding this issue, particularly as regards the perceived security value which it offers banks issuing documentary credits. With a traditional maritime term such as CIF, the seller delivers goods on board a vessel at a port of departure, and obtains from the carrier an

INCOTERMS® 1990 GENERAL QUESTIONS

ocean bill of lading. Possession of an ocean bill of lading is regarded by national laws and international customs of trade as representing control of delivery over the goods. Therefore, a credit which calls for provision of an ocean bill of lading appears to provide the issuing bank with additional security in the event the applicant should become insolvent. In such a case, the bank could theoretically obtain delivery of the goods, arrange for their re-sale, and use the proceeds to mitigate its exposure to credits issued on behalf of the insolvent applicant.

This explanation explains to some extent why some bankers have been cautious in accepting the 'new' Incoterms® rules which call for the use of transport documents other than the traditional bill of lading (e.g., FCA, CPT, CIP). In fact, these more modern transport documents, such as the sea waybill, multimodal transport document, air waybill (AWB), or FIATA bill of lading may provide banks with similar levels of security to that offered by the ocean bill of lading, or at least with an acceptable level of security. Nonetheless, in some countries, banks and their customers have clung to old practices based on FOB/CFR/CIF, and the use of ocean bills of lading, when it would appear that the multimodal or containerization aspects of particular transactions call instead for the Incoterms® rules, such as FCA/CPT/CIP and multimodal transport documents.

Should international trade bankers know about the Incoterms® rules and apply this knowledge in the opening or checking of documentary credits?

Strictly speaking, the Incoterms® rules do not play any mandatory role in the documentary credit process under the ICC standard rules which govern documentary credits (Uniform Customs and Practice for Documentary Credits – commonly referred to as the 'UCP 500' or simply 'UCP').

The UCP does not require trade bankers to apply a professional understanding of the Incoterms® rules, either in the issuance of the credit or in the verification of documents submitted under the credit. However, from a wider perspective, it is important that the bank understand the Incoterms® rules, because the bank's rights and obligations under a transport document, (e.g., in the event of the insolvency of the applicant), may be affected by the choice of Incoterms® rule in the contract of sale, and the protection or liability that this Incoterms® rule will in turn impose on the applicant. Bankers should also have some knowledge of the insurance requirements under the Incoterms® rule, because the insurance document is an extremely common and important component of the documentary credit process.

Conflict with documentary credits?

Can all 13 Incoterms® rules be used in transactions based on documentary credit payments? In practice, documentary credits have been most commonly issued in conjunction with sale contracts on FOB, CFR or CIF Incoterms® rules, which characterize the classic export 'shipment' contracts (referred to as such because the seller fulfils delivery obligations when the goods are shipped on board a vessel in the port of departure). Today, however, documentary credits are increasingly used in conjunction with sale contracts governed by a more modern set of Incoterms® rules specifically designed for multimodal or containerized shipments: FCA, CPT and CIP.

Traders should also be aware of the growth in usage of the so called 'D' Incoterms® rules: DAF, DES, DEQ, DDU and DDP, which are 'arrival' terms (the seller's obligations are completed upon the goods arrival in the buyer's country).

What happens if the parties choose the 'wrong' Incoterms® rule?

What should a banker do when asked to issue a credit on the basis of an inappropriate Incoterms® rule? For example: the banker may be requested by the applicant to issue a documentary credit based on an FOB contract, but the banker knows that transport will be by air, and that consequently the FCA Incoterms® rule is normally indicated.

First, it is highly inadvisable, although it appears to have happened on rare occasions, for the banker simply to suggest that the credit be issued on the basis of the FCA Incoterms® rule. Such an action could even force the applicant unwittingly into a breach of the contract of sale – documentary credits often originate in explicit provisions of the sale contract, and in such cases, under some systems of law the buyer is strictly required to have the credit issued precisely according to the terms of the sale contract.

In these jurisdictions, if the credit advised to the beneficiary differs materially from the terms negotiated in the contract of sale, the beneficiary may be able to use this mistake as a pretext for terminating the contract (e.g., in a rising market). Similarly, the FOB seller who receives a credit issued under the FCA rule may be able

INCOTERMS® 1990 GENERAL QUESTIONS

to claim that the non-conforming credit constitutes a breach of contract.

Note that the UCP does not strictly require a banker faced with a credit application containing an inappropriate or questionable Incoterm to act at all. However, if the banker does decide to offer advice, he may wish simply to alert the applicant to the inappropriate use of the Incoterms® rule. Neither the applicant nor the banker should ever act unilaterally (that is, without consulting the seller-beneficiary) to 'improve' the contract of sale as regards the choice of Incoterms® rule.

Can discrepancies arise in letter of credit presentations when a particular Incoterms® rule is stipulated in the credit and the beneficiary presents documents containing other Incoterms® rules or trade terms?

Example: the L/C advice features the words 'FOB Incoterms 1990', but the commercial invoice ultimately presented under the credit by the beneficiary refers only to 'FOB'. Could the issuing or confirming bank consider this a discrepancy when checking the documents? Most probably, yes, although there is no case law on the matter. Actually, there can be very much difference between a simple reference to 'FOB' (which may imply that interpretation of FOB will be that of the applicable national law) and the full and complete reference to 'FOB Incoterms 1990', which ensures that interpretation will be according to the standard definitions of the Incoterms® rules.

Since national law definitions of trade terms can differ markedly from the Incoterms® rules, such a discrepancy might be significant. For example, under US law, FOB has been accorded six separate possible interpretations, only one of which corresponds to the ICC definition. The ICC has suggested that the best way to avoid this problem is to either avoid mentioning the Incoterms® rules in the credit or to only refer to the Incoterms® rules in connection with a specified, particular document, such as the commercial invoice.

1990 Question 7: 'C + I' – Interpretation

Why is there no reference in the Incoterms® rules to the term 'C+i (destination)'?

Answer of the Panel of Incoterms® Experts:

Although this term is used in practice, it is outside the Incoterms® rules and always has been. The reference to 'C' may be most unfortunate if the intention is that the buyer should pay for the main carriage. This term can be interpreted as 'Cost and Insurance' or even 'Carriage and Insurance'. More details are needed on this question about what is involved in their use of 'C+1 destination'. If, as the question letter suggests, this term is 'effectively FCA plus transit insurance to the port of destination', then the following Incoterm alternative may be suitable: use FCA and add '+ insurance' (but specify quantity and kind of insurance coverage, i.e., Institute Cargo Clause A, SRCC, transit, etc.).

1990 Editor's notes and observations:

Why are some trade terms not Incoterms® rules?

This question points to the usage in practice of a wide range of variants of trade terms. The ICC position has been that many of these terms are ambiguous or are not used in standard ways worldwide, so that it is not possible to include them in a compendium of standard terms like the Incoterms® rules. However, in certain regions and in certain sectors it is not at all uncommon to find the frequent use of certain variants.

The question has been debated within the ICC for many years, and doubtless will be again during the Incoterms 2000 revision: should the ICC begin to include default definitions for some of the more common variants (e.g., Ex Works loaded, FOB stowed, etc.).

INCOTERMS® 1990 GENERAL QUESTIONS

1990 Question 8 'C' – family of Incoterms® rules v. 'D'-family of Incoterms® rules

Is the CIF Incoterms® rule, included in an international contract of sale, compatible with the seller's request to sign a disclaimer that releases him from liability as soon as the goods have been handed over to the freight forwarder at the port of departure? If this is the case, what Incoterms® rule should be used in order to render the seller liable until delivery of the goods in the country of destination?

Answer of the Panel of Incoterms® Experts:

The seller should have used the CIP Incoterms® rule. If the buyer does not want to bear the risks of transport, he should use a 'D' rule and, more precisely, DDU as he will pick up the delivery from the seller's works, in the buyer's country.

Analysis:

As the goods must be handed over to a freight forwarder, the contract of sale should have made reference to the CIP Incoterms® rule instead of CIF. Anyway, in both cases the seller must carry out, at his own expenses, the contract of carriage and must pay for the insurance of the goods. Under CIF, the transfer of risks takes place when the goods pass the ship's rail and thereafter, the buyer bears the risks of the sea carriage.

1990 Editor's notes and observations:

The above answer by the Incoterms® Panel emphasizes that CIF should be used exclusively in a maritime context. The statement in the question to the effect that goods would be delivered to a freight forwarder indicated to the Panel that transport would be multimodal, and therefore that CIP would be the most appropriate term. Usage of CIF places a documentary obligation upon the seller to provide an ocean bill of lading to the buyer, and this obligation may be difficult or awkward to fulfil when delivery is to an inland freight forwarder.

INCOTERMS® 2010 – MULTIMODAL QUESTIONS

2010 Question 17 'Seller's premises' in FCA

What is included in 'seller's premises' under FCA article A4(a)?

Guidance from ICC experts:

- 'Seller's premises' may be any place under the seller's control.

- In many cases, sellers consider a terminal contracted by the seller to be seller's premises, in which case, the seller would be obliged to load the goods on the buyer's transport (e.g. ship) and therefore the seller would be responsible for the terminal handling and loading costs.

- Therefore, if it is not obvious whether or not the place of delivery is the 'seller's premises', then it should be made clear in the contract of sale to avoid a dispute.

2010 Question 18 'Seller's means of transport' in FCA

What is included in 'seller's means of transport' under FCA article A4(b)?

Guidance from ICC experts:

- It may be a carrier contracted for by the seller.

- It need not literally be the seller's own vehicle.

2010 Question 19 'First carrier' in CPT and CIP

The Guidance Notes to CPT and CIP say that 'the default position is that risk passes when the goods have been delivered to the first carrier'. Who is the 'first carrier'?

Guidance from ICC experts:

The 'first carrier' is the very first carrier independent of the seller (i.e. not the seller's own vehicle/vessel) with whom the seller has contracted for carriage.

2010 Question 20 Seller using own means of transportation under DAT, DAP and DDP

Under article A3 of DAT, DAP and DDP, the seller must contract for carriage. May the seller use its own means of transportation rather than an outside carrier?

INCOTERMS® 2010 – MULTIMODAL QUESTIONS

Guidance from ICC experts:

Yes. The rule assigns the responsibility to the seller to arrange for carriage, which may be carried out using the seller's own means even though the text says 'must contract'.

2010 Question 21 'Terminal' in DAT

What is a 'terminal' in the new Incoterms® 2010 rule 'Delivered at Terminal' (DAT)?

Guidance from ICC experts:

'Terminal' is intended to have a broad meaning, as the Guidance Note to DAT indicates, including any place, whether covered or not, such as a quay, warehouse, container yard or road, rail or air cargo terminal. But a 'terminal' cannot be simply an open field; there must be some organization of the space for receiving goods.

2010 Question 22 Where to unload in DAT?

Under the Incoterms® 2010 rule 'Delivered at Terminal' (DAT), where does the seller unload the goods, at the terminal or in the terminal? For example, can the seller just leave commodities on a pallet on the street outside the terminal, or must the goods be brought inside?

Guidance from ICC experts:

- DAT in article A4 requires that the goods be delivered 'at the named terminal'. Whether the goods must be brought inside the terminal will depend on the particular physical circumstances of the terminal, on the customs of the trade and, perhaps most importantly, on where the seller will be able to obtain a delivery document that will allow the buyer to take delivery of the goods, as required under article A8.

- Nevertheless, as advised by the Guidance Note of the DAT term in the Incoterms® 2010 rules, it would be convenient for the parties to agree as clearly as possible upon a specific delivery point within the terminal.

2010 Question 23 Buyer doesn't arrive to collect goods under DAP

If a buyer doesn't arrive to collect the goods once they have been delivered under the Incoterms® 2010 rule 'Delivered at Place' (DAP) by being placed at buyer's disposal, what should seller do? And who pays for whatever is done?

Guidance from ICC experts:

- As stated in the query, delivery takes place by placing the goods at the disposal of the buyer on the arriving means of transport ready for unloading. The seller must give notice to the buyer to enable the buyer to take any measures necessary for taking delivery. Assuming this has been done, delivery has taken place, and any costs relating to the goods thereafter are for the buyer according to article B6(a). Moreover, the buyer must pay any additional costs if the buyer has failed to inform the seller of the relevant details of delivery mentioned in article B7.

- The Incoterms® 2010 rules do not deal with the consequences of a breach of contract, so the question as to what the seller should do with the goods where the buyer fails to take delivery as required in article B1, and what other consequences the breach would have, would be governed by the applicable law such as the CISG unless addressed in the contract of sale.

- Despite the above, it can be generally stated that both the carrier and the seller have a duty of care vis-à-vis the buyer regarding the goods, even when the buyer fails to take delivery in time. Normally, the consignee (i.e. the buyer or buyer's agent) is then contacted. The seller that has contracted with the carrier is in practice primarily responsible for compensating the carrier for any expenses, e.g. for storage of the goods on the consignee's account, but as between the seller and the buyer, these costs are for the buyer in accordance with the division of costs under DAP Incoterms®2010.

2010 Question 24 Documents under DAP and DDP

While article A8 in the Incoterms® 2010 rules DAP and DDP are identical, article B8 is different: in DAP, buyer must accept the 'delivery document' provided by seller, while in DDP, buyer must accept the 'proof of delivery' provided by seller. Why the difference?

Guidance from ICC experts:

The real obligation is on the seller and B8 only mirrors it. The buyer shall accept a document that meets the requirements of A8 in each case (not in EXW). For each rule, the drafting group chose suitable wording to reflect the circumstances. However, the buyer is not deemed to have accepted any goods as delivered because of accepting a mere proof of delivery.

INCOTERMS® 2010 – MULTIMODAL QUESTIONS

2010 Question 25 VAT and DDP

The Guidance Note to the Incoterms® 2010 rule DDP, states that 'any VAT or other taxes payable upon import are for the seller's account unless expressly agreed otherwise in the sale contract.'

Where an American exporter wants to deliver in Belgium, for example, using DDP Brussels, must that American seller pay the 21% VAT upon import of the goods? This is hard to believe, since European VAT is deductible on the importer's VAT declaration. Where a Belgian seller sells to an American, using, for example, DDP Chicago, would the Belgian company have to pay the American equivalent of VAT upon import?

Guidance from ICC experts:

- Article A6(c) of DDP Incoterms® 2010 states that the seller must pay (where applicable) the costs of customs formalities necessary for the export and import of the goods as well as all duties, taxes and other charges payable upon...import of the goods as well the costs of transit formalities. VAT payable upon importation is one of such taxes payable by the seller. The Guidance Note to DDP states that any VAT or other taxes payable upon import are for the seller's account unless expressly agreed otherwise in the contract.

- An American selling DDP Brussels takes responsibility for import and is therefore responsible for the taxes arising on import.

- The practicability of using DDP must be assessed by the parties. Some customers expect 'full service' from the seller, which means that goods must cleared through customs with all taxes paid. As the seller may not be able to deduct VAT, parties frequently agree that VAT is excluded. The problem does not arise when the seller has an establishment in the buyer's country or tax territory.

2010 Question 26 Does the need for an on board transport document rule out FCA for containers?

Users in South Africa have frequently underlined the importance of using on board bills of lading because otherwise the buyer is at risk for goods stranded at the port, for example because of strikes and the goods thereby never actually getting on board for transit. Depending on the circumstances and the Incoterms® 2010 rule concerned, the seller either obtains and hands over an on board document to the buyer or assists the buyer in obtaining one. The enquirers find that the recommendation that FCA be used for containers is untenable because of the need for an on board transport document. Please provide thoughts.

Guidance from ICC experts:

- There are certainly advantages of using on board negotiable transport documents as referred to by the South African users. However, on board transport documents reflect the reality of delivery only when goods are delivered on board the vessel by the seller, usually acting as the actual shipper as is done under FOB, CFR and CIF Incoterms® 2010, where the seller has to deliver the goods on board the vessel, which is only evidenced by an on board bill of lading (see Ramberg, *Guide to Incoterms® 2010*, ICC Publication No. 720, p. 74).

- On the other hand, containers are practically invariably delivered to the carrier prior to being loaded on board, and FCA is therefore more appropriate as it reflects the realities of the delivery. Containers are most often delivered to the carrier by placing them on a container stack in a container yard. The parties should agree on this at least implicitly. The problems referred to by the South African users may occur even when the carrier would exceptionally be prepared to issue an on board bill of lading under such circumstances since a strike might prevent the actual loading operation. The parties should consult with the carrier for measures to verify in the transport document that goods are actually on board e.g. by amending a received bill of lading by an on board notation. ICC does not have an 'off-the shelf' answer to solve the discrepancies between modern transport technology and the requirements of transport documentation based on old transport technology.

- • Containerized goods can be sold on an FOB basis. However, the seller needs to be aware that it takes a risk as seller will have lost control of the goods (as usually delivered into custody of the carrier prior to loading) but will still retain legal risk for loss of or damage to the goods.

INCOTERMS® 2010 – MULTIMODAL QUESTIONS

2010 Question 27
Can seller refuse to load buyer's arriving truck under FCA?

An FCA buyer has sent a truck to the seller's factory to collect the goods. The FCA seller has serious doubts regarding the safety of transportation when using this truck (insufficient straps, curtain-side, slippery steel deck, etc.). Can the seller refuse to load the truck?

Guidance from ICC experts:

- The risk of loss of or damage to the goods under the FCA Incoterms® 2010 rule passes pursuant to article A5, when the goods are delivered according to article A4. Pursuant to article A4(a), delivery is completed if the named place is the seller's premises, when the goods have been loaded on a means of transport provided by the buyer. This means that any loss of or damage to the goods caused by inadequate safety of transportation is in principle to be borne by the buyer.

- The F-family rules FCA, FAS and FOB do not contain any express requirement as to the means of transport sent to collect or receive the goods since it is the buyer's responsibility to see to it that the means of transport are adequate. FCA Incoterms® 2010 does not therefore regulate this matter concretely. However, some general observations can still be made.

- Under transport law, such as the CMR Convention applicable in Europe, gross negligence on the side of the carrier could deprive the carrier of the right to limit its liability in circumstances where safety deficiencies would amount to gross negligence. A shipper that is aware of the deficiencies might not be able to plead gross negligence. This might hamper the buyer at risk from seeking an effective recovery from the carrier.

- In addition, seller and buyer will have health and safety responsibilities under local law. The seller will not be able to load if in doing so it breaches local health and safety law. Whether this constitutes a breach of contract will depend on the contract in which an Incoterms® 2010 rule is being used. Typically, there will be an obligation (expressed or implied) to comply with applicable laws.

- In the most probable circumstances, it might become evident to the seller as the shipper that the buyer has contracted with a carrier without being aware of the vehicle's condition and equipment. In such circumstances, most legal systems would place a duty on the seller to take care of the buyer's interests to avoid an event leading to loss of or damage to the goods. A good piece of advice would be to contact the buyer for further instructions.

2010 Question 28 Who is the 'shipper' on transport document under FCA?

In a sale 'FCA seller's premises Incoterms® 2010', who should be the 'shipper' on the transport document?

Guidance from ICC experts:

- This matter is typically not governed by any provision of the contract of sale (FCA Incoterms® 2010 being silent on the matter) but rather by the relevant transport law regime, which is generally either statutory law based on international conventions for the relevant mode of transport, or (usually) a contractual regime for multimodal transport.

- A shipper can be a contractual shipper, who has contracted with the carrier, or an actual shipper simply handing over the goods to the carrier, or both. More detailed definitions are found in transport conventions and laws, but inconsistency generally exists in this field. Under normal situations envisaged under FCA, an actual shipper is concerned. Moreover, there exists a special legal regime for the shipment of dangerous goods, which confers obligations and liabilities on the actual shipper marked on special documents.

- It is therefore not feasible to give any recommendation to cover all FCA shipments.

2010 Question 29 Destination contract with the seller unloading, but not at a terminal

We want to use a delivered Incoterms® 2010 rule, but don't know whether to use DAP or DAT in the following situation: the seller and buyer agree that seller is to retain risk for the goods during transport, pay all transport costs to, and provide unloading at, the buyer's premises, which is not a terminal.

Guidance from ICC experts:

- This situation doesn't fit any of the 11 Incoterms® 2010 rules exactly - DAP (and DDP) anticipate delivery to buyer's premises but delivery not unloaded, and DAT is unloaded but anticipates delivery to a 'terminal'. However, the guidance note to DAT makes it clear that 'terminal' is defined broadly as, 'any place, whether covered or not'.

- We suggest then that either:
    - DAT is used but making clear in the contract that the place of destination is the buyer's premises; or
    - DAP is used but making clear in the contract that the seller shall provide for unloading at the buyer's premises and the seller shall pay all costs and bear all risks relating to unloading.

2010 Question 30 Domestic arrival contracts for pre-imported foreign goods – DAP or DDP?

For domestic arrival contracts covering pre-imported foreign-origin goods, should we use DAP or DDP?

Guidance from ICC experts:

DAP was developed to cater for this situation as it does not mention any duties or other charges in its name. However, either DAP or DDP can be used.

2010 Question 31 Seller doubts safety of buyer's arriving truck under EXW

An EXW buyer has sent a truck to the seller's factory to collect the goods. The EXW seller has serious doubts regarding the safety of transportation when using this truck (insufficient straps, curtain-side, slippery steel deck, etc.). Can the seller refuse to load the truck at the buyer's request, risk and expense?

Guidance from ICC experts:

- Under EXW the seller is not obliged to load the goods. It is at the seller's discretion whether to agree to load (and if the seller does agree to load the seller should make it clear in the contract that it does so at the buyer's risk, request and expense).

- Seller and buyer are obliged to comply with local laws relating to health and safety. This obligation is not an Incoterms® 2010 rule obligation but an obligation arising from the local law. The seller should not assist the buyer to load if that causes the seller to be in breach of the law.

2010 Question 32: Who pays 'container cleaning charges' under DAP?

Goods have been sold 'DAP Durban – South Africa Incoterms® 2010'. Due to the nature of the goods, the container needs to be cleaned. Who has to pay the 'container cleaning charges'?

Guidance from ICC experts:

- DAP does not deal with responsibilities for the container in which the goods are delivered.

- The legal responsibility for the container will be dealt with in the contract between the container owner (usually the carrier or a container lessor) and the seller. The seller will be responsible to the container owner for the container, including cleaning responsibilities. If the seller wants to pass these responsibilities to the buyer (and oblige the buyer to return the container) then the seller should specify so in the contract with the buyer.

2010 Question 33: Relation of risk passage and export formalities under FCA, CPT and CIP

According to article A5 of the Incoterms® 2010 rules FCA, CPT and CIP, risk of loss of or damage to the goods passes to the buyer when the goods have been delivered in accordance with article A4, that is, handed over to or placed at the disposal of the carrier. But the seller is also obliged to clear the goods for export under article A2, which may take place after the goods have been delivered.

What happens if the seller delivers the goods (and thus risk has passed to the buyer), but then the seller fails to satisfy the required export formalities? Does risk for the goods revert to the seller in that case? And if the goods are damaged or lost between the physical delivery and completion of export formalities, would the seller still go ahead and complete export formalities?

Guidance from ICC experts:

- Delivery of goods and passage of risk for the goods under articles A4 and A5 occur independently of the obligation of the seller under article A2 to undertake export formalities. If the seller fails to complete its export obligations, and assuming the buyer has provided any related assistance as required under article B10, then the buyer's recourse will be to seek remedies for contractual breach available under the applicable legal regime, outside the scope of the Incoterms® 2010 rules. For example, if as a result of the seller's breach the goods are stranded at the port and perish, then subject to the relevant law, the seller will be liable for that loss to the buyer. Therefore although 'risk' has passed, the seller may still be liable.

- Where goods are destroyed after delivery but before the seller has completed export formalities, seller will still be obliged under the Incoterms® 2010 rules to clear the goods for export, but the parties may want to consider other options by mutual agreement.

2010 Question 34 — Delivery date under CIP?

In a contract CIP (Antwerp) Incoterms® 2010, delivery date March 23, 2011, goods leave the Chinese seller's factory on March 15, 2011, arrive at the forwarder's terminal (COSCO) in Shanghai on March 22, 2011 (date of the freight cargo receipt) and are received by the ship on March 24, 2011 (date of bill of lading). When did the C-seller deliver?

Guidance from ICC experts:

In this question, the Incoterms® 2010 rule CIP is chosen by the parties. Therefore the delivery obligation is fulfilled by handing the goods over to the first carrier, unless agreed otherwise by the parties under the sale contract. In this case, the first carrier is the carrier taking goods from the seller's factory in China (assuming that the seller has not carried the goods itself). If the seller has carried the goods itself, then delivery will be to the first carrier – i.e. freight forwarder terminal at Shanghai). Therefore, the goods would be delivered on March 15, 2011.

INCOTERMS® 1990 – MULTIMODAL QUESTIONS

1990 Question 9

FCA – Forwarder's handling fees

For air shipments under FCA terms, who as between seller and buyer must pay for the freight forwarder's 'handling fee' (for export clearance and other services)? Who must pay for storage at the freight forwarder's warehouse (prior to loading on aircraft)?

Facts:
The goods are delivered, as per buyer's instructions, to the freight forwarders' warehouse.

Answer of the Panel of Incoterms® Experts:

1. To the extent that the 'handling fee' represents a charge for services related to export customs clearance, it should ultimately be paid by the seller. To the extent that this fee is a charge for physical handling of the goods after receipt from the seller, this is a freight element and should be charged to buyer.

2. Storage costs at the freight forwarder's terminal are transport costs which must be borne by the buyer.

3. In practice, considerable difficulties arise owing to the fact that the freight forwarders (particularly in connection with air transport) have a dual function. First, they could represent either the seller or the buyer. Second, they could also act as agent for the carrier. In connection with air transport, the freight forwarders usually hold the position as 'IATA agents'. This means that they may be authorized to receive the goods on behalf of their carrier. In answering this question, this has been assumed to be the case.

1990 Editor's notes and observations:

The above question deals with the issue of air shipments pursuant to the FCA Incoterms® rule. As with FOB, customs clearance is an obligation of the seller, and any charges that a freight forwarder may incur in obtaining export customs clearance will normally, under an FCA contract, be billed to the seller.

It is worth mentioning that this basic principle on customs should apply regardless of whether one uses FCA Incoterms® rule for an air shipment, or the formerly common 'FOB Airport', which is no longer one of the 13 valid Incoterms® rules. As regards the costs of storage in a warehouse prior to shipment, this would generally be

INCOTERMS® 1990 – MULTIMODAL QUESTIONS

for the buyer's account as a cost arising after the seller had complied with his delivery duty. However, the allocation of storage and handling costs is a frequent source of conflict, as will be seen in other queries, and it is recommended that the parties come to a clear, explicit understanding of any necessary splitting or allocation of terminal charges in those cases where the seller's delivery obligation is at a terminal.

1990 Question 10 FCA – Manner of delivery

1. With respect to the FCA rule, who must pay the export terminal handling charges?
2. Does 'handed over' mean the physical transfer of the goods to the carrier?
3. Who must unload the goods from the road truck by which delivery to the export terminal is made?

Answer of the Panel of Incoterms® Experts:

1. Specific stipulations in the contract of sale or in addition to the Incoterms® rule should be made with respect to the costs of loading, discharge, and division of Terminal Handling Charges (THC). If the THC are not fully absorbed by the carrier but split between him and the shipper, it may be correct to let the 'shipper's portion' fall upon the seller in the understanding that this is needed for the 'handing over' to be completed.

   However, no answer to this question can be derived from the Incoterms® rules themselves: in the absence of express provisions in the contract, custom of the export or trade usage will rule.

2. 'Handed over' means the physical transfer of the goods to the carrier.

3. Usually, the carrier owns the unloading equipment, and it therefore makes sense that the carrier should carry out the unloading and include the costs in the freight.

1990 Editor's comments and observations:

The Panel of Experts was studiously cautious in answering this question, refusing to go further than the general statements made in the text of Incoterms® rule FCA itself.

In particular, the Experts refrained from attempting an analysis of the possible splitting of Terminal Handling Charges ('THC'), sometimes also known as Container Service Charges ('CSC') or Destination Delivery Charges ('DDC').

As transport in containers has become the norm for a great deal of export goods, customs of trade based on delivery to ports have had to be replaced by customs based on delivery to container transport terminals. A practice has grown in some of these terminals, which may or may not be owned by the actual carrier, to split the charges incurred within the terminal, with some of the charges going to the 'shipper' – generally the exporter, although the buyer can technically also be shipper – and the other charges allocated to the consignee (generally the buyer). In some areas it would appear that an 80% / 20% split of charges was considered customary. Nonetheless, the ICC Experts felt that practice was too diverse and too unsettled for the ICC to state a final rule.

Rather, the onus is put back on the traders to achieve the necessary clarity in their contract. The ICC repeatedly reminds traders that they should not expect the Incoterms® rules to resolve all contractual uncertainties. In particular, when goods are to be delivered to a container terminal under FCA, traders would be well advised to specify how unloading at the terminal will take place and who will pay for it, and how any additional terminal charges are to be split.

1990 Question 11 — FCA – Import duties levied by seller's customs authorities

Under the FCA Incoterms® rule, who, as between the seller and the buyer, must pay for the import duties levied by seller's customs authorities (i.e., duties for importation, from a third country into the seller's country, of the same goods that are now sold to the buyer under FCA)?

Facts:
A Dutch seller sold goods produced in the US on FCA Delfzijl (Netherlands) terms to a Danish buyer. Upon collection of the goods, the Dutch company claimed that the Danish company had to pay the customs duty (the import duty from the US into the Netherlands).

Answer of the Panel of Incoterms® Experts:
The seller is under a duty to deliver the goods ready for export, which means *having already paid any customs duties still outstanding.*

In the absence of any special terms in the contract of sale, the matter is governed by A2 of the FCA Incoterms® rule, which places on the seller the duty to obtain at his expense any export licence or other official authorisation necessary for the export of the goods. On the assumption that the goods could not leave the seller's country before payment of levies charged on their import into that country, the seller is under a duty to deliver the goods to the buyer ready for export, with all prior import duties paid.

1990 Question 12 FCA – Port/airport handling charges not 'official' charges

According to the 'Guide to Incoterms 1990', under FCA, in the case of sea or air transport, charges incurred in ports or airports (trucking, handling, stevedoring, taxes levied by ports or airports authorities) are not 'official charges'. This would mean that these charges are for the buyer's account (since the seller must only pay for pre-delivery costs plus custom clearance, formalities and official charges). Is that statement correct?

Answer of the Panel of Incoterms® Experts:

Yes. Under FCA the seller must pay for the charges incurred before delivery including customs formalities.

In the case of air transport under the FCA term, for example, all airport charges arising after the goods have been delivered to the freight forwarder who will issue the waybill must be paid by the buyer, but the exact point should be clarified with the freight forwarder in order to avoid uncertainty or disputes.

In the case of sea transport, delivery may take place at the seller's premises, at a terminal gate or at the terminal itself. However, according to a certain custom of port, mainly in French ports, costs up to the ship's side are generally for the seller's account, unless the buyer instructs the carrier to include them in the freight.

Analysis:

Air and sea transport must be dealt with separately because the question has been formulated by a French company and in France the custom is different in these two kinds of transport.

In the case of air carriage, the goods are always delivered to a freight forwarder who will clear the goods for export if the clearance has not been carried out by the seller himself. If the freight forwarder is an IATA agent, he will fill in the air waybill and will often choose the carrier, because the buyer commonly forgets or neglects to do it. In practice, direct delivery to the carrier never occurs. Delivery is completed when the goods have been handed over to the agent who issued the

AWB, but the cost of customs clearance for export, if necessary, must be paid by the seller. Airport charges can be mentioned in the air waybill as disbursements, and they can be collected on arrival from the buyer along with the freight and AWB charges.

In the case of sea transport, there are several possibilities for the place of delivery: the seller's premises, the gate of the terminal or the terminal itself. In many ports the custom is to invoice the terminal costs to the shipper, i.e., the seller. The seller may have to pay the horizontal handling costs according to the custom of the place, but, in all cases, he will have to pay for the customs clearance.

1990 Editor's notes and observations:

In this question the Panel was asked whether a buyer could avoid all handling charges in the port/airport of departure under FCA/FOB airport on the grounds that such charges, not being 'official charges', are for seller's account. The Panel's answer is that the correct interpretation will depend on the circumstances of the transaction and the particular customs of the port or airport.

In practice, both FCA airport and FOB airport (not currently a valid Incoterms® rule) are commonly encountered. Readers should be aware that the basic 'problem' with FOB airport, and the reason is no longer a valid Incoterms® rule, is that the law and practice of international trade, built around the concept of delivery to ship's side or on board against a negotiable bill of lading, do not apply nicely to air shipments. A variety of charges can arise in connection with the delivery and handling of the goods by the freight forwarder, airport terminal, and/or air carrier. If parties are in doubt, additional drafting to achieve clarity may be advisable.

1990 Question 13 DDU – Wharfage fee

Who has to pay for a wharfage fee and a landing charge raised by the port of destination authority under the DDU delivery term?

Answer of the Panel of Incoterms® Experts:

The buyer must pay for all duties, taxes and official charges connected to the importation of the goods. The landing charge and the wharfage fee can be both considered as charges linked to the carriage and therefore should be paid by the seller.

Analysis:

Under DDU, the landing charge is a part of the carriage and the wharfage fee cannot be considered as a tax on the sole ground that it is customs value-based. The Incoterms® rules determine the nature of a cost according to the type of activity covered; in this case the use of the wharf. The criteria on which the cost is based are irrelevant. Moreover, the fact that it is levied by a public authority is not determining.

1990 Editor's notes and observations:

As a general rule under the Incoterms® rules, customs clearance responsibilities include payment of duties and other 'official charges' which are required for importation. The question that arose here was whether the seller could claim that the landing charges were 'official charges' because they were levied by a port authority, which in this case was a public or governmental authority. The Panel decided that the DDU seller could not pass on the buyer the wharfage and landing fees in the port of destination. The Panel thus appears to clarify the rule in DDU by requiring a clear linkage of 'official charges' to the customs clearance procedure before such charges can be considered part of the buyer's customs responsibility.

1990 Question 14 — DDU – Customs clearance

With respect to the DDU rule, since it is specified that this term means that import customs clearance and duties are for the buyer, why is it later stated that the Incoterm may be modified so that the duties or clearance is the responsibility of the seller?

Answer of the Panel of Incoterms® Experts:

Under DDU, import formalities fall upon the buyer. However, it must be understood that important responsibilities may be divided into two concepts:

1. custom clearance – administrative formalities, such as obtaining necessary licences, and
2. duties – import taxes and other official charges, such as VAT. Thus, although the seller is not responsible for either clearance or duties under DDU, he may agree to pay the costs of VAT, for example, which should be made clear by adding 'Delivered duty unpaid, VAT paid'.

1990 Editor's notes and observations:

All Incoterms® rules except EXW and FAS place some kind of customs clearance responsibilities upon the parties. In fact, these responsibilities can be subdivided further into three sub-parts:

1. payment of duties or other official charges,
2. effecting any required documentary formalities, and
3. taking the risk that it will be impossible to obtain customs clearance.

Theoretically, it is possible to split the above responsibilities between the parties, although as a general principle Incoterms always assign them entirely either to seller or buyer.

1990 Question 15 — DDU/DDP – Offloading and discharging

How should questions relating to offloading, discharging etc. be handled under DDU/DDP shipments when the contract is silent?

Facts:

The enquiry noted that under Incoterms 1953 and Incoterms 1980 it seemed clear that the seller would be responsible for discharging or landing the goods where it was necessary or customary to do so; however, this language was dropped from *Incoterms 1990*.

Answer of the Panel of Incoterms® Experts:

The issue here is the allocation of costs of discharge as between seller and buyer where the sale is contracted on DDU or DDP terms. The seller must pay all costs until the moment at which the goods reach the place of discharge under A3, and at which the goods are at the disposal of the buyer under A4.

The determining language under EXW A4 states that the seller must place the goods 'at the disposal of the buyer'. This is precisely the same language that is used under EXW, under which it is a well-accepted and long-established rule that the seller is not required to load the goods on vehicles provided by the buyer. Just as the buyer must take the goods, at his cost, from the seller's warehouse, so he must take goods, at his expense, from the seller's conveyance.

Therefore, under DDU/DDP *Incoterms 1990*, unless otherwise specified in the contract, unloading/offloading or discharge costs and risks are for buyer's account.

1990 Editor's notes and observations:

The above issue was decided by the Panel by looking to the following determinative language in the text of the Incoterms® rules: goods must be placed 'at the disposal of the buyer'. Since the identical language is found in EXW, and since the rule is well-established that the EXW seller does *not* have to load the goods, it was felt that the same result should be obtained under DDU/DD. When seller only has to place goods 'at the disposal' of the buyer this means that any further loading or unloading required in order for the buyer to take possession of the goods will be by the buyer's responsibility. Certain key phrases, such as this one, are used in several of the Incoterms® rules, and the Incoterms 2000 revision will seek further standardization of the meanings of these and other recurrent phrases or terms (another example is the 'handing over' terminology found in FCA, CPT and CIP).

1990 Question 16 — DDU – Customs clearance within reasonable time

Under the DDU Incoterms® rule, is the buyer obliged to make customs clearance possible within a reasonable period of time? Would late delivery be at the buyer's risk? Could the time for customs clearance be added to the contractual time for delivery under DDU?

Facts:

Under DDU terms, the seller fears that lengthy customs procedures may prevent him from delivering the goods in the time specified in the contract. Subsequent to the signing of the contract, it became clear that the goods had to pass through a customs prior to the delivery point.

Answer of the Panel of Incoterms® Experts:

1. The Incoterms® rules do not define the time for delivery, and in particular do not require that delivery be made within a reasonable time. The time for delivery must be found in the contractual provisions or by the application of legal principles under applicable law.

2. Despite the foregoing, the Incoterms® rules do state a rule as regards risks related to customs clearance under DDU: 'The buyer has to pay any additional costs and to bear any risks caused by his failure to clear the goods for import in time'. Thus, the risk of delay related to customs clearance is on the buyer under DDU. However, whether or not a delay in delivery is unreasonable in general, and in particular

whether or not such delayed delivery is the result of a delay in customs clearance will depend on the contract itself, the facts of the particular case, and on the applicable law; consequently, these further questions are not within the remit of the Panel of Experts.

3. Generally, interpretation of the contract will involve construing the intent of the parties on issues related to the time of delivery, such as the calculation of the time for delivery, the inclusion of a reasonable period of time for customs clearance, the condition upon which delivery time was agreed, and the consequences of delay.

4. This matter may well require contractual interpretation which is outside the scope of the Incoterms® rules and is therefore beyond the remit of the Panel of Experts.

1990 Editor's notes and observations:

The facts of this case, as suggested in the letter we received from the enquirer, were as follows: an exporter concludes a sales contract on DDU terms with delivery to an inland point, and with the understanding (which we assume was not made explicit contractually) that customs clearance would be handled at the delivery point. Subsequently, for reasons which were not made clear, it became understood that customs clearance must transpire at an earlier location, and the seller now feared that he would not be able to reach the ultimate delivery point in time.

We do not know if the seller had guaranteed a particular delivery time, or if he merely fears that he will now exceed a reasonable time. Consequently, we should consider both cases.

The further question raised is that of the buyer's cooperation; if, in order for the goods to pass through customs, it is necessary for the buyer to perform some minimal activity, such as by supplying information to the seller or the customs authorities, and the buyer fails to do so for a very prolonged time (let us say 10 months), out of a simple desire to escape the contract, has the buyer breached any provision of the Incoterms® rules?

Thus, the following further issues are raised by the above question:

1. If the DDU buyer 'stalls' customs clearance by refusing to cooperate, does the late-delivering seller have any excuse or remedy?

This Editor would personally argue that the DDU buyer should be considered under a duty to take timely delivery. Thus, if the lateness was to some extent caused by buyer's own failure to take the goods, such breach cannot be imputed to the seller.

2. If the contract was based on the understanding that customs clearance would be at the delivery point, and it subsequently becomes clear that customs clearance must take place at a different, distant point, which will add appreciably to the transit time, may the seller be allowed an extended period for delivery?

Several cases can be distinguished here. In one case, the seller alone has made a mistake. In another case, an intervening customs regulation has changed a previous clearance procedure. Would this make any difference? The answer to these types of questions generally lies in national laws which deal with the issues of the legal impact of unforeseeable or unpredictable events upon a commercial transaction.

3. If the contract is silent as to delivery time, is there a presumption under the Incoterms® rules that delivery must be made within a reasonable time?

The Incoterms® rules do place a delivery obligation on the seller, and a receipt obligation on the buyer. Although timeliness of performance of these obligations is not specifically covered by the Incoterms® rules, it is generally covered by national law, and as a general principle neither party must unduly or unreasonably delay the performance of delivery.

INCOTERMS® 2010 – MARITIME QUESTIONS

2010 Question 35

Ship and goods on different quays under FAS

Under FAS, if the seller has delivered on the quay, indicated by the buyer, but the boat arrives at another quay, must the seller agree to buyer's request that seller move the goods to this new quay? Article A4 provides delivery must be 'alongside the ship', but also allows seller to 'select the point within the named port of shipment that best suits its purpose'. Can the seller select a point other than physically 'alongside the ship'?

Guidance from ICC experts:

- Under article A4 FAS Incoterms® 2010, the seller delivers the goods by placing them alongside the ship nominated by the buyer at the loading point, if any, indicated by the buyer at the named port of shipment. Under article B7, the buyer must give the seller sufficient notice of the vessel name, loading point and, where necessary, selected delivery time within the agreed period. By providing this information, the buyer makes it possible for the seller to deliver alongside an arrived ship.

- Failing receipt of precise notice on the loading point and the selected delivery time, the seller may use its discretion to select a point that best suits its purpose, and the delivery time within the agreed period. Moreover, in the absence of precise information of place and time, the seller can deliver the goods even when the ship has not arrived.

- Where the buyer has given an indication as to the loading point but later wants to change these instructions, the seller is not obliged to cover the expenses of transferring the goods to a new loading point, provided the seller has acted in line with the buyer´s first instructions and the buyer´s new notice has arrived too late for seller to comply with it without extra cost.

INCOTERMS® 2010 – MARITIME QUESTIONS

2010 Question 36

Containerized shipments and FOB, CFR and CIF

It seems we can no longer use Incoterms® 2010 FOB/CFR/CIF rules for containerized shipments. Is this true? The Guidance Notes on the FOB, CFR and CIF rules say that they may not be appropriate for use where goods are handed over to the carrier before they are on board the vessel, such as goods in containers, which are typically delivered at a terminal.

But sometimes an exporter of goods in containers wants an ocean bill of lading (because the bank requires it in a Letter of Credit, for example). Can the parties agree to use FOB, CFR or CIF but stipulate in the contract of sale that risk passes to buyer when the goods are handed over at the terminal?

Guidance from ICC experts:

- Indeed, the Guidance Notes on FOB, CFR and CIF Incoterms® 2010 caution parties to consider carefully whether the delivery point under these rules makes using them for containerized shipments appropriate.

- For example, even where goods in a container are sold under FOB, a container is typically handed over by the seller at a container yard or warehouse, which is in practice the appropriate delivery point. Given that under FOB, CFR and CIF the seller would bear the risk of loss of or damage to the goods until they are delivered under article A4 by being placed on board the vessel, users are recommended to instead choose FCA, CPT or CIP in such circumstances. The reason is that, under these rules, risk is typically transferred to the buyer when the seller hands the goods over to the carrier, usually earlier than their being placed on board.

- In the case where an exporter of goods in containers wants an ocean bill of lading, the parties can agree as suggested above, stipulating in the contract of sale that risk passes to buyer when the goods are handed over at the terminal. FOB, CFR and CIF require the goods to be delivered on board the vessel and an ocean (shipped) bill of lading is evidence thereof, but that risk would pass at terminal. The better solution is to use FCA or CIP but agree in the sale contract that seller will tender an on board bill of lading and then ask from the carrier either the issue of a shipped bill or (more likely) an annotation on a received for shipment bill of the date of shipment.

- This question is a good example of how important it is that the chosen Incoterms® rule and payment terms are in accordance with each other. The parties could try to refrain from asking for an on board bill of lading in the described situation. If this is not possible, then solutions offered by pricing and/or insurance could be examined.

2010 Question 37 — What does 'on board' mean in FOB, CFR and CIF?

Regarding the delivery point under A4 of FOB, CFR and CIF, what is meant by 'placing' the goods 'on board' the vessel? Are securing, dunnage, and/or trimming of the cargo required? Who has the risk if the goods are dropped on board during loading and damage results?

Guidance from ICC experts:

- Article A4 provides that delivery must be completed 'in the manner customary at the port', and port customs may vary widely. For example, in some ports, goods are considered 'on board' for delivery purposes when they are under ship's tackle. Further, the nature of the cargo and the type of vessel frequently dictate how loading is accomplished.

- In the absence of custom of the port, or other relevant consideration such as practice between the parties, the default position is that goods may be considered to be delivered on board the vessel when first at rest on deck.

- If goods are dropped during loading and land on deck causing damage, the risk would still be considered to be with the seller, since placing goods on board does not contemplate a process that results in damage. If, however, the goods were considered to be already 'on board' when under ship's tackle, the risk would be with the buyer.

- Please also see Question 35, immediately below, on securing and trimming.

2010 Question 38 — Risk transfer in 'free in stowed and secured' under FOB, CFR and CIF

When does risk transfer under FOB/CFR/CIF in a 'free in stowed and secured (and even maybe trimmed)' shipment?

INCOTERMS® 2010 – MARITIME QUESTIONS

Guidance from ICC experts:

- If parties agree on a variant in their contract of sale by adding 'stowed, secured, trimmed', then the costs for the buyer would most likely be understood to begin only when the goods were safely stowed/secured/trimmed as set out in the contract, and passage of risk would likewise be delayed.

- In order to be sure about allocation of costs and risks, though, under any variant of an Incoterms® rule, parties are strongly encouraged to make their intent clear in their contract of sale.

2010 Question 39 Goods destroyed mid-loading under FOB

Under FOB, what happens if goods are destroyed during loading when only part of the goods has been put on board? Has delivery been made under article A4, so that risk for the goods already on board has passed to the buyer?

Guidance from ICC experts:

- Article A4 provides that the seller must deliver the goods by placing them on board – 'them' referring to all the goods.

- As all the goods have not yet been delivered, the risk (article A5) has not yet passed and the risk is for the seller.

- The answer will be different if partial delivery is agreed or allowed under the contract of sale.

2010 Question 40 Packaging, containers and break bulk under FOB

We are the seller under FOB contracts stating that the cargo must be shipped in fumigated wooden crates able to withstand the ocean transportation. The cargo is many times a mix of small and large wooden crates and the buyer sometimes insists that the smaller crates are to be containerized.

Are we obliged to ship in containers under FOB Incoterms® 2010? We take the position that the cargo is in wooden seaworthy crates and the contract does not mention containers, but the buyer insists that the FOB rule means the goods are to be shipped in containers. Our position is that we can ship FOB Break Bulk and if the buyer wants containers, all costs associated with containers are for the buyer.

Guidance from ICC experts:

- The FOB Incoterms® 2010 rule does not presuppose that goods are shipped in containers. On the contrary, the relevant Guidance Note indicates that FOB may not be appropriate for goods shipped in containers due to the fact that delivery of containers takes place prior to the goods are on board the vessel, and that frequently FCA is a better choice.

- Article A9 of FOB provides that the seller must package the goods (unless it is usual for the particular type of goods to be transported unpackaged) in a manner appropriate for transport, unless the buyer has notified the seller of specific packaging requirements prior to the conclusion of the sale contract. The Introduction ('*Explanation of terms used in the Incoterms® 2010 rules*') mentions that containerization is not included in the term 'packaging' as used in the Incoterms® 2010 rules. Therefore, the buyer could not strictly speaking base its requirements to stow the crates in containers on the provisions of FOB Incoterms® 2010, even if the requirement is made prior to the conclusion of the contract of sale. However, the unwritten rationale of article A9 of each of the Incoterms® 2010 rules — that the buyer can impose reasonable requirements on the safe packaging of the goods — could lead to the conclusion that such a requirement can validly be made under the applicable sales law. In case of the seller's containers (Full Container Load, FCL), transport law may treat containers not as a means of transport, as suggested by the Incoterms® 2010 rules, but as the goods (which means that they constitute packaging under transport law).

2010 Question 41 — Proof of delivery, bill of lading, under FOB

In FOB Incoterms® 2010

- Who pays the cost of the bill of lading?

- And what if the seller booked the freight at the buyer's request?

Guidance from ICC experts:

- Article A8 (Delivery document) of FOB Incoterms® 2010 states that: 'the seller must provide the buyer, at the seller's expense, with the usual proof that the goods have been delivered in accordance with A4'. The same article further provides that: 'unless such proof is a transport document, the seller must provide assistance to the buyer, at the buyer's request, risk, and expense, in obtaining a transport document'.

- The above quotations mean that in certain situations such as particular trades, ports or practices with ship owners, or even practices established between the parties, the usual proof of delivery is a transport document (usually an on board bill of lading) in which case the seller pays the costs of the bill of lading. Alternatively, there are situations where the usual proof may be a receipt only, and it is for the buyer to pay the costs of the bill.

- Article A3(a) of FOB Incoterms® 2010 now contains a possibility that: 'if requested by the buyer or if it is commercial practice and the buyer does not give an instruction to the contrary in due time, the seller may contract for carriage on usual terms at the buyer's risk and expense'.

- The Incoterms® 2010 Drafting Group did not consider in detail whether the reference to the buyer's costs would entail the costs of producing a bill of lading. On balance, it is submitted that the reference relates to the freight costs only, and that the seller may have to bear the costs of the carrier issuing a bill of lading in practices where a transport document is the usual proof of delivery. As the seller may even conclude a contract of carriage on the buyer's behalf, a bill of lading could easily be regarded as proof that goods have been delivered pursuant to FOB so modified.

2010 Question 42: Loading a ship under FOB, CFR and CIF

How to load a ship under the Incoterms® 2010 rules FOB, CFR and CIF?

Guidance from ICC experts:

This is a rather general question. One should carefully examine the obligations of the seller and buyer under the relevant Incoterms® 2010 rule, especially the A4 (Delivery) and B4 (Taking Delivery) provisions. The seller's obligation to place the goods on board the vessel in due time is the essence of the delivery obligation under these rules. If there is a different custom at the port of shipment, then the seller delivers the goods/loads the ship in the manner customary at that port. Moreover, loading may be subject to special conditions such as the provisions of the sales contract between the parties, nature of the product, type of vessel, etc.

2010 Question 43 — Formalities in intra-EU sale under FOB

The FOB Incoterms® 2010 rule requires the seller to clear the goods for export. For sea transport between Member States, there is no 'export' regime in the sense commonly accepted by the EU Customs regulation. However, a simplified (but similar procedure) is needed to prove the Community status of the goods in the port of arrival (that is, application for a T2L document).

Is it correct to say that a seller has the obligation to provide a T2L document to the buyer for goods delivered under FOB Incoterms® 2010 in case of sea transport between Member States?

Guidance from ICC experts:

- In order to be able to answer any specific questions regarding the parties' obligations in respect of export, transit or import formalities, we should examine what the formalities in question consist of. A T2L-document is used to confirm the Union status of the goods traded. A T2L is mentioned in paragraph 4 of the Single Administrative Document (see Commission Regulation No. 756/2012 and further legislation references contained therein). A T2L document can simply be a 'T2L' notion in the commercial invoice or transport document designated solely for that quantity of Union goods.

- Article A2 of FOB Incoterms® 2010 vests the task of export clearance with the seller and the transit formalities and import clearance with the buyer. Under articles A10 and B10, the seller and buyer are under a duty to render assistance to each other in carrying out the export and import formalities, as the case may be. This will depend on the relevant administrative provisions, and on which information and documents need to be furnished at which end. In the EU, the seller does not have transaction-specific clearance obligations but merely block reporting obligations of Intrastat and VAT. Practically speaking, however, the seller is in a position to include a T2L notion in the invoice that the seller will provide anyway (also pursuant to article A1 FOB Incoterms® 2010).

- Indeed, as a general rule, the Incoterms® rules have traditionally been used in international sale contracts. Nonetheless, the Incoterms® 2010 rules explicitly state that they are available for application to both international and domestic sale contracts, presumably because in various areas of the world, customs unions (such as the European Union) and

INCOTERMS® 2010 – MARITIME QUESTIONS

free market areas have made border formalities between countries less significant.

2010 Question 44 — Risk and port charges under FOB

In each of the two scenarios regarding Incoterms® 2010 rule FOB described below,

- Who bears risk of damage to the cargo, the buyer or the seller?

- Who should pay for the origin THC (terminal handling charge) – that is, a charge levied by the port of shipment that is invoiced to the shipping line?

Scenario 1: An exporter and importer have agreed upon the Incoterms® 2010 rule FOB Cape Town port. At the time the sales contract was agreed upon, it was unknown which shipping line or vessel would be used.

At the time of export, the exporter loads the container at its premises and its forwarding agent arranges for the container to be sent to the export stack for the vessel as advised by the importer/agent; the container is placed into the export stack and the importer is notified.

The vessel nominated by the buyer is delayed due to wind and collects the cargo only after the scheduled loading date.

During the time after the export agent has placed the container into the export stack, (which is customary in procuring the container so delivered in South African ports) and the placing of the container on board the vessel nominated by the buyer at the loading point, the goods are damaged.

Scenario 2: Same as above, except the vessel is not delayed due to wind, but the cargo is left behind on the quayside due to a 'short shipment' resulting from the vessel being overladen at the previous port of call.

The cargo is damaged between the time of delivery into the export stack and when the container is shipped on the next available vessel.

Guidance from ICC experts:

Scenario 1: The risk is for the buyer's account as per B5 (b), as the vessel failed to arrive on time. However, if the vessel had arrived on time, the risk would remain with the seller throughout the vessel loading.

Scenario 2: The same as for Scenario 1, except that the reason is not late arrival but that the vessel was unable to take on the goods.

Note that the Incoterms® 2010 rules strongly recommend that the marine-only rules (FAS, FOB, CFR and CIF) not be used for shipments of goods in containers because sellers typically hand over the goods to the buyer-appointed carriers at points prior to vessel loading.

Under FOB Incoterms® 2010, the seller is obliged to deliver the goods on board the vessel nominated by the buyer. At delivery, the risk passes from the seller to the buyer. The moment and method of delivering the goods on board under FOB depend on the custom of the port (see the answers to earlier queries addressing the custom of the port). As apparently necessary, the Panel of Experts would hesitantly stretch the reference to the custom of the port to cover ordinary methods (i.e. into stack) to deliver containers to the carrier at the loading terminal under FOB. Such a custom may not be universal since many ocean carriers would not cover expenses at the shore side. In lieu of the custom of the port, one may be able to refer to an agreement between the parties, express or implied, to deliver the goods to the carrier this way. Ideally, the parties should use such an agreement to amend FCA and not FOB.

INCOTERMS® 1990 – MARITIME QUESTIONS

1990 Question 17

FAS – Delivery period

In a FAS contract, delivery period is 'week 33'. During that week, on Tuesday, the seller places the goods on the quay where the ship will load on Thursday, but, on Wednesday, they are destroyed by a fire. There is no custom of the port or trade usage. Who must bear that risk?

Answer of the Panel of Incoterms® Experts:

Delivery can take place only alongside the vessel. According to B7, the buyer has the right to specify a required delivery time in the delivery period of the contract, which has been made. Since delivery did not take place, the risk of loss of the goods must be borne by the seller.

Analysis:

The text of the Incoterms® rules indicates that the seller must deliver the goods alongside the vessel, and the '*Guide to Incoterms 1990*' adds that the goods must be placed alongside the vessel. If the ship is not there, delivery cannot be performed. It can take place only when the ship is berthed, moored and cleared by health and customs officers, and in that case, ready to load on Thursday, since that day has been agreed upon.

As to the buyer, we can suppose that he has fulfilled his obligations and has given the notice of B7 about delivery time since it is agreed that the ship must load on Thursday, which is before the end of the delivery period. Concerning the insurance question raised in that question, A3 and B3 specify that there is no obligation. It is purely a matter of agreement between both partners. In fact, both of them should be insured, but Incoterms themselves do not have to deal with this problem.

1990 Editor's notes and observations:

The Panel of Incoterms® Experts' decision here sets forth the following rule for passage of risk in an FAS sale under particular circumstances: when goods are timely delivered to the quay but destroyed before ship's arrival and prior to expiry of the delivery period, the risk cannot be said to have passed from seller to buyer.

The Panel did not further consider the related question, what would happen if the ship were very late and the goods were destroyed one day after the expiry of the delivery period? The likely answer is that the buyer would have been held liable, for failing to take delivery within the allotted period. Although risk can normally be said to pass under FAS only when the ship has been berthed, as per the above Panel decision, some courts and legal commentators have argued for an exception allowing for what has been termed 'premature transfer' of the risk in those cases when the buyer fails to meet his obligation to receive delivery in a timely fashion.

1990 Question 18 — FAS – Who should be listed as shipper?

May a seller under FAS terms request that he not be indicated on the air waybill as shipper and that the freight forwarder be listed as the shipper on the air waybill and the shipper's export declaration?

Facts:

A US seller sells goods on an FAS basis to a South African buyer. The buyer arranges shipment by a US freight forwarder. The seller requests the freight forwarder not to include seller's name on waybill as shipper, nor on shipper's export declaration, but rather to put the freight forwarder as shipper of record.

Answer of the Panel of Incoterms® Experts:

Above all, it should be made clear that under *Incoterms 1990* FAS should only be used for purely maritime shipments.

In this case it would appear that the parties made an inappropriate reference to the FAS Incoterms® rule, which throws the entire question into doubt. If in fact the parties have completely misunderstood the Incoterms® rules requirements, the answer may depend on the interpretation of a contract involving a mistake by both of the parties; this is a matter which can only be decided under the applicable law, and is therefore beyond the remit of the Panel of Experts.

In any case, note that the seller is under an obligation to render the buyer any assistance necessary in obtaining export customs clearance.

1990 Editor's notes and observations:

The above cases brings to light an interesting anomaly in international trade: with FAS, FCA and FOB the transport document will frequently be initially handed over to the exporter as 'shipper', although from a strictly legal point of view it is the buyer who is the contractual 'shipper'.

It may happen that a particular seller does not want to appear upon the export documentation, or conversely, the buyer may wish to insist on the right to receive the transport document as the contractual shipper – perhaps the FAS buyer does not want the seller to know the ultimate destination of the goods. A shipper does have certain legal responsibilities, for example to report information to tax or customs authorities, and in some cases it may not be convenient for the seller to undertake these tasks.

In such cases it would seem that legal theory runs up against the hard rock of everyday practice, because so many traders assume that the seller must appear as shipper. If the parties wish to avoid any possibility that the seller may be considered an export 'shipper', they might consider selling Ex Works. Ex Works is the Incoterms® rule which is the least 'international', since it is from the seller's point of view virtually the same as a domestic sale.

1990 Question 19 — FAS/FOB – differences between the two rules

What is the difference, if any, between FAS and FOB as regards the following:

1. When does title transfer?
2. Who bears the cost of procuring export documentation?

Facts:
An exporter offers terms on FAS or FOB basis, nominating a freight forwarder to handle orders. The buyer, American, wants to know his rights under both rules.

Answer of the Panel of Incoterms® Experts:
Please note that the following answers apply unless there is a contractual stipulation to the contrary.

1. When does title transfer? The Incoterms® rules do not – and were never intended to – deal with the transfer of property rights. The issue depends upon the contract of sale and upon the law governing the passage of property.

2. Who bears the cost of procuring export documentation? Under FOB, the seller pays the cost of procuring export documentation. Under FAS, it is the buyer who pays these costs.

1990 Editor's notes and observations:

The Incoterms® rules and the transfer of title or transfer of property

The question is, when does title or ownership of the goods legally pass from seller to buyer? The question pre-supposes that there are various possibilities for the transfer of title, and indeed this appears to be the case in practice.

The transfer of property is a complex issue in international trade, which has resisted easy clarification or harmonization. Basic legal principles of property vary greatly from country to country. Nonetheless, the issue remains a very important one and one of crucial interest in particular cases. For example, if goods are delivered on open account to a buyer who becomes insolvent before paying the exporter, can the exporter seek to recover his property? It would appear that in some jurisdictions this is possible through the use of a so-called 'retention of title' or 'reservation of title' clause in the contract. In essence, the seller reserves title over the goods until he has received the purchase price in full.

1990 Question 20 FOB – Berthing and demurrage charges

Under an FOB contract:

1. Does responsibility for providing berthing at port of shipment lie with the seller or the buyer?

2. For whose account are demurrage charges on account of delay in berthing?

Facts:

An Indian seller sold methanol to a European buyer FOB Bombay, shipment to be by charter party arranged by the buyer.

Answer of the Panel of Incoterms® Experts:

1. Does the responsibility of providing berthing at the jetty in Bombay lie with the buyer or the seller?

In the absence of special stipulation in the contract of sale, the responsibility for making the shipping arrangements, including berthing, lies with the buyer. The seller's responsibility is to 'deliver the goods on board the vessel' (A4). The buyer's duty is to 'contract at his own expense for the carriage of the goods from the named port of shipment' (B3) and to give the seller 'sufficient notice of the … loading point …' (B7). It follows from these three articles that the naming of the loading point – and therefore its procurement – is a matter for the

INCOTERMS® 1990 – MARITIME QUESTIONS

buyer, saving contrary stipulation in the contract of sale.

2. Does the buyer or the seller bear the responsibility for paying the demurrage due because of delay cause in berthing at the loading port?

As between shipowner and charterer, it is clearly the charterer (buyer) who pays the charges.

However, can the buyer claim the demurrage (due by him under the charter party) from the seller (under the contract of sale)? Our opinion is that the buyer cannot, saving contrary contractual stipulation.

The Incoterms® rule FOB B3 states that buyer must 'contract at his own expense for the carriage of goods …'. The responsibility for transport arrangements is thus placed squarely on the buyer.

IFOB A6 states that seller 'must pay all costs relating to the goods until such time as they have passed the ship's rail'. Note that the reference is to costs 'relating to the goods' – which implies that costs related to transport are for the buyer.

1990 Editor's notes and observations:

Here, the Panel of Experts firmly closed the door on the possibility for an FOB buyer to escape his contractual obligations by claiming that berthing was difficult to obtain in timely manner.

Moreover, it was not felt that the buyer should be able to pass on demurrage charges to either seller or shipowner.

This rule simply points to one of the basic differences between the two sets of maritime terms, FOB and FAS on the one hand, and CFR and CIF on the other. With the 'F' rules, the buyer takes the risk that transport-related costs will turn out to be higher than he anticipated when he entered into the contract. For example, sudden rises in freight rates (after the signing of an FOB contract) will have a negative impact only on the buyer. With 'C' rules, sudden rises in freight rates are a problem for the seller. Thus, important fluctuations in the oil markets may have important repercussions on the different choice between 'F' rules and 'C' rules (because ocean freight is adjusted according to fluctuations in the cost of the oil which powers transport ships – this is known as the Bunker Adjustment Factor – BAF). Many transport contracts allow the carrier to adjust the freight quickly, in effect, by linking it to fluctuations in the bunker market.

1990 Question 21 FOB – Terminal handling charges

National carrier asks – how is FOB term defined in Germany, Holland, Belgium and UK? Main interest concerns the responsibilities of the carrier and the division of cost concerning terminal handling charges under A.M. rule (shipper/receiver – who pays what?).

Answer of the Panel of Incoterms® Experts:

The Incoterms® rules book makes clear the general division of costs under FOB, and this division should be similar in all the countries mentioned. However, under the terms of FOB, customs of the port may determine particular aspects of the division of costs, but this can only be studied in each port separately. Prior inquiry as to the particular customs of a port is the only practical solution. The members of the Panel were not aware of the A.M. rule.

1990 Editor's notes and observations:

The Panel did not choose to also note with respect to this instance that the FOB term can cause difficulties when goods are delivered to a seaport terminal for intermediate storage or handling prior to loading on board. The seller does not transfer costs and risk to the buyer under FOB until the goods pass the ship's rail, but in the case of delivery to a terminal the seller relinquishes control over the goods before they reach the ship's rail. Moreover, an FOB buyer does not expect to pay for any handling costs incurred prior to loading. Therefore, it would seem that the best solution for the seller is use the FCA rule and precisely specify the point of delivery at the seaport terminal.

For the buyer, there are advantages in remaining with the FOB rule, in that the buyer does not incur any costs or risks prior to the goods passing the ship's rail. One compromise is to use the FCA rule, but to add a notation that 'costs up to ship's rail for seller's account'. That way the seller transfers risk when he delivers the goods, but the buyer does not have to pay for unexpected overseas handling charges.

1990 Question 22

FOB – Transshipment

A freight forwarder is responsible for coordinating the shipment, taking delivery from vendors in Sweden (Helsingborg) and Finland based on the FOB Incoterms® rule, shipping the equipment to a port in Indonesia and carrying out custom clearance at the port of discharge. There is no direct shipment from Sweden to Indonesia and the goods have to go to Hamburg. Who has to pay for the Terminal Handling Charges which take place during the carriage of the goods; in this case in Hamburg? To what extent should the vendor pay for the loading cost? Is packaging included in a loading cost?

Answer of the Panel of Incoterms® Experts:

Under FOB, all horizontal charges connected with the delivery, before the critical point should be paid by the seller. The transshipment, including Terminal Handling Charges in Hamburg and all related costs, are for the buyer's account, according to section B3 and B6.

Analysis:

Firstly, we assume that the contract refers to the Incoterms® rules and not liner terms, and secondly, that the Incoterms® rules used are FOB Helsingborg and FOB named port in Finland. As far as the FOB Incoterms® rule is concerned, the buyer has to enter, at his own expenses, into a contract for the carriage of the goods from the named port of shipment. However, customs of the port, customs in the trade or previous course of dealing can always impose a different solution. As for loading costs, it is necessary to distinguish between the Incoterms® rules, which are found in the contract of sale between the buyer and the seller, and liner terms, found in the contract of carriage between the transporter and his client. Under the Incoterms® rules, loading the goods on board is the seller's responsibility. Note that packaging is generally not considered as part of the loading costs, although normal packaging is the seller's responsibility under section A9 of the Incoterms® rules to the extent that the circumstances relating to the transport are made known to the seller before the contract of sale is concluded. If liner terms were used the loading and unloading charges would generally be included in the freight and then would be paid by the buyer. However, the ICC cannot pronounce definitively upon an interpretation of liner terms, since those are not ICC products.

Finally, note that in case of a containerized shipment the term FCA should be used instead of FOB.

1990 Editor's notes and observations:

The Panel attempted to provide some general education in its response, apparently in the belief that the question was based to some extent on the very common misunderstanding amongst traders of failing to properly distinguish the contract of sale and the contract of transport. The Incoterms® rules should only appear in the contract of sale; that is the only place where they make sense.

It does happen (although the ICC opposes the practice) that a carrier will quote a freight rate on 'FOB' terms. Such a freight quote cannot involve Incoterms, which only regulate the relationship between the seller and buyer, and do not concern the carrier. However, when a dispute arises under a carriage contract which contains such an 'FOB' rule, it should not be surprising that some traders mistakenly assume that issues arising under the carriage contract are covered by the Incoterms® rules.

1990 Question 23 'FOB Airport' – Payment of dangerous goods fee

Under the FOB Incoterms® rule, who as between seller and buyer must pay the 'airline dangerous goods fee'?

Facts:

The seller believes that this fee should be paid by the buyer, because an FOB seller is not responsible for the main international transport.

Answer of the Panel of Incoterms® Experts:

Assuming that the contract is silent and that the charge is payable to the airline as part of the freight charges, *the fee should, as between seller and buyer, be borne by the buyer*. The Incoterms® rule FOB B3 makes it clear that the buyer must 'contract at his own expense for the carriage of the goods ...'.

Incoterms 1990 normally give guidance as to the precise division of costs in term 6 of each Incoterm, which in FOB talks of costs before and after passage of the goods across the ship's rail. This illustrates the difficulties caused when the FOB term is used for the sale of goods carried by air.

The better term for air shipments is FCA, which, under B6, obliges the buyer to pay all costs after delivery, which is in turn defined in A4 as 'when the goods have been handed over to the carrier or to another person acting on his behalf.' Thus, under the FCA rule, the airline dangerous goods charge would fall on the buyer (either when booking the space --under B3 – or when the

INCOTERMS® 1990 – MARITIME QUESTIONS

goods are handed over, depending on when the charges are levied by the airline).

1990 Editor's notes and observations:

Note that the Panel's answer is the same regardless of whether the parties have referred (as recommended) to FCA airport or whether they have referred to the term 'FOB' airport, which has been dropped from the list of valid Incoterms® rules.

Usage of FOB for airport shipments ('FOB airport') continues to be quite common, notwithstanding its absence from the roster of valid Incoterms® rules. The reason that FCA is preferable is that FOB may lend itself to an interpretation according to which the seller must load the goods 'on board' the aircraft. This can lead to disputes as to payment of charges incurred in the airport terminal. At least in this case, however, the costs are clearly related to transport; therefore, there would be no difference in result between FCA and FOB airport. The ICC continues to recommend that FCA be used in place of FOB for airport shipments, and that generally FOB be restricted to use in purely maritime contexts.

1990 Question 24 FOB – 'Deadfreight' claim

As between seller and buyer, under the FOB Incoterms® rule who must pay a 'deadfreight claim' by the buyer's shipbroker, resulting from the ship loading lightweight?

Facts:

A UK buyer bought solid fuel on terms FOB 'stowed' Incoterms®, payment by letter of credit negotiated in a London bank on basis of clean bill of lading. The buyer believes that the charge should be payable by the loadport freight forwarder, who was appointed by the seller.

Answer of the Panel of Incoterms® Experts:

Liability for deadfreight is imposed by the contract of carriage, and it therefore rests on the cargo interest who has contracted for the carriage of the goods, in this case the buyer.

Deadfreight is an incident of the contract of carriage and is a liquidated sum payable by a cargo interest, normally a voyage-charterer, for having failed to ship the quantity of goods which the cargo interest has undertaken to ship *under the contract of carriage*.

The buyer here is presumably attempting to recover from the seller deadfreight which he has paid or is bound to pay to the carrier under the contract of carriage. In the absence of any specific term in the contract of sale stipulating for such recourse – as is common, for example, with demurrage clauses – the buyer will have to bear this cost himself, and this for two reasons.

First, this is a liability under the contract of carriage, for which the cargo interest party to that contract is exclusively liable. Second, the division of costs in A6 and B6 provides no guidance, as a deadfreight charge can hardly be described as a cost 'relating to the goods': it is a liability under the contract of carriage for non-shipment of goods.

Finally, note that the term 'stowed' is not defined by the Incoterms® rules. Traders should be careful in using this type of provision that they understand the consequences --in terms of both division of cost and transfer of risk – of the modification.

1990 Question 25: FOB – What does it mean to 'effectively' pass ship's rail?

1. Under *Incoterms 1980*, the FOB seller was to bear all costs and risks of the goods until such time as they had 'effectively' passed the ship's rails, whereas under *Incoterms 1990* the word 'effectively' is dropped. What is the reason for this omission?

2. Under FOB, as under CFR and CIF, the risk of loss or damage is transferred from seller to buyer when the goods cross the ship's rail. What happens if the goods are damaged after crossing the ship's rail but prior to safe deposition in the ship's holds? For example, what would be the result if the goods were dropped into the hold and damaged in the process?

Answer of the Panel of Incoterms® Experts:

1. The word 'effectively' was not felt to add any useful substance to the definition of FOB and was, therefore, dropped.

As the Incoterms® rules are not published with an official legislative history and transcripts of the deliberations of the drafting committee are unavailable, we can only conjecture as to the meaning of the word 'effectively' in the above context. FOB was once applied more broadly than is counselled today, so that FOB was used even for those export shipments involving multimodal transport, roll-on roll-off ships (RO-RO), or containerized cargo (prior to *Incoterms 1976*). In the case of FOB shipments via RO-RO vessels, in particular, the issue of 'effectively' crossing the ship's rail was important because the goods passed *underneath* the ship's rail. However, since the advent of FCA it is no longer necessary today to specify 'effectively' for FOB, because *Incoterms 1990* make it quite clear that shipments via RO-RO vessel, or involving multimodal transport or containerized cargo, call for the use of the Incoterms specifically-designed for such circumstances: FCA, CPT and CIP.

2. Under FOB, if goods are damaged because they are dropped into the hold, after having crossed the ship's rail, the damages must be borne by the buyer.

Thus, Incoterms® rule article B5 places on buyer the duty to 'bear all risks of loss or damage to the goods from the time they have passed the ship's rail'. Clearly, the drafters could have chosen to state 'until the goods are safely deposited in the ship's hold' if that had been their intention. One could be confused here by the provision in the FOB Incoterms® rule A4 that the seller must 'deliver the goods on board the vessel', which could be interpreted wrongly to mean that the seller must safely deposit the goods on the ship's deck or in its holds. The correct interpretation is that in the context of FOB A4, the meaning of 'delivery' is that the seller must, at his cost and risk, make sure that the merchandise has, in good condition, been hoisted over the ship's side and is prepared to descend to the deck or the holds. The risks associated with the descent of the goods to the deck are for the buyer, as are all costs and risks associated with stowing and trimming the goods.

3. The question further raises two related issues: would the answer to point 2 above differ if the seller were also under a duty to tender an 'on-board' bill of lading for payment? And why does the FOB Incoterms® rule not require the tender of an on-board bill of lading by the seller?

i) First, why does the FOB Incoterms® rule not require the tender of an 'on-board' bill of lading by the seller?

In an FOB sale, the obligation to make the contract of carriage lies, not with the seller but with the buyer. Consequently, the seller is not contemplated by Incoterms 1990 as the party who is likely to receive a bill of lading from the carrier and who will then tender it to the buyer.

Nonetheless, the seller is under a duty to tender the buyer the 'usual document in proof of delivery' (A8) and not the usual transport document. This envisages the seller procuring from the carrier a document such as a mate's receipt, which the buyer will then exchange for a bill of lading by tender to the carrier.

It should be added, however, that the FOB contract is a flexible instrument. It is perfectly possible for the sale contract to stipulate, albeit incorporating *Incoterms 1990,* that the seller is to make the contract of carriage, or that he is to procure the bill of lading and then tender it to the buyer. This will nonetheless be an FOB contract, to which *Incoterms 1990* will apply if incorporated, with additional duties imposed explicitly by the contract.

ii) What happens if the goods are damaged during stowage across the ship's rail in a situation where the seller is under a contractual duty to tender an 'on-board' bill of lading?

We assume that the question means that the seller and buyer have agreed that payment will be made against tender of a 'clean on-board bill of lading'. Here, risk of loss or damage to the goods still passes across the ship's rail. However, if the seller has, in addition to his basic duties under *Incoterms 1990*, undertaken the duty to tender a 'clean on-board bill of lading', he will not be in a position to make such tender, and he will not be paid by the buyer. In these circumstances, the seller is under two types of duty: documentary duties and physical duties. Although he has delivered the goods across the ship's rail, he is not in a position to tender the documents stipulated for in the contract of sale and will not therefore be paid by the buyer.

1990 Editor's comments and observations:

Is the traditional interpretation of FOB well-adapted to current transport practice?

One of the first things students learn about the Incoterms® rules is that costs and risks are divided at the ship's rail. It is an ancient rule, the origins of which lie in early maritime practices. However, it is increasingly open to question whether this venerable rule actually reflects current practice. And if it does not reflect current practice, one should consider changing it, regardless of its venerable nature.

As for the practical division of costs in maritime transport, it is virtually never the case that these are split at the ship's rail, as the Incoterms® rule provides.

Generally, the cost of hoisting goods over the ship's rail and lowering them to the deck are considered as one indivisible cost, which is either included in the freight or not, and which is paid entirely either by seller or buyer. It is never the case that the cost of hoisting upward is divided from the cost of lowering to the deck. Moreover, the strict usage of the words 'on board' in FOB – 'Free on board' – can easily be misunderstood to mean that the seller's obligation is to deliver the goods on deck or into the ship's holds.

1990 Question 26 CFR – Transfer of risk point

A major Indonesian oil producer asks:

1. Under the CFR Incoterms® rule, is the seller at risk during international transport, to the point of discharge;

2. Is 'delivery date' to be interpreted as delivery at port of departure (or delivery at port of discharge)?

Facts:

Apparently, in the enquirer's experience, some counterparties are under the impression that the seller always remains responsible for loss or damage, throughout transport to port of discharge, and remains responsible for respecting a delivery date at port of discharge; moreover, the enquirer understands delivery date to refer to delivery in the port of departure and would like this interpretation confirmed.

Answer of the Panel of Incoterms® Experts:

1. Where does risk pass under CFR?

Clearly, risk under CFR passes in the port of loading. However, a contractual promise of delivery by a certain date to the port of discharge raises the possibility of contradicting the CFR term, in that it implies that risk does not pass until delivery at the port of discharge. The Incoterms® rules cannot resolve the issue. An answer will depend on an interpretation of the contract and the attendant circumstances.

2. Does the term 'delivery' in conjunction with the CFR rule refer to delivery on board the vessel in the port of shipment, or in the port of discharge?

Under the Incoterms® rules, goods are delivered on board the vessel in the port of shipment, and any date mentioned in connection thereto normally refers to the date of delivery in the *port of shipment*.

Despite this clear rule under the Incoterms® rules, it is nonetheless possible that the parties decide to use the term 'delivery' in a different sense in a particular contract (for example, if the contract spoke both of a 'date of shipment' and then a later 'date of delivery'). Thus, it could well be that a court would consider that the parties had mutually agreed to a modification of the meaning of term 'delivery' as defined in the provisions of Incoterms® rule CFR A4. Thus, if it could be established that the parties intended that the goods be delivered in the *port of discharge* by a certain date, then their express intention would supersede the Incoterms® rules. However, it would raise the further question of whether it was also the parties' intention to alter the transfer of risk accordingly. This example shows how careful parties must be when changing the basic scheme provided by the Incoterms® rules: a modification of a cost or delivery provision may also alter the transfer of risk provisions.

1990 Editor's notes and observations:

One of the most common misconceptions concerning the Incoterms® rules is to think that the transfer of risk under CFR or CIF takes place at *destination*. It does not: it takes place at the ship's rail in the port of *departure*, exactly as with FOB.

This misconception seems logical, because with CFR or CIF one identifies the name of the port of destination (e.g., CIF Singapore, for goods shipped from Los Angeles to Singapore), whereas with FOB one states the name of the port of departure (e.g., FOB Los Angeles, for goods a shipped from Los Angeles to Singapore). As a result, FOB is associated in the minds of traders with ports of shipment, CFR and CIF with ports of destination. But this leads to the erroneous conclusion that seller is at risk under CFR or CIF during the main international transport. Rather, the seller under CFR and CIF has precisely the same point of transfer of risk as under FOB: the ship's rail. Once the goods have crossed the ship's rail, all risks are for the buyer, equally true under FOB, CFR and CIF. In addition the CIF buyer will have obtained an insurance policy, but that does not eliminate the risk question or change the point of transfer of risk; moreover, there is always the question of whether the policy will be sufficient to satisfy any claims for damages.

1990 Question 27: CFR – Unloading 'liner out'

In the absence of any specific mention in the pro forma invoice or L/C, does a CFR price mean 'free out' or 'liner out'?

Answer of the Panel of Incoterms® Experts:

It is clear under sections A6 and B6 of CFR and CIF that the seller will pay 'any charges for unloading and discharge which may be levied regular shipping lines when contracting for carriage'. Thus, in the above question a factual determination would be required as to whether the transport was via 'regular shipping line'.

As is specified at page 29 in the *Guide to Incoterms 1990*, 'Liner shipping companies usually include costs of loading and discharge in their freight rates, but in charter party operations there may be provisions stipulating that the discharging operations should be wholly or partly 'free' to the carrier ('free out' stipulations)'.

As is further specified at page 79 of the *Guide to Incoterms 1990*, 'In any case, the expression 'liner terms' is vague and ambiguous, and it is recommended that the parties specifically deal with the conditions of the contract of carriage in the contract of sale when carriage is not be arranged by regular, well-known shipping lines'.

1990 Editor's notes and observations:

Once again, the very wording of the questions indicates that the inquirer may not have fully appreciated the distinction between the Incoterms® rules – as terms of *the contract of sale* – and 'liner terms' or 'free out' provisions, which are forms of quoting freight rates under *contracts of carriage*.

Although there is no official definition of 'liner terms', it is perhaps safe to say that the common meaning assigned to this term is that the freight includes a certain amount of loading and unloading services. 'Free out', in contrast, implies that the freight does not include any unloading services. Both of these terms apply only to carriage contracts.

It is essential that the transport responsibilities under the contract of sale match up with the transport responsibilities under the contract of carriage.

1990 Question 28: CFR – Unloading charges – Tramp vessels

Under the CFR Incoterms® rule, who must take care of unloading charges when tramp vessels are used?

Facts:
A Russian state agency sold steel coils on terms CFR Karachi, with shipment via tramp vessels. A dispute arose as the division of unloading costs in the port of destination.

Answer of the Panel of Incoterms® Experts:
Under the CFR Incoterms® rule A3/B3 and A6/B6, it is clear that unloading charges in the port of destination are for buyer's account **unless** they are levied by regular shipping lines as part of the freight.

1990 Question 29: CFR – Importer refusing to timely receive goods

In the event of CFR sales, is there anything a seller can do about the problem of an importer who does not accept the goods immediately upon arrival and seeks more or less to use the vessel as a floating warehouse?

Answer of the Panel of Incoterms® Experts:

1. First, it should be noted that CFR *Liner Terms* represents a combination of an Incoterms® rule with a term which is not subject to any precise, standard definition. By selecting CFR Liner Terms as the trade term, the parties run the risk that the lack of definition of this term will lead to ambiguities and disputes. It is therefore advisable that parties clearly state what they mean by CFR Liner Terms.

2. CFR A6 (*Incoterms 1990*) does in fact state that .. any charges for unloading at the port of discharge which may be levied by regular shipping lines when contracting for carriage' are to be paid by the seller. All costs relating to the goods and arising in the port of destination which are not part of the freight for the contract of carriage will have to be borne by the buyer. Whether this finding is somehow altered by the amendment 'Liner Terms' is something which cannot be considered by the ICC, since this addition is not part of the Incoterms® rules system.

3. It should further be noted that the costs resulting from a vessel being used as a floating warehouse might also be freight components such as demurrage charges. Those costs are for the seller according to the Incoterms® rules ('all other costs resulting from A3').

4. It is correct that the Incoterms® rules do not give any indication as to time for acceptance of delivery of goods in the port of discharge. Nevertheless, two remarks should be made. First, CFR B4 stipulates that the buyer must 'accept delivery of the goods when they have been delivered in accordance with A4 and receive them from the carrier at the named port of destination'. The buyer has thus an obligation to the seller to receive the goods. Unless the contract allows the buyer to use the ship as a 'floating warehouse', the buyer is in breach by failure to take delivery as set forth in B4. Second, protection for the seller in those circumstances is usually taken by introducing demurrage clauses into the contract of sale whereby the buyer undertakes to pay a specified demurrage sum to the seller after a defined laytime has elapsed. Those provisions in the contract of sale do however not release the seller from all obligations he has undertaken towards the carrier as the contracting party.

1990 Editor's notes and observations:

The Panel's opinion is simply that the CFR buyer is responsible for costs resulting from his failure to take timely delivery. The question did not state how in practice the buyer was able to defer delivery, and these facts may have been relevant.

1990 Question 30 — CIF – Unloading costs

Under CIF, section A6, 'Division of Costs', we see that the seller must 'pay all costs ... including ... charges for unloading at the port of discharge ...'. However, under CIF, section B6, we see that the buyer must '... pay all costs and charges ... as well as unloading costs including lighterage and wharfage charges'. Are these sections not contradictory with the respect to the seller's obligation to pay for unloading in the case of a CIF sale?

Answer of the Panel of Incoterms® Experts:

As set forth under CIF, A6, the seller only pays for unloading charges if those charges are 'levied by regular shipping lines when contracting for carriage'. That is to say, in the case of liner transport, if the unloading charges are included in the total freight paid by the seller, then the seller may not pass these on to the buyer.

1990 Question 31 'CIF landed'

In the case of a contract 'CIF landed Rotterdam Incoterms 1990', does the seller only have to pay for the discharging onto the quay, or does he also have to pay for discharging into the warehouse?

Answer of the Panel of Incoterms® Experts:

Aside from the observation that the definition of 'CIF landed' is not specified within the Incoterms® rules, the Panel did not set out a consensus decision as to allocation of such charges. It was noted that the only proof of 'custom of port' was a simple declaration of it.

1990 Editor's notes and observations:
What's wrong with using CIF landed?

Unloading charges related to transactions involving the CFR or CIF Incoterms® rules are the source of continual dispute. One way that parties have sought to resolve the potential uncertainties is to add the word 'landed' to CIF, e.g., 'CIF landed'.

The problem with this term is that it can lead one to wonder whether the parties did not intend to use a D rule, a delivered term which places all costs and risks of transport on the seller. 'CIF landed' seems to imply obligations on the part of the seller for actions after delivery, which is only consistent with a 'D' rule.

However, it is also possible that the parties clearly intended CIF landed simply to mean that the seller would be required to procure transport which covered any unloading costs at the port of destination.

1990 Question 32 CIF – Date of shipment

Under the *1980 Incoterms*, CIF rule A4, the seller was obliged to deliver the goods on board the vessel at the point of shipment:

'At the date or within the period fixed or, if neither date nor time has been stipulated, within a reasonable time...'

Under the *1990 Incoterms*, this provision has been altered so that the seller must deliver the goods on board the vessel at the port of shipment.

'On the date or within the period stipulated...'

It appears that the change places rather more emphasis on the specific date of shipment. In light of the trend in the oil trade towards contracts in which more significance is placed upon the date on which the cargo will be delivered, rather than the date of shipment, would the ICC please explain the reasoning behind the change in the 1990 text?

Answer of the Panel of Incoterms® Experts:
No change of substance was intended. A reference to 'reasonable time' does not add anything to what would apply anyway (cf. the 1980 Vienna Convention – if the parties fail to stipulate either a date or period, then the stipulation with respect to 'within a reasonable time' becomes applicable).

1990 Editor's notes and observations:
The *1990 Incoterms* omitted a reference to 'reasonable time' since it was not felt to be necessary (it was felt that a reasonable time rule would be applied in any event). The concern of the questioner is a vivid indication of the degree of interest that professional exporters and importers have in establishing an absolutely perfect understanding of every nuance in the Incoterms® rules. The Incoterms® rules are important. But in this case the questioner's concern was misplaced.

1990 Question 33: CIF – Customs costs

Certain Spanish importers who buy merchandise under CIF named point refuse to pay the costs that the transport company attempts to bill them via the transport company's customs agent. These costs are for: the transport company's intervention in the presentation custom declaration, verification and control of the merchandise, supervision of the transfer or unloading of the merchandise, etc.

It sometimes arises that the importer refuses to pay the customs agent for expenses the agent has undertaken, because the importer considers that said costs are included in the transport price. Under the Incoterms® rules, should the above operations realized by the transporter or his representative be paid by the importer of the merchandise?

Answer of the Panel of Incoterms® Experts:
C rules under the Incoterms® rules clearly place the costs or import clearance on the buyer. The operations of import clearance should not be considered as included in the transport price paid by the exporter of the merchandise. Strictly speaking, the term 'CIF named point' does not appear in the Incoterms® rules, since the only relevant point is the passing of the ship's rail in the port of loading (especially with inland destinations, CIP should be used instead of CIF). If something else is

intended, the CIF term should not be used. With respect to the allocation of custom costs and risk under D rules, see the '*Incoterms 1990*' themselves or the '*Guide to Incoterms 1990*'. 'Free delivered', 'CIF Spanish frontier' or 'Free Spanish frontier' are not Incoterms® rules.

1990 Editor's notes and observations:

Who pays the customs man under CIF?

Clearly, under the Incoterms® rules import customs duties and formalities are for the buyer. However, this question provides an interesting view on the way that disputes can arise under the Incoterms® rules. Small traders rely more and more often on all-purpose freight forwarders to arrange transport, and sometimes these forwarders will also perform customs formalities. The forwarders are constantly required in practice to discern the appropriate splitting of costs under the Incoterms® rules.

Sometimes the forwarder gets the appropriate division wrong, and sometimes (as in the above case) the forwarder or agent gets it right, but the trader does not understand why he is receiving a bill from a transport company (even though in this case it is appropriate for the buyer to receive a bill for customs clearance services performed by the forwarder). This question demonstrates why it is so important for the international freight forwarding community to understand the Incoterms® rules, and it is laudable that FIATA (the international federation of freight forwarding associations) has sought to play a more important role in the development and dissemination of the Incoterms® rules.

1990 Question 34 CIF – Additional 10% insurance cover

With respect to CIF, section A3, why is the minimum insurance cover specified to be the contract price plus 10% (i.e., 110%)? The purpose of the insurance coverage is to cover the value of the goods at destination. Therefore, the additional 10% represents a 'profit' to third parties. Why is this necessary?

Answer of the Panel of Incoterms® Experts:

The idea of an additional 10% goes back to 1906 and the Marine Insurance Act. The purpose is to cover the average profit which buyers of goods expect from the sale. In fact, this excess insurance is a general custom in certain trades and countries, and was incorporated in the very first edition of the Incoterms® rules in 1936.

For example, in the cocoa trade, the custom is to cover the invoice price plus 12.5%. In France, international sales contracts are sometimes insured for up to 20% over the invoice value (though this is only the case for contracts involving international transport). However, there is nothing in the Incoterms® rules that prevents the parties from agreeing to more or less than 110% coverage, provided that both parties to the contract of sale make an express agreement to that effect.

1990 Editor's notes and observations:

It should be noted that the CIF Incoterms® rule insurance requirement can have a major impact in a documentary credit situation.

1990 Question 35

CIF – 'Destination delivery charges' (DDC)

Under the CIF Incoterms® rule, who as between seller or buyer pays for 'DDC' ('Destination Delivery Charges') costs? BAF (Bunker Adjustment Fuel Surcharges) costs?

Facts:

Shipments of Chinese goods sold on a CIF Incoterms® rule basis, unloaded in US and Canadian ports. The bills of lading are marked 'DDC collect at destination' and 'BAF collect', and the total outstanding balance is listed in a box marked 'Freight amount to collect' or simply 'Collect'. The carrier requests payment from the buyer. The main freight was pre-paid. For the purposes of this answer, DDC are understood to be charges generally associated with unloading and handling charges in the port of destination, and BAF are understood be a freight adjustment factor used to account for fluctuations in the price of shipping fuel.

Answer of the Panel of Incoterms® Experts:

It is necessary to draw a distinction between two quite separate questions, i.e. whether the carrier can claim DDC and BAF charges from the buyer, and whether, if the buyer pays the carriage for these charges, he is entitled to recovery from the seller.

The first question is answered not by Incoterms 1990, nor indeed by the contract of sale, but by the contract of carriage between the carrier and buyer (although it is the seller who has arranged transport), presumably contained exclusively in the bill of lading.

The second question is more properly an incident of the contract of sale, and again, the starting point should be the contract itself rather than Incoterms 1990. Thus, if the contract expressly excludes the tender of documents 'collect', then the seller is clearly in breach, and if the buyer has reserved his right to damages on accepting the documents, then the buyer can recover these charges from the seller.

Guidance on the second question is to be sought in *Incoterms 1990* if the contract is silent, and the answer here is clear and as follows:

- DDC charges: From their description in the question, these charges appear to be 'charges for unloading … levied by regular shipping lines when contracting for carriage' within the wording of CIF A6. Subject, therefore, to the buyer having reserved his rights to damages on accepting the documents, the buyer can recover these charges from the seller.

- BAF charges: From their description in the question, these charges are effectively increased freight charges, connected more to the transit of the goods than to their handling. Consequently, the relevant articles are CIF A3(a) and A8, in terms of which the seller must contract for the carriage of the goods at his own expense and must tender a document which enables the buyer to claim the goods from the carrier.

1990 Question 36 CIF – Quay dues at destination

In CIF oil cargo shipments under Worldscale Charter party terms, may the seller pass on to buyer those quay dues ('taxes d'accostage' – charges for the use of oil docks) which, under Worldscale provisions, are for charterer's account rather than shipowners?

Answer of the Panel of Incoterms® Experts:

The Incoterms® Panel is of the opinion that a seller wishing to pass on quay dues as above to the seller should specifically stipulate to that effect in the contract of sale, e.g. 'CIF Incoterms 1990 quay dues for buyer's account'. Failing such a stipulation, it is possible that the facts in a given case (custom of trade, prior course of dealing, port custom, etc.) may justify passing these costs on to buyer, but such factual determinations are not within the ambit of the Incoterms® Panel.

Analysis:

The instant case is a difficult one in that the situation is not explicitly addressed in *Incoterms 1990*. In attempting to interpret the general terms of Incoterms, and particularly the wording of sections A4/B4 and A6/B6 of the CIF Incoterms® 1990 rule, it is in fact possible to arrive at different conclusions. Indeed, the initial response of the Incoterms® Panel on this question was not unanimous. Nonetheless, after due reflection the

INCOTERMS® 1990 – MARITIME QUESTIONS

Incoterms® Panel is of the opinion that the better interpretation of Incoterms is that the seller may not pass on quay dues to the buyer (provided, as stated above, that the factual situation does not indicate an implicit agreement to the contrary).

Let us now examine the reasoning underlying the two opposed points of view, so as to explain the basis for the decision of the Incoterms® Panel.

■ Worldscale Terms

In the basic case referred to the Incoterms® Panel, an oil cargo is shipped under Worldscale Charter party terms to a particular port. Worldscale terms represent a standard framework for charter-parties in the oil trade. Under Worldscale terms, quay dues are allocated between charterer and shipowner depending upon the port of discharge. In the case we are considering here, the Worldscale terms indicate that the quay dues are for the charterer's account. The Incoterms® rules, however, only govern the sales contract between the seller and the buyer, whereas the charter party is an entirely separate contract, with different parties and different terminology. The buyer, for example, is not a party to the charter party contract. Thus, the fact that the charter party allocates certain charges to the charter (who is for our purposes the same party referred to as the 'seller' in the contract of sale governed by Incoterms) does not necessarily preclude the seller from passing these charges on the buyer, provided the seller is justified in doing so according to the Incoterms® rules. In this case, as we have stated above, we believe this justification to be lacking.

■ Seller's arguments for passing on charges

In the case considered here, the arguments that the seller makes in order to justify transferring the quay dues to buyer are as follows:

1. Quay dues in these oil cargo cases are essentially costs associated with discharging the merchandise. The Incoterms® rules specify that the seller must only pay charges for unloading at the port of discharge if such charges are levied by shipping lines (presumably, as part of the freight). Thus, Incoterms® rule CIF A6 reads as follows:

The seller must 'pay ... any charges for unloading at the port of discharge which may be levied by regular shipping lines when contracting for carriage';

and CIF B6 reads:

The buyer must 'pay all costs relating to the goods from the time they have been delivered and, unless such costs … have been levied by regular shipping lines … pay all costs and charges related to the goods … as well as unloading costs in question including lighterage and wharfage charges'.

2. The implication for the foregoing is that the buyer must pay for unloading costs unless these are included in the freight charged by shipping lines. In the herein case, we are not dealing with shipping lines; moreover, the unloading costs in question (quay dues) are generally not included in the pre-paid freight.

3. The general rule of cost division in the Incoterms® rules is that the seller pays all costs up until the point of delivery, and the buyer pays all costs incurred thereafter. Since, under CIF terms, the point of delivery is over the ship's rail in the port of shipment, and the quay dues in question are incurred at the port of discharge, the charges clearly arise after delivery and should be for regular shipping lines nor part of the pre-paid freight under the Worldscale Charter party, sections A6 and B6 of CIF indicate that they should be for buyer's account.

■ Buyer's arguments for refusing to accept charges

Buyer's arguments are as follows:

1. It is the seller's responsibility to obtain the contract of carriage and to pay all costs associated therewith. If the seller wishes to transfer any of these costs to the buyer, he should specifically stipulate to that effect in the contract of sale.

Thus, under CIF A3(a):

The seller must 'contract … at his own expense for the carriage of the goods to the named port of destination';

and under CIF A6:

The seller must 'pay all costs relating to the goods until they have been delivered … as well as the freight and all other costs resulting from A3(a)';

2. The quay dues in question clearly fall under 'all other costs resulting from A3(a)', that is to say, costs arising under the contract of carriage.

Therefore, the costs are for seller's account unless he has specifically allocated them to buyer in the contract of sale.

3. Seller's reliance on CIF B6 is misplaced. In fact, B6 provides that the buyer must pay 'all costs *relating to the goods* from the time they have delivered' (emphasis added). The operative words are 'relating to the goods'. The quay dues in question are not related to the goods: rather, they are levied upon the ship, and therefore are for the seller's account as costs arising under the contract of carriage. Even in ports where the quay dues are calculated upon the tonnage discharged, the quay dues are still considered by port authorities to be levied upon the ship.

4. Any other conclusion would establish the principle that the CIF buyer can be liable for charges levied upon the ship, which would open the door for unacceptable uncertainties. For example, what if the ship, for whatever reason, were to make unscheduled intermediate stops in ports prior to the port of discharge? It would be unacceptable to permit the seller to pass these additional charges on to the buyer. If the seller contracted for a ship which turned out to be inconveniently large for the port of discharge, with the result that dredging was required to allow the ship to dock, could such dredging charges be passed on to buyer? Of course not; to do so would defeat one of the essential purposes of the CIF rule, which is to enable the buyer to easily compare the prices of sellers from different locations without having to calculate the effect of the differing transport costs.

As stated above, the Incoterms® Panel finds that the buyer's arguments are more persuasive than the seller's. To allow the seller to pass the quay dues on to the buyer would require a hypothetical, excessively technical reading of the CIF rule's provisions, one which the unsuspecting CIF buyer would not likely have noticed from an initial perusal of the Incoterms® rules prior to signing the sales contract. Given the uncertainty surrounding the interpretation of the CIF rule in a charter party context, we feel that the best solution for a seller wishing to pass quay dues on the buyer in the above-stated context is to explicitly put the buyer on notice of this intention, as by specifying in the contract of sale: 'CIF Incoterms 1990 quay dues for buyer's account'.

However, this does not at all imply that a given fact situation may not indicate a different outcome. If the two parties have a long history of trading in which the buyer/receiver has always paid, or if it is a custom of trade or of port for the buyer to do so, then factual determinations are beyond the scope of this Panel, and therefore the above opinion is only intended a general interpretation of the Incoterms for future reference, and is not meant to apply to or prejudice any specific case currently or previously in dispute.

1990 Editor's notes and observations:

The depth of analysis required to answer the above question indicates that the rule of interpretation in the Incoterms® rules is probably not yet sufficiently clear; in fact, the Panel of Experts was not unanimous in supporting the above answer.

1990 Question 37 CFR/CIF – Transfer of risk point/insurance

Why is the point of transfer of risk the same under CFR and CIF?

Answer of the Panel of Incoterms® Experts:

The only intended distinction between CFR and CIF is that with CIF the cost and obligation of procuring an insurance policy are the responsibility of the seller, and are therefore included in the price. However, the point of transfer of risk is indeed supposed to be the same in both cases.

1990 Editor's notes and observations:

What is the difference between risk and insurance?

Traders frequently fail to appreciate that usage of the CIF rule does NOT mean that transport risk is transferred to the buyer; rather, it merely means that the buyer is protected against transport-related risks by the seller's provision of the required insurance policy. But keep in mind that the insurance policy may not be sufficient to cover potential damages, or may contain exclusions for common types of losses, such as those due to theft. So it is not correct to think that CFR and CIF involve different points of transfer or risk, as the questioner apparently did.

1990 Question 38

DES – Legal obligation to insure v. Commercial need to insure

With respect to the DES Incoterms® rule, section A3(b), stating 'Contract of Insurance – no obligation (on seller's part)' is this provision not misleading, in that the seller clearly does have an obligation to himself to insure for risk of loss or damage until the goods arrive at ship's rail at the discharge port?

Answer of the Panel of Incoterms® Experts:

As is clearly explained in the '*Guide to Incoterms 1990*', the Incoterms® rules only specify those obligations owed by one party to the other party; the Incoterms® rules do not specify those actions which may be prudent or practical for a party to carry out in his own interest. Obviously, in the case of DES, it may very well be prudent for the seller to take out insurance, but he has no 'obligation' to the buyer to do so. (See *Incoterms 1990* book, page 8, under No. 5.)

1990 Editor's notes and observations:

Particularly with regard to insurance, traders frequently misunderstand the absence of an Incoterms® rule requirement (in all the Incoterms® rules except CIP and CIF). Traders mistakenly think that the absence of the legal requirement suggests that there is no need to self-insure. This is a result of failing to distinguish legal obligations from commercial necessities. Both are necessary considerations for the business person, but Incoterms only deal with bi-lateral legal obligations in an international sale transaction.

1990 Question 39: DES – Quay dues

In the case of a gasoil shipment under the Incoterms® rule DES at destination Fos, who must pay for quay dues (taxes d'accostage) levied upon the ship?

Answer of the Panel of Incoterms® Experts:

The seller should pay quay dues because DES requires the seller to berth the ship and quay dues are levied upon the berthed ship.

Analysis:

As a general principle charges levied upon the cargo are for buyer's account, whereas charges levied upon the ship are for seller's account.

With the DES Incoterms® rule, the point of delivery (and therefore of transfer of costs and risks) is on board the ship at the port of destination. As compared to CIF, where the point of transfer is at the ship's rail in the port of departure, with DES there is greater reason to allocate quay dues to the seller. However, in specific cases, customs of port or trade or prior course of dealing may override the above principles and indicate a different outcome.

1990 Editor's notes and observations:

Compare with Question No. 36, which dealt with a similar issue. It is also interesting to note the number of Incoterms® rule queries that arrived from the petroleum or gasoil sector – this would seem to make sense because petroleum shipments are very often large bulk transfers, so that issues of loading, berthing, etc., that might not be 'worth fighting about' for small exporters, can assume major proportions when the cargo in question is a large petroleum shipment.

ANNEX 1

GLOSSARY – INTERNATIONAL TRADE AND TRANSPORT TERMS

A

AAA – *See* American Arbitration Association.

aar – against all risks.

acceptance (also, acc.) **–** The agreement written on a draft and signed by the drawee – who becomes the acceptor – to pay the specified amount on the due date. The term is also applied to the accepted time draft itself. *See* bill of exchange.

acceptance credit – A documentary credit that requires, amongst the documents stipulated, provision of a term bill of exchange. The bill is then generally accepted by the bank on which it is drawn or discounted. The practical result is that the beneficiary is paid promptly at a discount.

act.wt. – Actual weight.

A/d – *See* After date.

ad valorem duty – A duty assessed as a percentage rate of the value of the imported merchandise. *See* customs duty.

ADR – *See* alternative dispute resolution.

advance payment guarantee/bond – A guarantee that advance payments will be returned if the party having received such payments does not perform its part of the contract.

advising bank – The bank that notifies the exporter of the opening of a letter of credit in his or her favour. The advising bank, usually located in the exporter's country, fully informs the exporter of the conditions of the letter of credit without itself making a payment commitment. See generally letter of credit.

after date – Payment on a negotiable instrument such as a bank draft, becomes due a certain number of days after the date shown on the instrument.

GLOSSARY – INTERNATIONAL TRADE AND TRANSPORT TERMS

after sight – Payment on a negotiable instrument, such as a bank draft, becomes due a certain number of days after presentation and acceptance of the instrument.

agent/agency agreement – An agent is an independent person or legal entity that acts on behalf of another (the 'principal'). In international transactions, generally refers to a sales representative who prospects on behalf of a foreign principal, earning commission on sales eventually concluded between the principal and the ultimate client. See Foreign sales agent. To be distinguished from sales through employees and subsidiaries – who are not independent, or through distributorship relations, which involve the distributor's buying and re-selling in its own name. Sales agents should also be distinguished from buying or purchasing agents, as the respective rights and obligations are quite different.

agio – The extra amount over and above the market price that is paid in countertrade transactions and results from the particular costs of counter-trade.

air waybill (airbill) (AWB) – A non-negotiable shipping document used by the airlines for air freight. It is a contract for carriage that includes carrier conditions, such as limits of liability and claims procedures. In addition, it contains shipping instructions to airlines, a description of the commodity and applicable transportation charges. It performs the functions of a bill of lading in land surface transport. *See* bill of lading.

all risks (AR) – A type of insurance coverage providing somewhat more than the minimum coverage, at a premium above the base amount paid under a particular policy. Unfortunately, 'all risks' coverage does not in fact cover all risks – thus, for example, coverage of war, riots and strikes is not usually included; moreover, there is no standard nomenclature for all risks coverage. Traders should understand what exactly is covered in all risks coverage, and decide whether or not they need additional coverage, before agreeing to such a term.

alternative dispute resolution (ADR) – A general term for a variety of dispute-resolution mechanisms that may be used as alternatives to traditional litigation before governmental courts or tribunals. May be said to include such techniques as conciliation, mediation, arbitration, re-negotiation and mini-trial.

American Arbitration Association (AAA) – Perhaps the world's largest arbitration forum and institution; the great bulk of cases handled under its rules and procedures are domestic US cases, although the AAA does have specific rules for international cases.

AN – *See* Arrival notice.

applicant – In the documentary credit process, normally the buyer or importer, who applies (thus, the applicant) for a letter of credit in favour of the beneficiary, the seller.

AQ – Any quantity.

arbitration – A process of dispute resolution in which a neutral third party (arbitrator) renders a decision after a hearing at which both parties have an opportunity to be heard. Arbitration may be voluntary or contractually required. The advantages of arbitration – compared to litigation – are neutrality, confidentiality, reduced costs, faster procedures and the arbitrator's expertise. Internationally, the main arbitration body is the International Chamber of Commerce. Other arbitration institutions include the London Court of International Arbitration, the Stockholm Court of Arbitration, and the American Arbitration Association (AAA).

arrival notice (AN) – Communication from a carrier to the intended receiver that an international shipment will soon arrive.

at sight – A term used in international banking practice to indicate that payment is due immediately upon presentation of given documents.

ATA Carnet – 'Admission Temporaire/Temporary Admission'. An international customs document for the temporary duty-free admission of goods into a country for display, demonstration or similar purposes. ATA Carnets are issued by national chambers of commerce, which guarantee the payment of duties to local customs authorities should the goods not be ultimately re-exported.

Av. – Average

aval – A guarantee to pay a bill of exchange. An irrevocable, unconditional promise to pay on the due date. The use of avals is common in the practice of forfaiting.

AWB – *See* Air waybill.

B

back-to-back credit – A commercial device under which a middleman uses a documentary credit to open a second credit in favour of a supplier. Should be distinguished from a transferable credit. *See* letters of credit.

BAF – *See* bunker adjustment factor.

bank guarantee – Contract between a bank as guarantor and a beneficiary in which the bank commits itself to pay a certain sum under certain specified conditions. Thus, a demand guarantee is one in which the bank agrees to pay against the simple written demand of the beneficiary.

banker's acceptance – A bill of exchange accepted by a bank usually for the purpose of financing the sale of goods to or by the bank's customer. The bill may be drawn, for example, by an exporter on the importer's bank and be sold on the open market at a discount. *See* bill of exchange.

bareboat charter – The lease (charter) of an entire vessel under an agreement whereby the lessor only provides the 'bare' vessel – that is, operation of the vessel is not included in the lease, and the charterer must arrange to hire a ship's master and crew itself.

barter – The direct exchange of goods and/or services for other goods and/or services without the use of money and without the involvement of a third party. Bartering is an important means of trade with countries using currency that is not readily convertible. *See* countertrade.

basis points – One thousandths; 1/100 of 1%; i.e., 100 basis points is equal to 1%.

B/B – Breakbulk (cargo).

B/D – Bank draft.

beneficiary – Documentary credit context: generally, the exporter-seller; the one on whose behalf the documentary credit is opened by the applicant (the importer–buyer). Guarantee/bond context: the one who will receive payment under the bond should the specified documents or contingencies be produced.

Berne Union – International Union of Credit and Investment Insurers.

B/G – Bonded goods. *See* bonded warehouse.

bill of exchange (B/E) – A draft. An unconditional order addressed by the exporter to the importer for the payment of a specific sum. A sight draft requires immediate payment, while usance or term drafts indicate payment at a specified future date.

bill of lading (B/L) – A document issued when goods are entrusted to a shipping company for carriage. It can serve as a formal receipt for the goods by the shipowner, a memorandum of the contract of carriage and documentary evidence of control over the goods. The holder or consignee of the bill has the right to claim delivery of the goods from the shipping company when they arrive at the port of destination. Bills of lading may be negotiable (order B/L) or non-negotiable (straight B/L). Bills of lading may also be distinguished by the mode of transport used for the shipment. *See* marine bill of lading, multimodal transport bill of lading, air waybill, railway consignment note and sea waybill.

GLOSSARY – INTERNATIONAL TRADE AND TRANSPORT TERMS

B/L terminology:

- **clean –** a B/L that contains no notation indicating that the goods have been wholly or partially lost/damaged.
- **direct –** a B/L for direct transport between loading and discharging ports.
- **dirty/foul/claused –** a B/L with a notation to the effect that the goods have been partially/wholly lost or damaged.
- **FIATA FBL (FBL) –** a standard-form B/L issued by a freight forwarder; considered under the UCP 600 – along with other forwarder bills in which the agents accept full responsibility as a carrier – as acceptable as a clean on board B/L issued by a carrier.
- **freight pre-paid –** a B/L indicating on it that the freight has been paid.
- **full set of originals –** for documentary credit or collection purposes, the buyer may require the seller to produce a full set (commonly up to three) of signed originals – that is, B/Ls that bear the original signature of the ship's master or agent.
- **house –** a B/L issued by a forwarder in its own name ('house') covering grouped consignments.
- **liner –** a B/L issued subject to the terms and conditions of a shipping line.
- **multimodal/combined transport –** a B/L issued to cover transport involving successive stages via different transport modes, e.g. road transport followed by sea followed again by road transport.
- **ocean/marine –** the classic B/L, a negotiable instrument used for goods shipped on board ocean-going vessels.
- **on board/shipped –** a B/L evidencing the loading on board of cargo in good condition.
- **order –** a negotiable B/L, issued 'to the order' of a particular party, commonly the shipper.
- **received for shipment –** a B/L that only evidences that goods have been received, not that they have been loaded on board; common with container shipments delivered to port terminal; must be converted by subsequent 'on board' notation if shipper needs an 'on board' or 'shipped' document for payment under a letter of credit.
- **short-form –** a B/L that does not contain the full terms and conditions of the contract of carriage; instead, it contains an abbreviated version of the carrier's condition, with a reference to the full set of conditions.
- **stale –** a B/L that is presented late (for documentary credit

purposes, a B/L must be presented within a certain number of days after shipment).

- **straight –** a non-negotiable B/L; the consignee only needs to identify itself to pick up the goods.
- **through –** a B/L used when shipment will involve successive transport stages with different carriers.
- **waybill –** a non-negotiable transport document.

bolero (www.bolero.net) – An Internet platform for processing trade–related electronic documents.

bonded warehouse – A warehouse authorized by customs authorities for storage of goods on which payment of duties is deferred until the goods are removed for domestic consumption. If the goods are re-exported, no duty has to be paid at all. *See* foreign trade zone.

breakbulk (BB) – Non-containerized cargo that is grouped or consolidated for shipment, and then is later broken down, sub-divided or distributed at a further destination point. Breakbulk cargo is often unitized cargo on pallets or packed in boxes; specialized breakbulk vessels tend to carry their own loading/unloading machinery.

bunker adjustment factor (also, BAF) – A surcharge charged by ocean carriers to account for fluctuations in the cost of shipping fuel, which is known as bunker fuel.

buy-back (compensation) – A form of countertrade under which exporters of, e.g., heavy equipment, technology, or plant facilities agree to purchase a certain percentage of the output of the new facility once it is in production. *See* countertrade.

C

c & f (C&F) – Warning: common but non-standard version of Cost and Freight – CFR *Incoterms® 2010* (Cost and Freight). See *Incoterms® 2010*.

CAD – Cash against documents.

call – A demand for payment under a loan or guarantee. In the case of demand guarantees, the abusive resort to the guarantee (i.e. in the absence of non-compliance by the principal) is sometimes referred to as an unfair call.

cash on delivery (COD) – A term specifying that the receiver of goods will make payment for them to the carrier upon delivery; common in domestic trade, unusual in international trade.

CBD – Cash before delivery.

certificate of inspection (also, certificate of quality) – A document certifying the quality, quantity and/or price of a

GLOSSARY – INTERNATIONAL TRADE AND TRANSPORT TERMS

given shipment of goods. The inspection certificate is often required by buyers, especially those paying via documentary credit, from sellers, in order to assure that the goods are of contract quality. Generally, the buyer will designate a neutral, independent inspection company.

certificate of origin – A document certifying the country of origin of specified goods. It is often required by the customs authorities of a country as part of the entry process, for instance to grant preferential tariff treatment on imports of goods originating in a particular country. Such certificates are usually obtained through a semi-official organization in the country of origin, such as a local chamber of commerce or a consular office.

CFR – Cost and Freight. See *Incoterms® 2010*.

charter party – A contract under which a charterer agrees to rent/hire the use of a ship or part of a ship from a shipowner. The charterer in some cases will be empowered to issue its own bills of lading, known as charter party bills of lading, subject to the conditions of the original charter party contract. Note that the charter party itself is not a bill of lading, but rather a contract between the shipowner and charterer under which the shipowner hires out all or part of its ship for a given period to the charterer.

CIA – Cash in Advance.

CIF (also, c.i.f.) – Cost, Insurance and Freight. See *Incoterms® 2010*.

CIF & C – Cost, insurance, freight and commission. (also, CIF & I – Cost, insurance, freight and interest); and CIF & CI (Cost, insurance, freight, commission and interest). Warning: these are variants on the standard Incoterms® 2010 rule, so the additional abbreviations are not covered by international standard definitions. Traders may, therefore, wish to inquire and expressly stipulate as to the precise requirements implied by the additional 'C' or 'CI'.

CIP – Carriage and Insurance Paid To (named point). *See Incoterms® 2010*.

claused bill of lading – A claused, or foul, bill of lading contains notations or remarks as to defects in the goods and/or packaging. *See* bill of lading *and* clean bill of lading.

cld – Cleared (through customs).

clean bill of lading – A bill of lading indicating that the goods were received in apparent good order and condition. A clean bill is one that contains no notations of defect, damage or loss, and is signed by the carrier or its authorized representative. Note that a clean bill does not have to have any positive affirmation or mention to the effect, e.g. 'clean bill' or 'merchandise in

GLOSSARY – INTERNATIONAL TRADE AND TRANSPORT TERMS

good order'. If a bill does contain a notation of damaged or missing merchandise, the bill of lading is called 'claused', 'foul' or 'dirty'. *See* bill of lading and claused bill of lading.

clean report of findings – A document issued by a pre-shipment inspection agency stating that a particular shipment conforms to specified criteria (usually relating to the quality, quantity or price of the goods).

CMR – International road transport convention (treaty).

collecting bank – In a documentary collection, the bank acting as an agent for the seller's bank in collecting payment or acceptance of a time draft from the buyer to be forwarded to the seller's bank (the remitting bank). *See* documentary collection.

combined transport document (CTD) – A transport document similar to a bill of lading but that is issued to cover shipments carried by more than one mode of transport.

commercial invoice – A document containing a record of the transaction between a seller (exporter) and a buyer (importer), containing information such as a complete listing and description of the goods including prices, discounts and quantities, and the delivery and payment terms. A commercial invoice is often used by governments to determine the true value of goods for the assessment of customs duties, and must therefore conform to the regulations of the importing country.

commission agent – A foreign sales representative who is paid a percentage of the sales he or she generates. See agent and foreign sales agent.

common carrier – In some jurisdictions, a legal term referring to carriers who offer transport services to the general consumer or business public. In contrast, for example, to carriers who may work as employees, sub-contractors or agents of the manufacturer/shipper.

compound duty – A combination of both a specific rate of duty and an ad valorem rate of duty. Whereas specific duties are based on factors such as weight or quantity, ad valorem duties are based on the value of the goods. *See* customs duty.

conference (also, steamship conference, shipping conference) – A group of steamship companies or shipping lines that have associated to offer regular service on specific routes at publicly announced prices. Conferences generally offer specific rebates for regular or high-volume shipments. Shipping lines that are not members of a conference for a particular route are known as outsiders, independent lines, or non-conference liners.

GLOSSARY – INTERNATIONAL TRADE AND TRANSPORT TERMS

confirmed letter of credit – A documentary credit issued by a foreign bank that has been confirmed by another bank (usually a local bank or an international leading bank), the confirmation consisting of an additional irrevocable undertaking to pay according to the terms of the credit.

confirming bank – In letter of credit transactions, the bank that adds its own irrevocable undertaking for payment in addition to that given by the issuing bank. The confirming bank is usually located in the exporter's country. *See* letter of credit.

consignee – In international export transactions: the intended receiver of a cargo shipment. The named person or legal entity having the right to claim the merchandise from the carrier at destination, and is generally recognized as the legal owner for customs purposes. In international representation or distributorship relations (viz., consignment sales): the holder and re-seller of merchandise who receives payment in the form of commission or a discount as and when sales are made but does not have to purchase the goods in advance.

consular declaration – A description of goods to be shipped, made in official form to a consulate.

consular invoice – An invoice covering a shipment of goods certified by the consul of the country for which the merchandise is destined. The invoice is used by customs officials of the country to verify the value, quantity, and nature of the merchandise imported to determine the import duty. In addition, the export price may be examined in the light of the current market price in the exporter's country to ensure that dumping is not taking place.

contingency insurance (also, 'difference in conditions') – Insurance coverage taken out by one party to an international transaction to complement and fill in any gaps in the coverage taken out by the counterparty. Thus, the open account exporter using the Incoterms rule FOB does not have an obligation to insure the goods during the main international transport, but may wish in any event to take out contingency insurance so that if the goods are lost or damaged there will be no loss to the buyer (such a loss might lead to disagreements or disruption of commercial relations with the buyer, even if the seller was not legally at fault).

correspondent bank – A bank that performs certain operations on behalf of another bank, usually in a different country. Correspondent banks hold deposits with each other, and accept and collect items on a reciprocal basis. It is through networks of correspondent banks that trade banks are able to service and support international business transactions.

counterpurchase – The agreement of an exporter to purchase a quantity of unrelated goods or services from a country in exchange for, and approximate in value to, the goods exported.

countertrade – All foreign trade transactions resulting from exporters' commitments to take products from the importers or from their respective countries in full or part payment for their exports. Countertrade is typical of trade with developing countries, which often suffer from a lack of foreign exchange and/or credit facilities. Countertrade transactions include barter, buy-back or compensation, counterpurchase, offset requirements, and swap. *See* respective terms.

courtage (French) – Brokerage, brokerage fee.

cover note (also, broker's cover note) – An insurance document indicating coverage of a particular shipment under an open cover policy. To be distinguished, particularly as regards to presentation under a documentary credit, from an insurance policy or an insurance certificate.

CPT – Carriage Paid To…(named point). *See Incoterms® 2010*.

credit risk insurance – An exporter's insurance against non-payment by the importer.

c/s – Case(s).

CSC – Container service charge.

currency future – A contract for the future delivery of a commodity, currency or security on a specific date. In contrast to forward contracts, futures contracts are for standard quantities and for standard periods of time and are primarily traded on an exchange. Forward transactions enable importers and exporters who will have to make, or will receive, payment in a foreign currency at a future time to protect themselves against the risk of fluctuations in the spot rate.

currency option – The contractually agreed right to buy (call option) or to sell (put option) a specific amount of a foreign currency at a predetermined price on a specific date (European option) or up to a future date (American option).

customs broker – Licensed agent or broker (licensing may not be required in all jurisdictions) whose function is to handle the process of clearing goods through customs for importers.

customs duty – Tax levied by the government on goods crossing the customs border, usually a tax imposed on imports. Duties, or tariffs, are either based on the value of the goods (ad valorem duties), some other factors such as weight or quantity (specific duties), or a combination of value and other factors (compound duties).

customs union – An association between two or more countries to eliminate tariffs and other import restrictions on each other's goods and establish a common tariff on the goods from all other countries. The European Union is the best-known example of a customs union.

cw – Commercial weight.

CWO – Cash with order.

cwt – Hundredweight; unit of measurement.

date draft – A draft that matures a specified number of days after issuance.

D

DAF (deleted from the Incoterms® rules in 2010) – Delivered at Frontier. An obsolete Incoterms® rule that was discontinued in the 2010 edition.

DAP – Delivered at Place. *See Incoterms® 2010*.

DAT – Delivered at Terminal. *See Incoterms® 2010*.

D/D – Delivered.

ddc (also, DDC) – Sometimes said to be 'delivered destination charges', referring to various miscellaneous charges in the port of destination; alternatively said to refer to dispatch money at discharge. *See* dispatch money.

DDP – Delivered Duty Paid. *See Incoterms® 2010*.

DDU (deleted from the Incoterms® rules in 2010) – Delivered Duty Unpaid. An obsolete Incoterms® rule that was discontinued in the 2010 edition.

deadfreight – Freight charge to be paid even when shipment was not made, owing to failure by the shipper or charterer to actually ship goods in the shipping space for which a reservation was made.

deadweight – Total carrying capacity of a vessel.

deck cargo – Goods shipped on the deck of a ship rather than in its holds. Since deck cargo is more exposed to the elements, traders may wish to stipulate that goods not be carried on deck (except in such cases as transport of hazardous materials, in which case carriage on deck may be mandatory).

deferred air freight – Air freight offered at cheaper rates for non-urgent shipments.

del. – Delivery.

del credere – As relates to international commercial agency relationships: a del credere agent is one who guarantees the ability to pay prospective clients he has brought to the

GLOSSARY – INTERNATIONAL TRADE AND TRANSPORT TERMS

principal; in exchange, the del credere agent is usually accorded a higher percentage commission than is a regular agent. As relates to risk in general: del credere risk is the risk that a party will be unable to meet its financial obligations.

delivery order – An order, commonly addressed to a terminal superintendent or warehouse manager, directing the release of specified cargo to a particular receiver. The order may in some cases be issued by the seller, shipper or consignee, while in other contexts the order will be issued by the shipping line or carrier. Commonly, a delivery order directs delivery of part of a larger consignment, which is itself covered by a single bill of lading; i.e. the issuance of several delivery orders 'splits up' the cargo covered by the bill of lading. In any event, delivery orders should be clearly distinguished from bills of lading: the delivery order is not a negotiable document, nor does it evidence receipt of goods, nor does it contain the provisions of the transport contract under which the goods were shipped.

demand guarantee – A guarantee usually issued by a bank, under which the beneficiary is only required to make a demand in order to receive payment. In contrast to the conditional or suretyship guarantee – which require the beneficiary to provide proof of the principal's default – a demand guarantee only requires that the beneficiary make a simple demand, and therefore the latter guarantee is relatively risky in terms of exposure to an unjustified demand on the part of the beneficiary. Some protection against such an unfair demand can be obtained by making the guarantee subject to the ICC Uniform Rules for Demand Guarantees (URDG, ICC Publication 758).

demurrage – The extra charges paid to a shipowner or carrier when a specified period for loading/unloading is exceeded. The demurrage may, depending on the context, be paid by the charterer or shipper.

DEQ (deleted from the Incoterms® rules in 2010) – Delivered Ex Quay. An obsolete Incoterms® rule that was discontinued in the 2010 edition.

DES (deleted from the Incoterms® rules in 2010) – Delivered Ex Ship. An obsolete Incoterms® rule that was discontinued in the 2010 edition.

destuffing (also, stripping) – Unloading goods from a container.

devanning (also, stripping) – Unloading goods from a container.

discount – The purchase by a bank or finance house of a bill of exchange at face value less interest. It is used as a financing tool should the holder of an accepted bill of exchange require the money before the bill matures. *See* bill of exchange.

GLOSSARY – INTERNATIONAL TRADE AND TRANSPORT TERMS

discrepancy – In the context of documentary credits: a discrepancy arises when documents presented under a documentary credit do not conform to the terms of the credit; generally, an error, contradiction or omission related to the documents constitutes the discrepancy. The bank will refuse to pay against the documents unless the applicant (buyer) agrees to amend the credit or otherwise waive objections to payment under the credit.

dispatch money (also, despatch) – An incentive payment offered by a shipowner to a charterer in exchange for completing loading or unloading in less time than is specified in the charter party contract (this time is often calculated as a number of 'lay days'). *See* charter party and demurrage.

distributor – An independent person or legal entity that sells goods locally on behalf of a foreign principal. Distributors can be distinguished from agents as distributors buy the goods in their own name, then re-sell them at prices that they have some liberty to set. Distributorship is frequently based on a contract that grants the distributor exclusivity for a specific territory. *See* for comparison, foreign sales agent.

Dk. – Dock.

D/O – *See* delivery order.

dock receipt – A document certifying receipt of goods by the international carrier at the port of departure.

documentary collection – A method of payment under which the shipping documents relating to a particular cargo are released to the importer on payment (documents against payment: 'D/P') or acceptance (documents against acceptance: 'D/A') of a documentary draft drawn on the importer by the exporter. Under collections, the exporter presents a draft together with shipping documents to a bank (the remitting bank) in the exporter's country, which then forwards the documents and draft to the collecting bank in the buyer's country. The documents enabling the buyer to take possession of the goods will only be released by the collecting bank when the buyer either pays or accepts the draft.

documentary credit (D/C) – *See* letter of credit.

documents against acceptance (D/A) – The documents transferring title to goods are delivered to the buyer (drawee) only upon the buyer's acceptance of the attached draft guaranteeing payment at a later date. *See* documentary collection.

documents against payment (D/P) – In the case of a sight draft, the documents transferring title to goods are released to the buyer/importer only against cash payment. *See* documentary collection.

GLOSSARY – INTERNATIONAL TRADE AND TRANSPORT TERMS

door-to-door – A transport service covering carriage from the seller's premises to the buyer's premises. Note that this term refers to a freight charge in a carriage contract between a carrier and a shipper and thus is distinct from the issue of the Incoterms rule chosen in the contract of sale (an agreement between seller and buyer). Depending on the circumstances of the transaction, it could be possible to quote prices on either EXW, FCA, CPT, CIP, DAP, or DDP Incoterms rules in conjunction with so-called 'house-to-house' transport services. Attention should be given to the inclusion of loading/unloading charges in the 'house to house' rate, especially in comparison with the responsibility under the respective Incoterms rule for loading or unloading. The shipper should make sure that the transport service corresponds to the contractual obligations under the chosen Incoterms rule. It is sometimes said that 'door-to-door' services imply that loading and unloading are not included in the freight charge, but this is not a standard rule and traders should inquire in each particular case. Door-to-door is sometimes used synonymously with house-to-house, but it is claimed by some that there is a distinction between the two, namely that 'house-to-house' only refers to rental rates for containers from container yard to container yard. *See* house-to-house.

draft – An unconditional order in writing, signed by a person (drawer) such as a seller, and drawn on another person (drawee), typically sent through a bank, ordering the drawee to pay a stated sum of money to yet another person (payee), often a seller. A draft, also called a bill of exchange, may be payable to a named person or his or her order (order draft), or to bearer (bearer draft). The most common versions of a draft are the sight draft, which is payable on presentation or demand, and the time (or usance) draft, which is payable at a future fixed (specific) or determinable (30, 60, 90 days etc.) date. Should the beneficiary under a time draft require the money before the bill matures, he or she may discount his or her claim for immediate payment with his or her bank. *See* bill of exchange.

drawee – The individual or firm on whom a draft is drawn. The drawee is instructed by the drawer to pay a specified sum of money to, or to the order of, the payee, or to bearer. In a documentary collection, the drawee is generally the buyer. See bill of exchange.

drawer – The individual or firm that issues or signs a draft, instructing the drawee to pay a specified sum of money to, or to the order of, a named person (payee), or to bearer. In the case of a draft to one's own order, the drawer is also the payee. Like the endorser(s), the drawer is secondarily liable on the draft. In a documentary collection, the drawer is the seller. *See* bill of exchange.

GLOSSARY - INTERNATIONAL TRADE AND TRANSPORT TERMS

D/S – Days after sight (payment term often used in conjunction with bank drafts and documentary credits).

dumping – The practice of selling a product in a foreign market at an unfairly low price (a price that is lower than the cost in the home market, or that is lower than the cost of production) in order to gain a competitive advantage over other suppliers. Dumping is considered an unfair trade practice under the GATT and World Trade Organization agreements; it is regulated by national governments through the imposition of anti-dumping duties, in some cases calculated to equal the difference between the product's price in the importing and the exporting country.

E

E&OE – Errors and Omissions Excepted: when appended to a signature on a shipping document, indicates a disclaimer of responsibility for spelling, typographical or clerical errors.

EDI (also, edi) – *See* electronic data interchange.

electronic data interchange (EDI) – The computer-to-computer transmission of business messages (such as purchase orders, invoices, booking instructions, etc.) using standard, industry-accepted, message formats.

EMC – *See* export management company.

est. – Estimated.

ETA – Estimated time of arrival.

ETD – Estimated time of departure.

ETS – Estimated time of sailing.

EU – European Union.

eUCP – A supplementary set of rules to the UCP 600 (see Uniform Customs and Practice for Documentary Credits) specifically tailored to the presentation of electronic documents in relation to a documentary credit.

Eurocurrency – A currency being used or traded outside the country that issued the currency. The most widely used Eurocurrency is the Eurodollar.

Ex factory – Warning: this is a non-standard trade term, a variation of the preferred formulation: EXW Incoterms® 2010.

export broker – An individual or firm that brings together buyers and sellers for a fee without taking part in actual sales transactions.

export credit insurance – Special insurance coverage for exporters to protect against non-payment by the importer (coverage may extend to certain other risks, depending on the policy). Export credit insurance is available from private insurance underwriters as well as from government agencies. Examples of well-known public export credit agencies include the US Eximbank, the UK Export Credits Guarantee Department and France's COFACE.

export licence – A government document granting the 'licensee' the right to export a specified quantity of a commodity to a specified country. This licence may be required in some countries for most or all exports and in other countries only under special circumstances.

export management company (EMC) – A private firm serving as the export department for several manufacturers, soliciting and transacting export business on behalf of its clients in return for a commission, salary, or retainer plus commission.

EXW – Ex Works. *See Incoterms® 2010.*

F

F&D – Freight and demurrage.

factoring – In the context of export trade: the financial service consisting of the granting of a cash advance against accounts receivable from foreign customers. More generally, a range of financing and risk management services offered by specialized firms, called factors, to sellers/exporters, particularly those who deal with a stream of low-value, short-term foreign accounts receivable. The exporter transfers title to its foreign accounts receivable to a factoring house in exchange for cash at a discount from the face value. Other basic services offered by factors include: foreign credit risk assessment, collection of overdue foreign accounts and administration of accounting ledgers.

FAK – *See* freight all kinds.

FAS– Free Alongside Ship. *See Incoterms® 2010.*

FB – Freight bill.

FCA – Free Carrier. See *Incoterms® 2010.*

FCL – Full container load.

FI – Free in. *See* free in and out.

FIO – *See* free in and out.

FO – Free out. *See* free in and out.

FOB – Free on Board. *See Incoterms® 2010.*

fob airport – Warning: no longer a valid Incoterms rule, see FCA, I*ncoterms® 2010*. Free on board airport: a trade or delivery term used when delivery is effected at an airport. It was withdrawn from use as a valid Incoterms® rule in 1980 because it was felt that the term was the source of much potential disagreement, especially as regards to allocation of customs clearance and export handling charges.

foc. – Free of charge.

fod. – Free of damage.

FOR – Free on rail. Warning: no longer a valid Incoterms® rule, but still used by some traders. The problem is that there is on occasion confusion as to whether it only applies to rail shipments. The suitable rule from *Incoterms® 2010* is FCA. *See Incoterms® 2010.*

force majeure – A clause that protects the parties to a contract in the event that a part of the contract cannot be performed due to causes that are outside the control of the parties and could not be avoided by exercise of due care. These causes may be earthquakes, floods, storms or war.

foreign sales agent – An individual or firm that serves as the foreign representative of a domestic supplier and seeks sales abroad for the supplier.

foreign trade zone (FTZ) – Special commercial and industrial areas in or near ports of entry where foreign and domestic merchandise may be brought in without being subject to payment of customs duties. Merchandise, including raw materials, components and finished goods, may be stored, sold, exhibited, repacked, assembled, sorted, graded, cleaned or otherwise manipulated prior to re-export or entry into the national customs authority. Duties are imposed on the merchandise (or items manufactured from the merchandise) only when the goods pass from the zone into an area of the country subject to the Customs Authority. Foreign trade zones are also called free trade zones, free zones, free ports or bonded warehouses.

forfaiting – The purchase by the forfaiter of an exporter's accounts receivable that are based on negotiable instruments such as bills of exchange and promissory notes. In contrast to factoring, forfaiting involves a series of independent, medium- to longer-term obligations of higher value. Since the forfaiter purchases the bills on a non-recourse basis, he assumes both commercial and political risk.

forward rate – The price of a foreign currency that is bought or sold for delivery and payment at a fixed future time, usually 30, 60 or 90 days. Forward transactions enable importers and exporters who will have to make, or will receive, payment in a foreign currency at a future time to protect themselves against the risk of fluctuations in the spot rate.

FOT – Free on truck. Warning: no longer a valid Incoterms® rule, but still used by some traders. The term may create confusion as to whether it applies to motor vehicle or to rail shipments. The suitable rule from *Incoterms® 2010* is FCA. *See Incoterms® 2010*.

foul transport document (also, 'dirty' or 'claused' transport document) – A transport document (such as a bill of lading) that indicates that the goods to be shipped have been received in a damaged condition or in a lesser quantity than expected. Documents that are not foul are termed 'clean'.

franchising – A system based on the licensing of the right to duplicate a successful business format or industrial process. The franchisor (licensor) permits the franchisee (licensee) to employ its business processes, trademarks, trade secrets and know-how in a contractually specified manner for the marketing of goods or services. The franchisor usually supports the operation of the franchisee's business through the provision of advertising, accounting, training and related services and in many instances also supplies products required by the franchisee for the operation of the franchise. The franchisee, in return, pays certain moneys to the franchisor (in terms of fees and percentage commissions) and agrees to respect contractual provisions dealing, inter alia, with quality of performance. The two principal kinds of franchise contracts are master franchise agreements, under which the franchisor grants another party the right to sub-franchise within a given territory, and direct or unit franchise agreements, which are direct contracts between the franchisor or sub-franchisor and the operator of the franchise unit.

Franco (French, European shipping) – 'Free delivered': the shipper pays all charges to a particular point. Warning: non-standard term; for preferred formulation, *see Incoterms® 2010*.

Free in and out ('FIO') – A transport or freight term that indicates that loading/discharging costs are not included in the freight. In the charter party context this means that loading/discharging are not the shipowner's responsibility – the charterer is responsible for loading/discharging. Also possible to use either Free in ('FI') or Free out ('FO') independently. May be used with the addition of stowed and/or trimmed: e.g. 'FIOS', or 'FIOST'.

free of particular average ('FPA') – A type of marine cargo insurance providing minimal coverage; it corresponds to the Institute of London Underwriters 'C' clauses.

free trade area – A group of countries that agree to eliminate tariffs and other import restrictions on each other's goods, while each participating country applies its own independent schedule of tariffs to imports from countries that are not members. Well-known examples are the North American Free Trade Association (NAFTA), the European Free Trade Association (EFTA) and Mercosur.

freight all kinds (FAK) – Freight rate applicable to all types of goods.

freight forwarder – A person or company that arranges transportation, usually on behalf of the party contracting for main carriage. Many forwarders provide additional services, such as assistance with country-specific documentary requirements, insurance, storage, and even customs brokerage. Some forwarders also act as carriers (air freight consolidators or NVOCCs). Typically, forwarders obtain brokerage commission income from the carrier(s) they select. This minimizes the fees that they charge their clients, and makes using forwarders cost-competitive. Some countries require that forwarders obtain a licence, at least to be eligible for brokerage income.

FTZ – *See* foreign trade zone.

G

general average – A voluntary sacrifice or extraordinary expense incurred during waterborne transit to protect all interests from an impending peril. The main principle behind general average is that when a sacrifice is made to save the interests of all parties involved in transportation, the party who makes the sacrifice must be compensated by all the parties who stand to benefit from the sacrifice or expenditure. For instance, when cargo is jettisoned to save a vessel from sinking, all parties whose cargo was not thrown overboard must contribute to reimburse those parties whose cargo was. Carriers will require some form of security (promissory note or insurance company guarantee bond) prior to releasing cargo, in order to enforce each party's contribution. While this can be a burden for owners of uninsured cargo, insurance companies provide such guarantees for cargoes they insure.

gross weight – Total weight of a shipment including packing.

H

Hague Rules – International Convention for the Unification of Certain Rules relating to Bills of Lading – Brussels Convention of 1924. A set of rules for international transport contained in an international treaty first published in 1924 and subsequently implemented by the greater part of world trading nations. The Hague Rules were revised and updated in the so-called Hague-Visby Rules, published in 1968, which have not received so universal an implementation as their predecessors.

GLOSSARY – INTERNATIONAL TRADE AND TRANSPORT TERMS

Hague-Visby Rules – Set of rules amending the Hague rules, published in 1968, which have not been implemented by as many countries as their predecessor, the Hague Rules.

Harmonized System (HS) – An international standard system for classifying goods for customs purposes, developed by the World Customs Organization.

hazardous materials (HAZMAT) – Materials that may be dangerous, such as explosives or toxic chemicals.

house air waybill (house AWB or, HAWB) – A transport document issued by an air freight consolidator.

house bill of lading (house B/L) – A bill of lading issued by a freight forwarder. Often covers a consignment of parcels from various shippers that has been grouped or consolidated by the forwarder. The forwarder may, for example, receive a single groupage bill of lading from the carrier, then issue a series of house B/Ls to the respective shippers.

house-to-house – This term generally refers to a container-yard-to-container-yard (CY/CY) shipment (in which case it may be used merely to quote the rental rate for the container itself), but is also used in some cases synonymously with 'door-to-door', a term that more generally refers to overall transport services from seller's premises to buyer's premises. *See* door-to-door.

I

IATA (International Air Transport Association) – Air transport industry association and issuer of standard air waybill form.

ICC (International Chamber of Commerce) – The world business organization, headquartered in Paris.

ICC Arbitration – Refers either to ICC Arbitration and ADR Rules or the process of submitting an arbitral complaint to the ICC Court of International Arbitration.

ICPO (Irrevocable Corporate Purchase Order) – An offer to buy stated goods under specified terms and conditions.

Incoterms® 2010 **–** A set of 11 international standard trade terms (also known as delivery terms). The Incoterms® 2010 rules allow the parties to designate a point at which the costs and risks of transport are precisely divided between the seller and the buyer. Incoterms rules also allocate responsibility for customs clearance/duties between the parties. Since Incoterms rules are not law but are contractual standard terms, they do not apply to a given transaction unless the parties specifically incorporate them by referring to the Incoterms rules, e.g.: '100£/tonne Liverpool port *Incoterms® 2010*' (in exceptional cases, the Incoterms rules apply regardless of explicit mention in the contract, if there is a custom of trade or prior course of dealing that indicates reliance on the Incoterms rules, or if the local jurisprudence creates a presumption in favour of applicability of the Incoterms rules). Incoterms rules are elements of the contract of sale, which may be derived from the seller's tender or pro forma invoice. Thus, the Incoterms rules apply to only the seller and buyer, one of whom will assume the role of shipper and enter into a contract of carriage. The contract of carriage should dovetail with the chosen Incoterms rule in terms of allocation of transport costs and risks, but this will depend on the shipper giving precise directions to the carrier to ship according to the constraints of the given Incoterms rule. For a definition of the 11 currently valid Incoterms rules, and their standard abbreviations, *see* 'Documents for reference' in Chapter One.

inland clearance depot (inland dry port) – A combination transport terminal and customs clearance centre.

institute clauses – Standard international transport insurance clauses, published by the Institute of London Underwriters. The Institute Cargo Clauses (LMU/IUA) are three sets of clauses providing different levels of protection: the 'A' Clauses correspond to the general notion that is commonly referred to in trade as 'all risks' coverage, while clauses 'B' and 'C' indicate a lower level of coverage and a greater number of exclusions.

integrated carrier – A carrier that can provide shipment by air, road and sea, facilitating control of 'door-to-door' shipments.

inv. – Invoice.

ISO 9000 – Series of production quality standards established by ISO (International Standards Organization). Certification that an exporter meets ISO 9000 manufacturing standards, for example, may be a minimum requirement for competing in certain markets or for certain tenders.

issuing bank – The buyer's bank that establishes a letter of credit at the request of the buyer, in favour of the beneficiary (seller/exporter). It is also called the buyer's bank or opening bank. *See* letter of credit.

GLOSSARY – INTERNATIONAL TRADE AND TRANSPORT TERMS

L

laydays/laytime – The time allowed by the shipowner to the charterer or shipper in which to load or discharge the cargo. May be expressed in days or hours, or tonnes per day. Laydays may be set in running days (every calendar day), working days (excludes Sundays and holidays observed by the port), or weather working days (excludes in addition days where operations are prevented by bad weather). It may be contractually provided that if the charterer or shipper loads/unloads more quickly than is necessary, it will be eligible for payment of an incentive called dispatch money; if the loading/unloading time is excessive however, the charterer or shipper may have to pay a penalty known as demurrage.

LCL (Less than container load) – Refers to shipments of goods that will have to be packed together with other consignments in order to fill up a container.

LCL/FCL – A way of quoting container freight rates in which the carrier agrees to pack the container at the outset (LCL) but the unpacking at destination must be carried out by the receiver or consignee. It is a common approach for buyers who wish to consolidate small purchases from multiple suppliers in a foreign market into container shipments.

LCL/LCL – A way of quoting container freight rates in which the carrier agrees to pack the container on departure as well as unpack the container at destination.

ldg – Loading.

letter of credit (L/C; also, documentary credit, D/C) – A document issued by the importer's bank stating its commitment to honour a draft, or otherwise pay, on presentation of specific documents by the exporter within a stated period of time. The documents the importer requires in the credit usually include, at a minimum, a commercial invoice and clean transport document, but may also include a certificate of origin, consular invoice, inspection certificate, and other documents. The most widely used type of credit in international trade is the irrevocable credit, which cannot be changed or cancelled without the consent of both the importer and the exporter. In a confirmed irrevocable credit, the confirming bank adds its irrevocable commitment to pay the beneficiary (the confirmation is an additional guarantee of payment).

Types of L/C:

- **advised –** a credit the opening of which the beneficiary has been informed by a local bank.
- **back-to-back –** a system used by middlemen/intermediaries to finance a single transaction through the use of two L/Cs

GLOSSARY – INTERNATIONAL TRADE AND TRANSPORT TERMS

opened in succession (e.g. 'back-to-back') in order to permit the middleman/broker to use the proceeds from the first credit to pay off his or her supplier under the second credit.

- **confirmed –** a credit that has received an additional guarantee of payment by a second bank, often in the beneficiary's country.
- **deferred –** an L/C under which payment is made at an agreed time after compliant documents are presented.
- **import –** an L/C used to finance importation of goods.
- **irrevocable –** a credit that cannot be retracted or revoked once the beneficiary has been notified; there is a presumption under the UCP 600 that a credit is irrevocable.
- **red clause –** an L/C allowing payments of advances to the beneficiary (originating in the wool trade in Australia, these clauses used to be printed in red ink).
- **revolving –** a credit that can be drawn against repeatedly by the beneficiary; it can take a variety of different forms depending on whether the credit is limited in terms of time, number of possible drafts, maximum quantity per draft, or maximum total quantity.
- **cumulative revolving –** revolving L/C under which unused amounts can be carried forward and become available under the next draft.
- **sight –** an L/C under which the beneficiary is entitled to present a sight draft or sight bill of exchange, which is a call for immediate payment upon presentation of conforming documents.
- **standby –** akin to a demand guarantee or bank guarantee, the standby L/C is generally used to assure performance or payment by the counterparty.
- **transferable –** an L/C that allows the beneficiary to make part or all of its credit payable to another supplier; used in middleman/brokerage contexts; distinguishable from back-to-back L/Cs as the transferable credit requires the knowledge and authorization of the importer (applicant/principal).

letter of indemnity (LOI) – A document commonly used in international trade to allow a carrier to release goods to a receiver who is not yet in possession of the bill of lading (exceedingly common in the oil trade, for example). The letter of indemnity is, in essence, a guarantee that the receiver provides to the carrier, assuring the carrier that it will not suffer any financial loss by having released the goods in the absence of a bill of lading. Also referred to as a steamer guarantee.

GLOSSARY – INTERNATIONAL TRADE AND TRANSPORT TERMS

lex mercatoria – Internationally accepted general trade practices; the international, informal law of merchants.

licensing – A contractual arrangement in which the licensor's patents, trademarks, service marks, copyrights, or know-how may be sold or otherwise made available to a licensee for compensation negotiated in advance between the parties. Such compensation may consist of a lump sum royalty, a 'running' royalty (based on volume of production), or a combination of both. Licensing enables a firm to enter a foreign market quickly and poses fewer risks than setting up a foreign manufacturing facility. Furthermore, it allows parties to overcome tariff and non-tariff barriers of trade.

LIFO – In international trade: liner in free out; referring to a freight charge that includes the cost of loading in the port of departure but does not include unloading costs in the port of destination. In accounting practice: last in first out.

lighters – Barges used for unloading sea vessels when normal harbour facilities are non-existent or unavailable.

liner shipping – Services provided by a shipping line, under which cargo vessels operate according to a fixed schedule and publicly advertised freight rates.

liner terms – Carriage terms that include vessel loading charges according to the custom of the respective ports – which unfortunately widely varies. 'Liner terms' is, thus, not yet a standard designation, and may or may not include cargo handling charges or the costs of moving cargo between the ship's hold and the quay; traders are therefore well advised to require full details in advance from carriers.

Lkg. & Bkg. – Leakage and breakage.

LOI – *See* letter of indemnity.

LTL – Less than truck load.

M

marine bill of lading (also, ocean bill of lading) – The classic document of the traditional export trade, it plays three potential roles: 1) as a receipt for the cargo and evidence that the goods have been received in apparent good order; 2) as evidence of the terms of the contract of carriage between the shipper and the ocean carrier; and 3) as an instrument enabling transfer of control over delivery of the goods ('negotiability'), which allows the holder of the bill to trade the goods in transit by simple endorsement and physical transfer of the bill. *See* bill of lading, B/L.

marine insurance – Generic term for insurance covering international transport of export transactions; used even in cases where ocean transport is not a predominant leg in the transport chain. Marine insurance can be provided either in terms of a specific policy or certificate (exporters should pay attention to which of the two is required under a documentary credit), or by open cover, under which the insurer covers an indefinite number of future shipments; the shipper declares each shipment to the insurer as they are made.

Policy terms:

- **Average –** loss or damage.
- **General Average –** loss occurring when extraordinary measures are taken to preserve the safety of the vessel.
- **Particular Average –** partial loss or damage; loss to an individual cargo interest rather than entire vessel.
- **With Average (WA) or With Particular Average (WPA) –** coverage of partial loss provided the claim amounts to at least 3% of the cargo's insured value.
- **Free of Particular Average (FPA) –** coverage does not include partial loss; a very restrictive form of policy.
- **Free of Particular Average American Conditions (FPAAC) –** coverage only of losses resulting from vessel's sinking, collision, stranding or fire.
- **Free of Particular Average English Conditions (FPAEC) –** coverage only of losses resulting from or connected to a vessel's sinking, collision, stranding or fire.

master document/form – Central document in export administrative systems under which all necessary information is entered into a single master document or computer file, which is then used to generate all shipping and export documents. Also known as aligned export documentation systems.

mate's receipt – A document issued by the carrier to the shipper, indicating receipt of the goods, but not loading on board. Like a B/L, a mate's receipt can be either clean or claused/dirty/foul, depending on whether or not the goods have been received in apparent good condition. The mate's receipt can later be exchanged for the bill of lading.

MO – Money order.

MTO – *See* multimodal transport operator.

multimodal transport document – Issued by a carrier whenever a bill of lading is used for carriage and there are at least two different forms of transport, such as shipping by rail and by sea.

GLOSSARY – INTERNATIONAL TRADE AND TRANSPORT TERMS

multimodal transport operator (MTO) – A carrier who concludes multimodal transport contracts; i.e. contracts involving transport by more than one mode of carriage, and for which the MTO accepts liability as a carrier.

M/V – motor vessel

N

N/A – Not applicable.

NCV – No commercial value.

NE (ne) – Not exceeding.

negotiable instrument – A written document that can be used to transfer the rights embodied in it by mere delivery (in the case of instruments made out to bearer) or by endorsement and delivery (in the case of instruments made out to order). Some instruments, such as the bill of exchange and the cheque, are negotiable unless their negotiability is explicitly excluded, while the bill of lading is negotiable only if made negotiable by the shipper.

N/F – No funds

non-circumvention non-disclosure agreement (NCND) – A type of contract frequently requested by brokers or middlemen under which buyers agree to refrain from going around the broker to deal directly with suppliers. Warning: these agreements sometimes refer erroneously to 'ICC Rules for Non-Circumvention Non-Disclosure Agreements', which do not exist. ICC has issued a Model Contract for Occasional Intermediaries, which deals with the confidentiality issues involved in middleman transactions.

non-vessel-operating common carrier (NVOCC) – A company providing point-to-point international transport of goods although it does not necessarily operate or own transport vehicles or equipment. NVOCCs will commonly contract with a shipper to move goods from the exporter's premises to the importer's premises and will issue their own door-to-door transport document, although they will in fact sub-contract the different stages of the transport chain to various road hauliers and ocean carriers.

nostro account – A bank account held by a bank with its foreign correspondent bank, in the currency of that foreign country.

N/S/F – Not sufficient funds.

NVOCC – *See* non-vessel-operating common carrier.

O

ocean bill of lading – *See* marine bill of lading.

offset – A type of countertrade transaction. In an offset contract, which may be required by importers' governments as a condition for approval of major sales agreements, the exporter makes an additional agreement to buy goods and services from the importer's country. In a 'direct offset' transaction, an exporter may be required to establish manufacturing facilities in the importing country or to use a specified percentage of the components in the product sold from the importer's country. In an indirect offset, an exporter may be obliged to buy goods or services from the importing country without any link to the product sold. *See* countertrade.

O/N – Order notify.

O/o – Order of.

OP – See open policy.

open account trading – The exporter allows the buyer to pay within a specified time after receiving the shipment.

open policy (OP) – A type of insurance policy intended to cover an indefinite number of future individual shipments. The insurance contract remains in force until cancelled. Under the open policy, individual successive shipments are periodically reported or declared to the insurer and automatically covered on or after the inception date. Open policies can provide efficiency and savings for all parties concerned, especially when the insured conducts a significant volume of highly similar transactions.

order bill of lading – A negotiable bill of lading, which is made out to the order of a particular person and can be transferred by endorsement and delivery of the bill. In practice, the bill is made out either to the shipper's order or to that of the consignee or to its order. *See* bill of lading.

owner's risk (OR) – Also: ORB – owner's risk of breakage; ORF – owner's risk of fire; ORL – owner's risk of loss (or leakage).

P

P & I Club (Protection and Indemnity Club) – A shipowners' insurance association.

P/A – Power of attorney.

PA – Particular average.

pallet – Flat support of wood or steel on which goods can be stacked and that can be easily moved by forklift trucks.

paramount clause – The clause in a bill of lading or charter party invoking coverage by the Hague Rules, Hague-Visby Rules, or by the particular enactment of these rules in the country with jurisdiction over the contract.

PD – Port dues.

performance bond (guarantee) – A bond or guarantee that has been issued as security for one party's performance: if that party (the principal) fails to perform, the beneficiary under the bond/guarantee may obtain payment. A performance bond may be of either the demand or conditional variety, which means that the beneficiary may or may not be required to prove default by the principal in order to obtain payment.

pick up and delivery (PU & D) – Freight quote includes service of picking cargo up at shipper's premises and delivering it at consignee's premises.

pier-to-pier (quay-to-quay) – Freight quote that only covers from export pier to import pier (i.e. excludes handling charges to bring cargo to and from piers).

P/N – *See* promissory note.

POD – Pay on delivery.

ppd (or PP) – Pre-paid.

pre-shipment inspection (PSI) – An inspection of contract goods prior to shipment so as to ascertain their quality, quantity or price. Importers may insist on PSI, requiring the exporter to furnish a certificate of inspection (commonly issued by neutral, internationally respected firms such as SGS or Bureau Veritas), so that the importer is assured of receiving goods of contract quality/quantity. Government agencies may require inspection certificates as regards price, so as to prevent parties from under- or over-invoicing in an attempt to pay lower customs duties or evade foreign-exchange restrictions.

pro forma invoice – A sample invoice provided by an exporter prior to a sale or shipment of merchandise, informing the buyer of the price, kinds and quantities of goods to be sent, and important specifications (weight, size, and similar

GLOSSARY – INTERNATIONAL TRADE AND TRANSPORT TERMS

characteristics). The pro forma invoice not only acts as the contractual offer (that may be accepted by the importer's transmission of a purchase order), it is intended to be exactly replicated in the final commercial invoice, so that the buyer receives no surprises as regards either the goods or the price. Importers may need a pro forma invoice to be able to apply for an import licence or a foreign exchange permit. In the case of a letter of credit, the pro forma invoice is frequently used to inform the importer of the amount for which the letter of credit has to be opened.

promissory note – An unconditional written promise to pay a specified sum of money on demand or at a specified date to, or to the order of, a specified person, or to the bearer. Promissory notes are negotiable instruments and perform more or less the same function as an accepted bill of exchange.

PSI – *See* pre-shipment inspection.

PSV – Post-shipment verification. *See* pre-shipment inspection.

PU & D – *See* pick up and delivery.

purchasing agent – An agent who purchases goods on behalf of foreign buyers.

R

r & cc – Insurance clause: riots and civil commotion. Also: srcc – strikes, riots and civil commotion.

railway consignment note – A freight document indicating that goods have been received for shipment by rail. *See* bill of lading.

red clause L/C – A letter of credit provision allowing the beneficiary to draw partial advance payments under the credit. This provision used to be set out in red ink, therefore the 'red clause' designation. Generally, the beneficiary is only required, in order to receive payment of the authorized advances, to present drafts along with a statement that shipping documents will be provided in due time.

reefer box/container/ship – A refrigerated container or ship. Refrigeration may either be mechanical, which means involving an external power supply, or by expendable refrigerant (dry ice, liquefied gases, etc.), which requires no external power supply.

remitting bank – In a documentary collection, the bank forwarding the exporter's documents and the draft to, and receiving payments from, the buyer's bank (collecting bank). *See* documentary collection.

retention of title (reservation of title) clause – A contract clause whereby a seller declares its intention to retain title or ownership over the contract goods until payment by the buyer is complete.

roll-on/roll-off (RoRo) – A combination of road and sea transport, where loaded road vehicles are driven on to a ferry or ship (roll-on/roll-off ship) and off at the port of destination. Major benefits of RoRo are reduced handling of the actual goods and packages, competitive costs for unit loads and scheduled services.

ROT – *See* retention of title.

S

S & C – *See* shipper's load and count.

S & T – Shipper's load and tally. *See* shipper's load and count.

S.A. – abbreviation after names of corporations in French- and Spanish-speaking countries: Société Anonyme (Fr.); Sociedad Anonima (Sp.).

SAD – Single Administrative Document; European administrative document for intra-European trade.

SD – *See* short delivery.

sea waybill – A transport document for maritime shipment that serves as evidence of the contract of carriage and as a receipt for the goods, but is not a document of title. To take delivery of the goods, presentation of the sea waybill is not required; generally, the receiver is only required to identify itself, which can speed up processing at the port of destination. *See* bill of lading.

shipper – In the export trade: the party (as between exporter and importer) who enters into a contract of carriage for the international transport of goods. The party receiving the goods (the importer or buyer) may be called the receiver or the consignee. Depending on the Incoterms rule chosen, either the exporter or importer (or a middleman) can be the shipper.

shipper's load and count (S & C) – A carrier's notation disclaiming responsibility for the quantity of the cargo's contents; the quantity declared is thus purely the shipper's statement. If there is a dispute because less than contract quantity is delivered, the carrier wishes to be free from liability and the receiver will have to claim directly against the shipper or insurer.

short delivery (SD) also, short-landed cargo – Non-delivery of cargo at the intended port. When reported, it will result in the

GLOSSARY – INTERNATIONAL TRADE AND TRANSPORT TERMS

ship's agent sending a cargo tracer to see if the cargo has been mis-delivered to another port.

short-form bill of lading (B/L) – A simplified B/L that contains a reference to or an abbreviation of the carrier's full B/L or carriage conditions.

sight draft (also, sight bill) – A financial instrument payable upon presentation or demand. It must be presented for payment by its holder (payee, endorsee, or bearer) within reasonable time. *See* draft.

specific duty – A duty based on some measure of quantity, such as weight, length, or number of units. *See* customs duty.

spot rate – Rate of exchange quoted for purchases and sales of a foreign currency for immediate delivery and payment.

standby credit (also, standby letter of credit, standby L/C) – A form of guarantee, usually indistinguishable from a demand guarantee. Origin lies in the fact that US legislation prevented US banks from directly issuing guarantees, so they resorted to the device of the 'standby credit'. In function the standby is usually used more as a security device, like a bank guarantee, than as a payment device, like a documentary credit. Under a standby credit the beneficiary usually obtains payment by presentation to a bank of a draft and some form of written demand, which may include a statement that the principal is in breach of its contractual obligations. Standby credits may be issued so as to be governed by any of the International Standby Practices ISP98, the UCP 600 or the URDG 758 (to the extent permitted by national law). A standby credit can be used to back up a payment commitment – therefore, an exporter may agree to sell on open account terms granting the importer 90-day credit terms on the condition that the importer open a standby credit in the exporter's favour. If the importer fails to honour the exporter's invoices, the exporter simply draws against the standby.

STC (said to contain) / STW (said to weigh) – Notations on transport documents by which carriers give notice that they do not wish to accept responsibility for the accuracy of a shipper's declarations as to the content, weight or quantity of a particular shipment. *See* shipper's load and count.

steamer guarantee – *See* letter of indemnity.

stowage – The placing of cargo in a ship's hold in such a fashion so as to assure safe and stable transport.

straight bill of lading – A non-negotiable bill of lading that specifies the consignee to whom the goods are to be delivered. The carrier is contractually obliged to deliver the goods to that person only. It is often used with open account

GLOSSARY – INTERNATIONAL TRADE AND TRANSPORT TERMS

or when payment for the goods has been made in advance. *See* bill of lading.

stripping – Unloading goods from a container. See devanning and destuffing.

stuffing – Loading goods inside a container.

surcharge – Charges added to ocean freight, variously, for bunker (fuel), currency fluctuation, congestion, port detention or extra risk insurance.

surety/surety-ship bond/guarantee – A surety bond is a guarantee, usually issued by an insurance or surety company, that a particular company will perform according to a contract. In order to collect payment under such a bond, the beneficiary normally must prove actual default on the part of the counterparty, as by furnishing a court judgement, arbitral award or official certificate. Suretyship bonds may be issued subject to the ICC Uniform Rules for Contract Bonds.

swap – The trading of almost identical products (such as oil) from different locations to save transportation costs. *See* countertrade.

SWIFT payment – International electronic funds transfer via the system known as SWIFT (Society for Worldwide Inter-bank Financial Telecommunications), offered by most major banks.

T

tare – Weight of packaging/container, without merchandise.

tender bond/guarantee – A guarantee provided by a company responding to an international invitation to submit bids or tenders (as for a large construction project). The tender bond is submitted along with the tender and is required with the purpose of discouraging frivolous bids and ensuring that the winning bidder will actually sign and execute the contract.

TEU – Twenty-foot equivalent units; a means of measuring the carrying capacity of container ships; e.g. a ship can be said to be capable of 3,000 TEUs, which is roughly equivalent to saying it could carry 3,000 standard containers.

THC – *See* terminal handling charge.

through bill of lading – A B/L issued to cover transport by at least two successive modes of transport.

time draft (time bill) – A financial instrument demanding payment at a future fixed date, or a specified period of time after sight (30, 60, 90 days etc.), or after the date of issue. It is also called a usance draft (usance bill). *See* draft.

TIR – TIR Carnets are transport documents used to cover

GLOSSARY – INTERNATIONAL TRADE AND TRANSPORT TERMS

international transport shipments on road vehicles such as trucks/lorries. TIR Carnets, issued pursuant to the 1949 TIR Convention, allow the truck or other vehicle to pass through all TIR-member countries without having to go through customs inspection until reaching the country of destination.

T/L – Total loss.

trade acceptance – A bill of exchange drawn by the seller/exporter on the purchaser/importer of goods sold, and accepted by such purchaser. *See* bill of exchange.

tramp vessel – A 'freelance' seagoing cargo vessel, available on a contract basis to carry cargoes to any given port. To be distinguished from liner ships, operating according to advertised routes, schedules and rates.

trimming – The operation of shovelling and spreading, within the ship's hold, dry bulk cargoes such as cement, ore or grains, so as to avoid weight imbalances that might hinder the ship's handling or unloading.

T/T – Telegraphic transfer. Refers to an electronic wire transfer, usually in connection with payment in advance or payment by open account.

U

UCC – (US) Uniform Commercial Code, the codification of American commercial law, followed in substantially uniform fashion by the US states. Article 5 of the UCC deals with letters of credit.

UCP 600 – *Uniform Customs and Practice for Documentary Credits,* ICC Publication 600, the set of rules that govern international documentary credit practice. UCP 600 are generally considered contractually incorporated into the documentary credit transaction by virtue of a mention in the credit application form; the UCP 600 may also have additional force as a trade custom, and in some countries UCP are even recognized as having legal effect generally. In other countries, the UCP 600 is complementary to national law and jurisprudence on documentary credits.

UNCITRAL (United Nations Commission on International Trade Law) – UN Agency based in Vienna, specializing in the development of model legal instruments and conventions in the area of international trade law. Most notable success is perhaps the so-called 1980 Vienna Convention, the Convention on the International Sale of Goods (CISG). Also, UNCITRAL Rules for Arbitration, which provide a procedural framework for international commercial arbitration but which, unlike the ICC Rules, do not provide direct administrative supervision of the arbitral process.

UNCTAD (United Nations Commission for Trade and Development) – UN Agency based in Geneva, which has developed numerous international instruments as regards trade with developing or transition economies. Notably, UNCTAD houses the ITC (International Trade Centre), a developer of useful guides and manuals for small- to medium-sized exporters.

undercarrier – a carrier that has been subcontracted to carry out part of the transport operation.

UNECE – United Nations Economic Commission for Europe.

unfair calling insurance – Insurance coverage to protect principals who have issued demand guarantees or bonds against an unfair or abusive call of the bond/guarantee (i.e. one that is not truly based on non-performance by the principal).

UNIDROIT (Institute for the Unification of Private Law) – International governmental organization headquartered in Rome. Administrative organization of treaties, conventions, model instruments, legal guides and research.

usance draft (usance bill) – Time draft; a written demand for payment that comes due at a specified future date.

V

VAT – Value-added tax.

Vienna Convention on the International Sale of Goods (CISG) – International treaty signed by approximately 76 nations, including most leading trading nations. Amounts to a commercial code for international sales transactions, but excludes contracts for services, securities, electricity, and some others. Parties may 'opt out' of coverage by the Vienna Convention by explicitly stating so in the contract of sale.

vostro account – An account held by a bank with its foreign correspondent bank, in the currency of the bank's domestic country.

W

W – A tonne of one thousand kilogrammes.

WA – *See* with average.

warehouse receipt (WR) – A document issued by a warehouse operator acknowledging receipt of goods; also referred to as a dock warrant or shed receipt. A warehouse warrant, in contrast, generally connotes a document of ownership/control over goods stored in a particular warehouse.

warehouse-to-warehouse clause – Insurance coverage of international cargo from export warehouse to import warehouse; coverage may also be substantially extended or limited according to time.

waybill (WB) – A non-negotiable transport document, issued for either ocean transport (sea waybill) or air transport (air waybill).

wharfage (WFG) – Charge for the use of docks.

wharfinger – (also wharf inspector, wharf superintendent, dock superintendent) Personnel in charge of receiving and registering goods in a port on behalf of the carrier. The wharfinger's signature of the shipping note assures the shipper that it can proceed to draw up bills of lading pursuant to the terms of the note.

with Average (WA) – Marine insurance term meaning that coverage includes partial loss (and not just total loss) of the cargo. *See* marine insurance.

World Chambers Federation (WCF) – ICC's specialized division for its chamber of commerce members worldwide. WCF has taken over from the International Bureau of Chambers of Commerce (IBCC). WCF also manages the ATA Carnet System and its guarantee chain for temporary duty-free imports.

World Chambers Network (WCN) – A global Internet platform run by the WCF, fostering a comprehensive exchange of business information between chambers and their member companies throughout the world.

Worldscale – A scale for quoting freight rates for oil tankers.

WP (w/o p) – Without prejudice.

WPA – With particular average. *See* marine insurance.

ANNEX 2
SAMPLE INCOTERMS® 2010 DECISION FLOWCHARTS

Note that any flowchart is by necessity very general and should be considered only as a starting point for thinking about which Incoterms® rule to choose. As noted in point 4 of the checklist on page 37, in any given real-life transaction, there are a number of considerations particular to that deal that parties must factor in to their final decision on which Incoterms® 2010 rule to choose. A flowchart alone cannot provide the answer.

SAMPLE INCOTERMS® 2010 DECISION FLOWCHART – SELLER'S POINT OF VIEW

The following procedure is provided merely to give an example of an analysis that could lead a seller to choose one Incoterms® 2010 rule over another in a particular case. There are many possible flowcharts for the making of an Incoterms® 2010 decision, and the following are intended only as examples:

You are the SELLER and –
1. You wish to sell directly from your factory or place of business. Are you willing to carry out export clearance formalities?
    a. If No, choose EXW, which simply requires the seller to make the goods available to the buyer at the seller's factory or place of business. Note that EXW is suitable primarily for domestic trade. See possible difficulties in using EXW at the Guidance Note on page 15.
    b. If Yes, you may use FCA, which in this case requires the seller to deliver the goods, by loading them onto the buyer's vehicle at the seller's premises and clearing them for export.

If the above does not apply, go to:

2. You wish to deliver the goods in your country (or in any event prior to subsequent international transport) and you do not wish to include the cost of the main (international) transport in your quoted price. The Incoterms® 2010 rules you have available are the 'F' or 'free' rules: FCA, FOB, FAS.

   a. If the goods are to travel in containers or by multimodal transport, or if delivery is to be made to an inland or port terminal, choose FCA. The goods are delivered to the first carrier, either at seller's premises or at a transport terminal.

   b. If the goods are general cargo or bulk commodities to be loaded onboard the vessel (or are containers that will be loaded directly by seller in such a traditional fashion) or if for any other reason you wish to transfer risks and divide costs once the goods are onboard the ship, choose FOB.

   c. If the goods are to be delivered alongside the ship, choose FAS (export clearance is the buyer's responsibility).

      If the above does not apply, go to:

3. You wish to include the cost of main international transport in your quoted price. You must choose between 'C' and 'D' rules, which means you must decide whether you want the risk of loss to be transferred to the buyer upon shipment or only upon arrival.

   a. 'Shipment' contract – you want the risk of loss to be transferred to the buyer at the time and place of delivery in the seller's country. Seller must choose a 'C' rule.

      i) If shipment is containerized or multimodal, or delivery is to an inland or port terminal:
         ‣ choose CPT if you do not want to include the cost of insurance in the quoted price;
         ‣ choose CIP if you do want to include insurance.

      ii) If shipment is of traditional commodities lifted onboard the ship, or you otherwise wish to divide risks once the goods are onboard the ship:
         ‣ choose CFR if you do not want to include insurance;
         ‣ choose CIF if you do want to include insurance.

   b. 'Arrival' contract – you want to be entirely responsible for costs and risks up to delivery in the buyer's country (or your buyer has insisted upon such risk coverage):

      i) choose DDP if you want to accept total responsibility up to delivery at the buyer's premises or the named delivery point;

SAMPLE INCOTERMS® 2010 DECISION FLOWCHARTS

ii) choose DAT if you want to be responsible for costs and risks including the cost of unloading the goods at destination, but do not want to pay duties or be otherwise responsible for customs formalities; or

iii) choose DAP if you want to be responsible for costs and risks – NOT including the unloading of the goods at destination – but do not want to pay duties or be otherwise responsible for customs formalities.

SAMPLE INCOTERMS® 2010 DECISION FLOWCHART – BUYER'S POINT OF VIEW

You are the BUYER and –

1. You wish to receive the goods directly at your place of business or other point in the country of destination, and you are unwilling to accept any transport risks. You must choose an 'arrival' contract (see above).

Are you willing to carry out import clearance formalities?

If No;

a. choose DDP, which gives the seller total responsibility up to delivery at the buyer's premises or the named delivery point if the shipment is containerized or multimodal, or delivery is to be made to an inland or port terminal. But note that practical realities may prevent a seller from being able to undertake import clearance, so choose this rule with caution. See the Guidance Note at page 20.

If Yes, you may use:

b. DAT, which imposes upon seller total transport responsibility and risk, except as regards import clearance formalities and duties, which are for the buyer's account. Note that DAT requires the seller to unload the goods at destination; or

c. DAP which imposes upon seller total transport responsibility and risk, except as regards import clearance formalities and duties, which are for the buyer's account. Note that DAP differs from DAT in that DAP does NOT require the seller to unload the goods at destination.

If the above does not apply, go to:

2. You wish to purchase on the basis of a sale price that includes the cost of the international carriage of the goods, but you accept to bear the risks of such transport. The seller will pay export clearance formalities, whereas you will pay import clearance formalities. The costs of main (international)

SAMPLE INCOTERMS® 2010 DECISION FLOWCHARTS

transport will be borne by the seller. Delivery of the goods takes place in the seller's country. The buyer must choose a 'C' rule.

a. If shipment is containerized or multimodal, or delivery is to an inland or port terminal:

   i) choose CPT if you do not want the seller to pay for an insurance cover;

   ii) choose CIP if you do want to include insurance costs in the price paid by the seller. Note the seller's insurance obligation under CIP is limited to minimum cover.

b. If shipment is of traditional commodities lifted onboard the ship, or you otherwise wish to divide risks once the goods are onboard the ship:

   i) choose CFR if you do not want the seller to pay for an insurance cover;

   ii) choose CIF if you do want to include insurance costs in the price paid by the seller. Note the seller's insurance obligation under CIF is limited to minimum cover.

If the above does not apply, go to:

3. You accept to arrange and pay directly for the international carriage of the goods and also to bear the risks of such transport. The costs and risks of main (international) transport will be borne by the buyer. Delivery of the goods takes place in the seller's country. Buyer must choose an 'F' or 'free' rule.

   a. If you are willing to be responsible only for import customs clearance, but not for export clearance:

      i) choose FCA if the goods are to travel in containers or by multimodal transport, or if delivery is to be made to an inland or port terminal. The goods are delivered to the first carrier, either at seller's premises or at a transport terminal. (Export clearance is the seller's responsibility);

      ii) choose FOB if the goods are general cargo or bulk commodities to be loaded directly onboard the ship or if for any other reason you wish to set the transfer of risks and divide costs once the goods are onboard the ship. (Export clearance is the seller's responsibility);

   b. If you are willing to be responsible for both export and import clearance formalities:

      ▪ choose EXW if the goods are to be delivered at the seller's premises. All costs and risks are transferred from the seller to the buyer after the goods have been made available to the buyer (not cleared for export) at the seller's premises. Note that EXW is suitable primarily for domestic trade. See possible difficulties in using EXW at the Guidance Note on page 15.

INCOTERMS® 2010 Q&A | 173

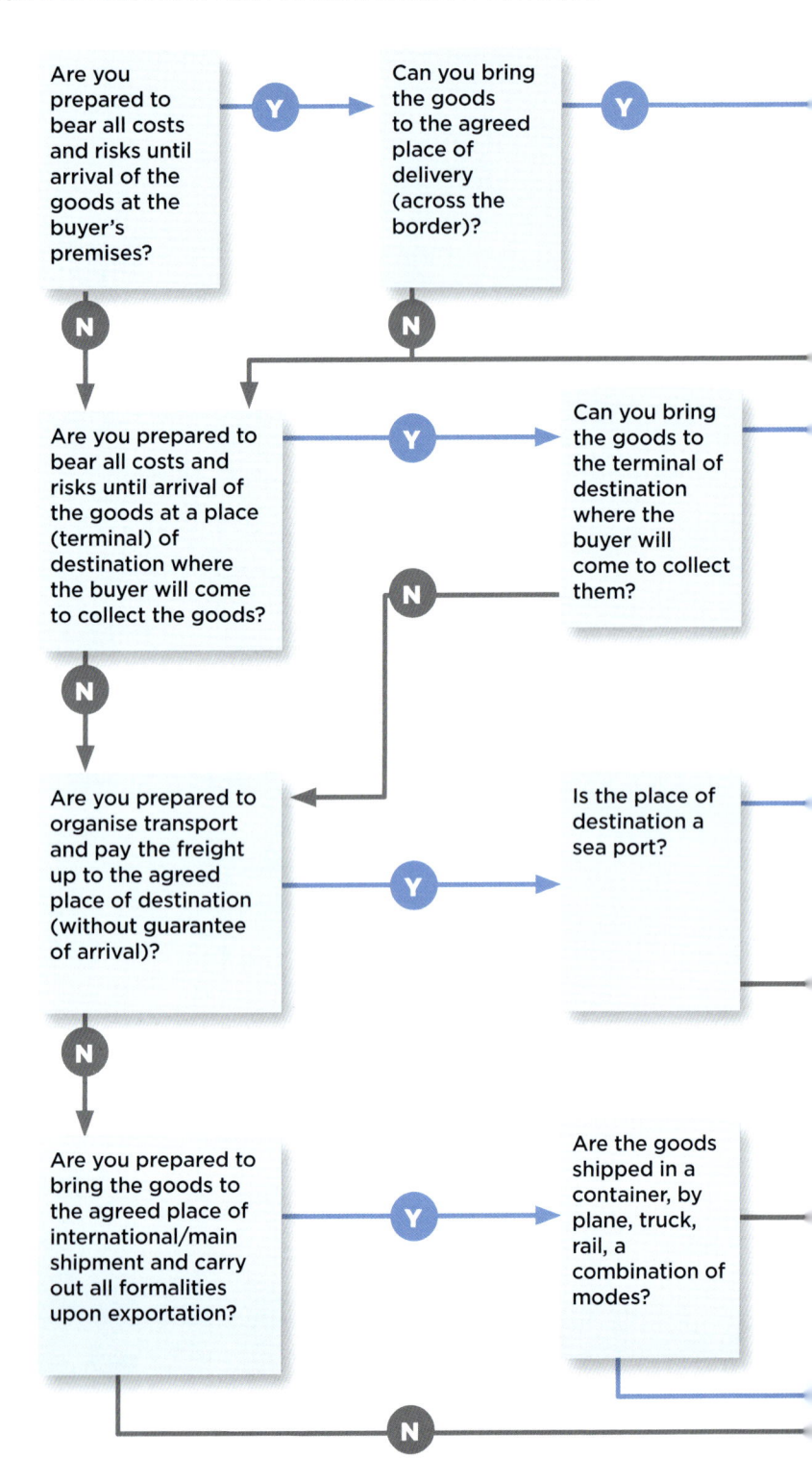

SAMPLE INCOTERMS® 2010 PICTORIAL DECISION FLOWCHART

```
┌─────────────────────┐         ┌─────────────────────┐
│ Are you prepared    │         │ Can you bring       │
│ to bear all costs   │──Y──▶   │ the goods to the    │──Y──▶
│ and risks until     │         │ agreed place of     │
│ arrival of the      │         │ delivery (across    │
│ goods at the        │         │ the border)?        │
│ buyer's premises?   │         │                     │
└──────────┬──────────┘         └──────────┬──────────┘
           N                               N
           ▼                               ▼
┌─────────────────────┐                                  ┌─────────────────────┐
│ Are you prepared to │                                  │ Can you bring the   │
│ bear all costs and  │────────────Y────────────────▶    │ goods to the        │
│ risks until arrival │                                  │ terminal of         │
│ of the goods at a   │                                  │ destination where   │
│ place (terminal) of │                                  │ the buyer will come │
│ destination where   │                                  │ to collect them?    │
│ the buyer will come │                              ┌───┤                     │
│ to collect the      │                              N   │                     │
│ goods?              │                                  │                     │
└──────────┬──────────┘                                  └─────────────────────┘
           N
           ▼
┌─────────────────────┐                                  ┌─────────────────────┐
│ Are you prepared to │◀─────────────────────────────────┤ Is the place of     │
│ organise transport  │                                  │ destination a sea   │
│ and pay the freight │                                  │ port?               │
│ up to the agreed    │────────────Y────────────────▶    │                     │
│ place of            │                                  │                     │
│ destination         │                                  │                     │
│ (without guarantee  │                                  │                     │
│ of arrival)?        │                                  │                     │
└──────────┬──────────┘                                  └─────────────────────┘
           N
           ▼
┌─────────────────────┐                                  ┌─────────────────────┐
│ Are you prepared to │                                  │ Are the goods       │
│ bring the goods to  │                                  │ shipped in a        │
│ the agreed place of │                                  │ container, by       │
│ international/main  │────────────Y────────────────▶    │ plane, truck, rail, │
│ shipment and carry  │                                  │ a combination of    │
│ out all formalities │                                  │ modes?              │
│ upon exportation?   │                                  │                     │
└──────────┬──────────┘                                  └─────────────────────┘
           N
```

SELLER'S POINT OF VIEW

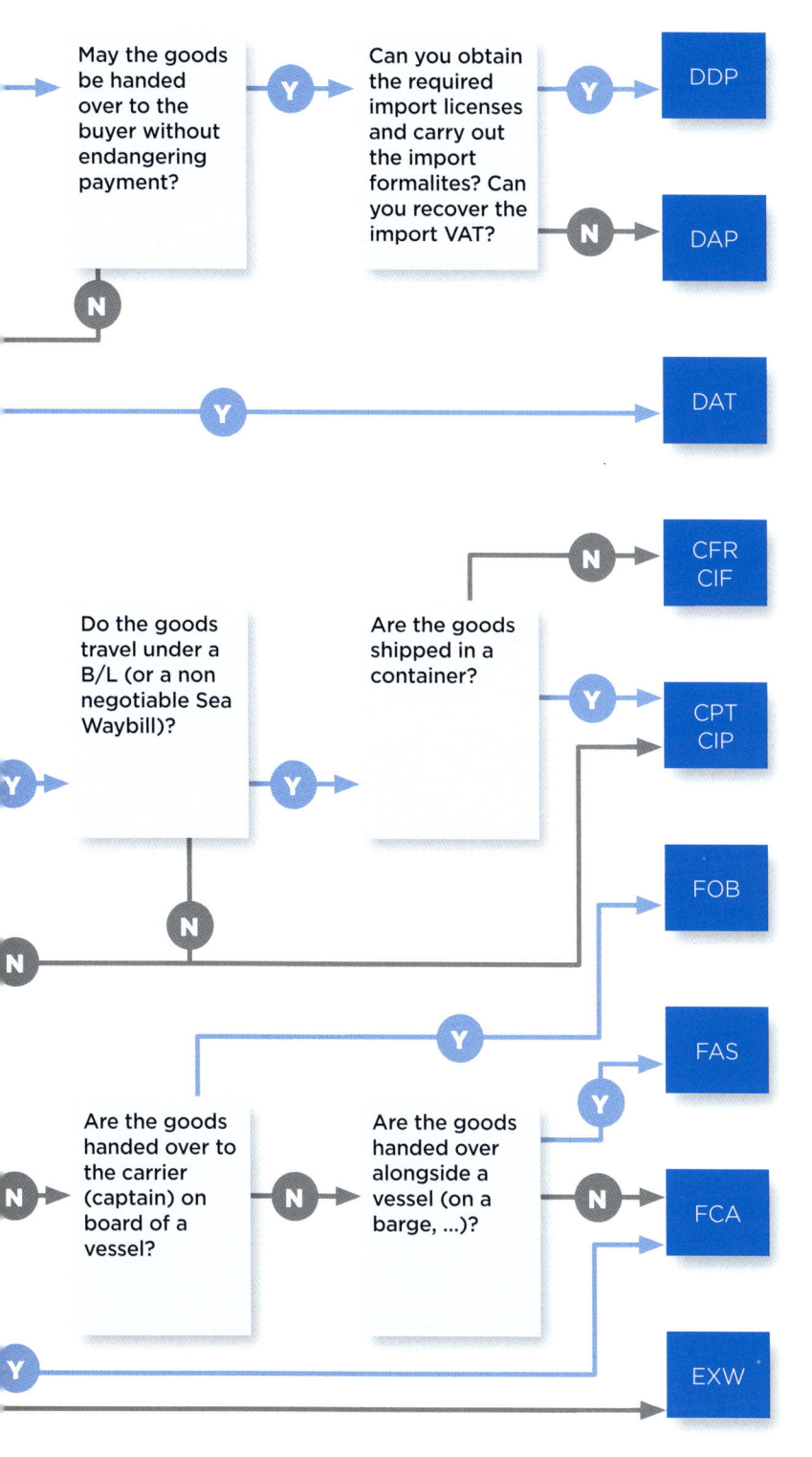

May the goods be handed over to the buyer without endangering payment?
- Y → **Can you obtain the required import licenses and carry out the import formalites? Can you recover the import VAT?**
  - Y → DDP
  - N → DAP
- N → (Y) → DAT

Do the goods travel under a B/L (or a non negotiable Sea Waybill)?
- Y → **Are the goods shipped in a container?**
  - N → CFR / CIF
  - Y → CPT / CIP
- N → (continues below)

Are the goods handed over to the carrier (captain) on board of a vessel?
- Y → FOB
- N → **Are the goods handed over alongside a vessel (on a barge, ...)?**
  - Y → FAS
  - N → FCA
- (N, overall) → EXW

INCOTERMS® 2010 Q&A | 175

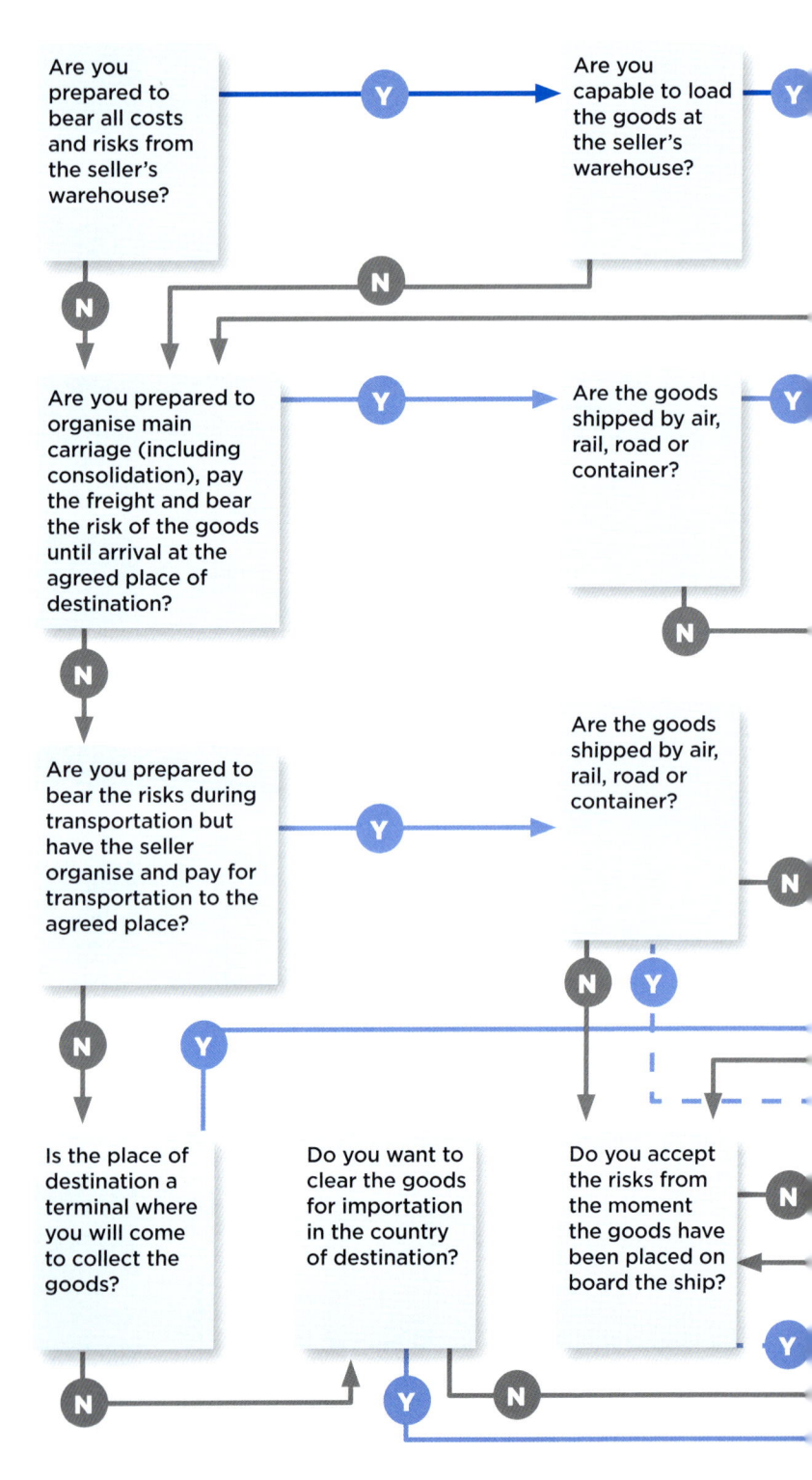

SAMPLE INCOTERMS(R) 2010 PICTORIAL DECISION FLOWCHART

- Are you prepared to bear all costs and risks from the seller's warehouse? — Y → Are you capable to load the goods at the seller's warehouse? — Y
- N ↓
- Are you prepared to organise main carriage (including consolidation), pay the freight and bear the risk of the goods until arrival at the agreed place of destination? — Y → Are the goods shipped by air, rail, road or container? — Y
- N ↓
- Are you prepared to bear the risks during transportation but have the seller organise and pay for transportation to the agreed place? — Y → Are the goods shipped by air, rail, road or container?
- N ↓
- Is the place of destination a terminal where you will come to collect the goods?
- Do you want to clear the goods for importation in the country of destination?
- Do you accept the risks from the moment the goods have been placed on board the ship?

BUYER'S POINT OF VIEW

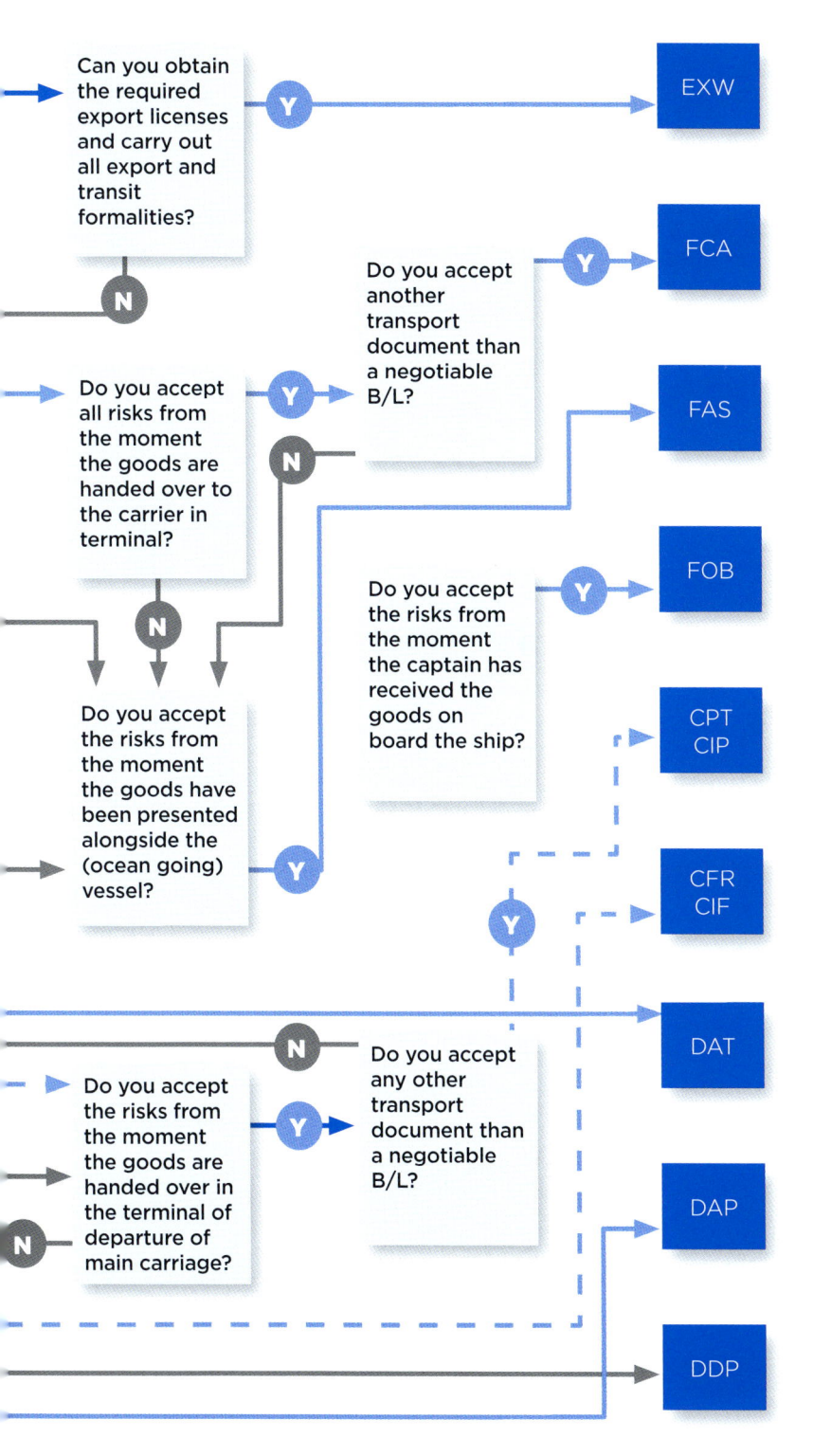

INCOTERMS® 2010 Q&A | 177

ANNEX 3
COMMONLY-USED DOCUMENTS IN INCOTERMS® 2010 SALES

EX WORKS
EXW (insert named place of delivery) Incoterms® 2010

Proof of Delivery
- Documents: Article A7 requires the seller to give the buyer any notice needed to enable the buyer to take delivery of the goods and article B8 requires the buyer to provide with appropriate evidence of having taken delivery.
- Issues: Article A4 situates delivery upon placing the goods at the disposal of the buyer (or the buyer-appointed carrier) prior to loading on the collecting vehicle. This may be between the notification of Article A7 and the evidence of Article B8. A Preshipment Inspection Certificate may well be the most appropriate document proving that the goods are at disposal and 'ready for collection' but not yet loaded.

Customs
- Documents: Article B2 contractually obliges the buyer to carry out all customs formalities and to obtain all documents licences and authorizations, not only upon transit and import in his own country, but also for the export of the goods from the seller's country. The seller is only required to give assistance to the buyer at the latter's request, risk and expense.
- Issues:
1. Article 788,2 of the implementing provisions of the Community Customs Code (CCIP) prohibits non-EU companies from exporting. A non-EU company may give instructions to a customs agent regarding export formalities and may pay the customs clearance costs, but for administrative purposes, the EU seller will always be indicated as the exporter on the customs clearance form and thus be administratively liable.

2. Non-resident companies cannot apply for export licences, health certificates, etc.

3. Article A1 of the Incoterms® rule EXW only requires the seller to provide the buyer with an invoice and evidence of conformity (packing list) in accordance with the seller's law (thus usually supporting the export formalities). As the seller is not supposed to know the final destination of the goods, the seller's obligations to obtain other documents are limited to assistance at the buyer's request, risk and expense.

4. As delivery is inland and not cleared, national VAT-regulations may prohibit exemption of the seller's invoice of VAT. Moreover, the seller depends on the buyer's willingness to return a proof of exportation, justifying the VAT-exemption for export (if allowed).

Transport
- Documents:

1. In application of Article A3 a) EXW, the seller has no obligation to make a contract of carriage and article A4 situates delivery prior to loading. Therefore, if an independent carrier is used, the buyer should be the shipper on the transport document, both as 'sender' (contracting party) and 'loader'.

2. Article A7 requires the buyer to notify the buyer when and where the goods can be collected. If the 'when and where' is left to the decision of the buyer, Article B7 requires the buyer to give the seller sufficient notice.

- Issues:

1. Loading is normally not part of 'transport under the contract of carriage'. The buyer should therefore instruct the carrier (or any other person) to load the goods as the buyer's agent and, when applicable, indicate the carrier as the loader on the transport document.

2. As the buyer loads the goods, the buyer is responsible for securing the shipment and dangerous goods declarations (when applicable).

Financing

- Documents: Article A1 requires the seller to provide the buyer with an (export) invoice. As the seller, in accordance with A9, also has to package the goods in the manner appropriate for their transport, the provision of a packing list will usually also be understood.
- Issues:

1. The Incoterms® rules as such do not impose conclusive documentation for document-driven payment terms. A preshipment inspection certificate may nevertheless provide a solution, as it is a document established by a third party upon delivery at the place of departure/collection.
2. In general not suitable if payment is to be executed under a documentary credit or documentary collection.

Insurance

- Documents: None required (Article A3 b)/B3 b)).
- Issues:

1. Buyer has the risk and should examine the need for insurance.
2. As the seller is at risk of not being paid, should the buyer not have sufficient insurance to cover possible transport damage to the goods, and as in such situations a credit insurance will normally not intervene, the seller might want to consider an insurance 'seller's contingency.

FREE CARRIER

FCA (insert named place of delivery) Incoterms® 2010

Proof of Delivery

- Documents:

A8 requires the seller to provide the buyer with the usual proof that the goods have been delivered.

1. If the named place is the seller's premises this would be a freight collect transport document (could be a pre-carriage or multimodal document).

2. If the named place is another location prior to main carriage, a freight prepaid pre-carriage transport document, signed off by the buyer or anyone acting on his behalf upon arrival, or a receipt document (FCR, terminal receipt, etc.), could provide this proof.

- Issues: Buyer contracts for carriage and therefore controls the disposition of any freight-collect documents.

Customs

- Documents: Article A2 requires the seller to carry out all customs formalities and to obtain all documents, licences and authorizations upon export (including export preshipment inspection – Article A9). Article B2 charges the buyer with transit and the import into its own country (including import preshipment inspection – Article B9). Parties must give each other assistance.

- Issues:

1. Article A2 contractually obliges the seller to carry out all customs formalities upon export at the named place, even though delivery is prior to passing the customs border. Article 788,(1) of the implementing provisions of the Community Customs Code (CCIP) however imposes the export formalities upon the EU-company '*who is the owner of the goods or has a similar right of disposal at the time when the declaration is accepted*'. If the goods are to be shipped to a destination outside the EU, the FCA buyer, *when established in the EU*, will thus have to be the exporter of record (and assume the liabilities), regardless of the contractual Incoterms provisions. This often complicates string sales.

2. When selling from countries requiring advance export customs reporting, the FCA buyer is in a better position than the FCA seller to communicate the required information in good time, as he appoints the forwarder and/or carrier.

3. Article A1 of the Incoterms® rule FCA only requires the seller to provide the buyer with documents (invoice and evidence of conformity) in support of the export declaration (article A2). The destination country of the shipment (that the seller is not supposed to know) may subject these documents to specific, different formal requirements. The FCA seller's obligations to adapt the said documents or to obtain other documents are limited to assistance at the buyer's request, risk and expense.

4. As delivery is inland, prior to leaving the customs territory, national VAT regulations may prohibit exempting the seller's invoice from VAT. Moreover, the seller depends on the buyer's willingness to return a proof of physical exportation, justifying the VAT exemption for export (if allowed).

Transport

- Documents: As the buyer contracts for carriage (Article B3 a)), article Article B7 requires the buyer to notify the seller in good time of the name of the carrier, when necessary, of the time when the carrier will take the goods, of the mode of transport and of the point of taking delivery. The seller, under Article A7 has an obligation to inform the buyer when the carrier has received the goods. A8 limits the seller's obligation to assisting the buyer, at the buyer's request, risk and expense, in obtaining a transport document.

- Issues:

1. If the named place is the seller's premises, carriage will often be door-to-door with the seller being the 'loader' and the buyer being the 'sender' on the transport document (when applicable). In this situation, the seller will be responsible for securing the load, and will have to provide a Dangerous Goods Declaration etc.

2. If the named place is another location prior to main carriage, the buyer should be the 'loader' as well as the 'sender' (= shipper) of the main carriage. In this situation, it is normally up to the buyer to provide a Dangerous Goods Declaration etc.

3. Article A3 a) imposes no obligation on the seller to contract for carriage but allows the seller to do so '*if requested by the buyer or if it is commercial practice [...]on usual terms at the buyer's risk and expense*'. In such situations, the seller will become the 'shipper' and be the contracting party with the carrier under the contract of carriage (freight collect) and will control the transport documents.

COMMONLY-USED DOCUMENTS IN INCOTERMS® 2010 SALES

Financing

- Documents: In addition to the documents mentioned under 'Proof of Delivery', 'Customs' and 'Transport', Article A1 requires the seller to provide the buyer with an (export) invoice. As the seller, in accordance with A9, also has to package the goods in the manner appropriate for their transport, the provision of a packing list will usually also be understood.

- Issues:

1. As the delivery document is '*the usual proof that the goods have been delivered in accordance with A4*', this document may not be a transport document but a receipt document. If this is the case:
   - the liability of the person receiving the goods (on behalf of the buyer) may not be of a mandatory nature (Hague/Visby, Hamburg, CMR, COTIF, Montreal, etc.) and may be contractually excluded;
   - the presentation of the document is not settled by UCP 600 and ISBP (regarding signing, presentation, emission, cleanliness, etc.);
   - the document is not a title document, and therefore not very appropriate for structuring the financing of the operation.

2. As the FCA buyer in principle is supposed to book the freight, he will control the transport documentation process. This might make it difficult for sellers to find protection in document-driven payment terms.

3. In general not suitable if payment is to be executed under a documentary collection, as delivery and the passing of risk will normally occur prior to presentation of the document and collection.

Insurance

- Documents: None required (Article A3 b)/B3b)).
- Issues:
   a. Buyer has the risk from the agreed point of departure and should examine the need for insurance.

1. As the seller is at risk of not being paid, should the buyer not have taken sufficient insurance to cover possible transport damage to the goods, and as in such situations a credit insurance will normally not intervene, the seller might want to consider an insurance 'seller's contingency'

CARRIAGE PAID TO
CPT (insert named place of destination) Incoterms® 2010

Proof of Delivery
- Documents: Article A8 requires the seller to provide the buyer with the usual transport document to the agreed point at the agreed place, freight prepaid (or freight for shipper's account).

- Issues: As the Incoterms® rule CPT only refers to the 'ship to'-place, the parties are well advised to identify as precisely as possible in the contract also the 'ship-from'-place where the risk passes to the buyer. If several carriers are used for the carriage to the agreed destination and the parties do not agree on a specific point of delivery, discussion might arise regarding the place where the risk actually passes.

Customs
- Documents: Article A2 requires the seller to carry out all customs formalities and to obtain all documents, licences and authorizations upon export (including export preshipment inspection – Article A9). Article B2 charges the buyer with transit and the import into its own country (including import preshipment inspection – Article B9). Parties have to give each other assistance.

- Issues:
1. Article A1 of the Incoterms® rule CPT only requires the seller to provide the buyer with documents (invoice and evidence of conformity) in support of the export declaration (Article A2). The destination country of the shipment might submit these documents to specific, different formal requirements. The CPT seller's obligations to adapt the said documents or to obtain additional documents are limited to assistance at the buyer's request, risk and expense.

2. The seller is required to provide the buyer with a freight-paid transport document. In some countries this document is needed to establish the customs value or to establish 'direct transportation' for tariff preference purposes.

Transport
- Documents:
1. Article A8 requires the seller to provide the buyer with the usual transport document to the agreed point at the agreed place, freight prepaid (or freight for shipper's account).
2. Article A7 moreover requires the seller to notify the buyer when the goods have been shipped so that the buyer can take reception of the goods upon arrival.

- Issues:

1. Buyers bear the transport risk for carriers that they have not selected and with which they have not contracted. However, they inherit sellers' contractual rights against carriers.
2. The seller has contract for the carriage on usual terms, freight paid by the usual route and in a customary manner.
3. The transport document may be road, rail, air or combined but may also be a port-to-port Bill of Lading.
4. The Incoterms rules do not require the transport document to be 'clean'.

Financing

- Documents: Freight prepaid transport document (see 'Proof of Delivery' and 'Transport'), export documents (see 'Customs') and (export) invoice (Article A1).
- Issues:

1. Sellers control the documentation process, and can obtain effective protection when financing the operation with a documentary credit.
2. In general not suitable if payment is to be executed under a documentary collection as delivery and passing of the risk will normally occur prior to presentation of the documents and collection.

Insurance

- Documents: None required (Articles A3 b)/B3 b)).
- Issues:

1. Buyers are at risk from the delivery point, which can be as early as the first carrier, and should provide adequate insurance, preferably on a warehouse-to-warehouse basis.
2. As the seller is at risk of not being paid, should the buyer not have sufficient insurance to cover possible transport damage to the goods, and as in such situations a credit insurance will normally not intervene, the seller might want to consider an insurance 'seller's contingency'

CARRIAGE AND INSURANCE PAID TO
CIP (insert named place of destination) Incoterms® 2010

Proof of Delivery
- **Documents**: Article A8 requires the seller to provide the buyer with the usual transport document to the agreed point at the agreed place, freight prepaid (or freight for shipper's account).

- Issues: As the Incoterms® rule CIP only refers to the 'ship to'-place, the parties are well advised to also identify as precisely as possible in the contract the 'ship-from' place where the risk passes to the buyer. If several carriers are used for the carriage to the agreed destination and the parties do not agree on a specific point of delivery, discussion might arise regarding the place where the risk actually passes.

Customs
- Documents: Article A2 requires the seller to carry out all customs formalities and to obtain all documents, licences and authorizations upon export (including export preshipment inspection – Article A9). Article B2 charges the buyer with transit and the import into its own country (including import preshipment inspection – Article B9). Parties must give each other assistance.

- Issues:

1. Article A1 of the Incoterms® rule CIP only requires the seller to provide the buyer with documents (invoice and evidence of conformity) in support of the export declaration (Article A2). The country of destination of the shipment might submit these documents to specific, different formal requirements. The CIP seller's obligations to adapt the said documents or to obtain additional documents are limited to assistance at the buyer's request, risk and expense.

2. The seller is required to provide the buyer with a freight-paid transport document. In some countries this document is needed to establish the customs value or to establish 'direct transportation' for tariff preference purposes.

Transport
- Documents:

1. Article A8 requires the seller to provide the buyer with the usual transport document to the agreed point at the agreed place, freight prepaid (or freight for shipper's account).

2. Article A7 moreover requires the seller to notify the buyer when the goods have been shipped so that the buyer can take reception of the goods upon arrival.

- Issues:

1. Buyers bear the transport risk for carriers that they have not selected and with which they have not contracted. However, they inherit the sellers' contractual rights against carriers.
2. The seller has contract for the carriage on usual terms, freight paid by the usual route and in a customary manner.
3. The transport document may be road, rail, air or combined but may also be a port-to-port Bill of Lading.
4. The Incoterms rules do not require the transport document to be 'clean'.

Financing

- Documents: Freight prepaid transport document (see 'Proof of Delivery' and 'Transport'), export documents (see 'Customs') and (export) invoice (Article A1).
- Issues:

1. Sellers control the documentation process, and can obtain effective protection when financing the operation with a documentary credit.
2. In general not suitable if payment is to be executed under a documentary collection as delivery and passing of the risk will normally occur prior to presentation of the documents and collection.
3. The seller-provided insurance cover might be of interest for structuring the buyer's financing.

Insurance

- Documents: Article A3 b) requires the seller to provide the buyer with evidence of insurance for at least 110% of the value of the goods in the currency of the contract with Institute Cargo Clauses C cover, enabling the buyer or anyone else with an insurable interest to claim directly from the insurer.
- Issues:

1. The seller is the applicant of the insurance policy, the buyer is the beneficiary.
2. In some countries the insurance certificate is required to establish the customs value.
3. C Clauses cover is seldom adequate. Parties should consider additional cover (A or B plus war, strike (SRCC)), and possibly warehouse-to-warehouse.

4. Some countries require exporters to contract for insurance with a national insurance company. If the buyer doubts the quality of this insurance, he might consider an umbrella insurance policy.

DELIVERED AT TERMINAL

DAT (insert named terminal at port or place of destination) Incoterms® 2010

Proof of Delivery

- Documents: Article A8 requires the seller to provide the buyer with a document enabling the buyer to take delivery of the goods at (the agreed point in) the agreed terminal of destination.
- Issues: The delivery document might be a delivery order, a release notice or warehouse warrant but might also be the transport document (freight prepaid), signed by the consignee upon collection in the terminal.

Customs

- Documents: Article A2 requires the seller to carry out all customs formalities and to obtain all documents, licences and authorizations upon export (including export preshipment inspection – Article A9) and transit to the agreed point of destination. Article B2 charges the buyer only with the import into its own country (including import preshipment inspection – Article B9). Parties must give each other assistance.
- Issues:
1. As the seller delivers the goods in a terminal within the country of destination, it will also have to carry out transit formalities (and post the required bonds) up to that place (when applicable) and formalities regarding advance warning of the customs authorities of this country, safety of the goods (REACH, ISPM 15, etc.).
2. As the place of delivery is inland in the country of destination, certain inland charges in this country such as carriage, warehousing, THC, etc. might be subject to local indirect taxes (VAT, etc.). If the seller has no place of business in the country he might not be able to apply for a refund or deduction of these taxes.
3. In order to avoid inclusion of these inland costs in the customs value, the seller is advised to indicate these costs separately on the invoice.
4. The seller should be able to provide a freight-paid transport document, which in some countries is needed to establish the entered value.

COMMONLY-USED DOCUMENTS IN INCOTERMS® 2010 SALES

5. Article A1 of the Incoterms® rule DAT only requires the seller to provide the buyer with documents (invoice and evidence of conformity) in support of the export and transit declaration up to the agreed place of destination (Article A2). The country of importation of the goods might submit these documents to different, specific formal requirements. The DAT seller's obligations to adapt the said documents or to obtain additional documents in view of the import procedures are limited to assistance at the buyer's request, risk and expense.

Transport:

■ Documents:

1. As Article A3 a) requires the seller to contract for carriage, the seller will always be able to provide with a freight-paid transport document (if an independent carrier is used).

2. Article A7 requires the seller to notify the buyer in order to prepare collection at the terminal.

■ Issues:

1. The seller is the shipper on the transport document.

2. DAT requires the seller to deliver the goods by placing them at the disposal of the buyer after unloading the arriving means of transportation. DAT thus is the only Incoterms® rule that requires the seller to unload at destination.

3. Certain logistical costs in the country of destination (such as THC, cartage, etc.) are at the expense of the seller to the extent they are made prior to the point where the buyer or its agent can take delivery of the goods.

Financing

■ Documents: Freight prepaid transport document (see 'Proof of Delivery' and 'Transport'), export and transit documents (see 'Customs') and (export/transit) invoice (Article A1).

■ Issues:

1. As the risk passes at destination, this Incoterms rule is not suitable if payment is made with a letter of credit. In a DAT sale the conclusive document should indeed be issued only after the goods have arrived, are unloaded and made available. This is hardly conceivable in a documentary credit.

2. Very suitable for documentary collections, as the delivery, passing of risk and presentation/collection of the documents can coincide.

Insurance

- Documents: None required (Article A3 b)/B3 b)).

- Issues: Sellers should consider obtaining adequate insurance cover as they are at risk through the arrival terminal. The seller will be the applicant as well as the beneficiary of the policy.

DELIVERED AT PLACE

DAP (insert named place of destination) Incoterms® 2010

Proof of Delivery

- Documents: Article A8 requires the seller to provide the buyer with a document enabling the buyer to take delivery of the goods at the agreed point in the agreed place of destination, not unloaded from the arriving means of transportation.

- Issues: As the goods are to be delivered 'ready for unloading' the delivery document will usually be the transport document (freight prepaid), signed by the consignee upon arrival.

Customs

- Documents: Article A2 requires the seller to carry out all customs formalities and to obtain all documents, licences and authorizations upon export (including export preshipment inspection – Article A9) and transit to the agreed point of destination. Article B2 charges the buyer only with the import into its own country (including import preshipment inspection – Article B9). Parties must give each other assistance.

- Issues:

1. As the seller delivers the goods at a location within the country of destination, he will also have to carry out transit formalities (and post the required bonds) up to that place (when applicable) and formalities regarding advance warning to the customs authorities of this country and safety of the goods (REACH, ISPM 15, etc.).

2. As the place of delivery is inland in the country of destination, certain inland charges in this country such as carriage, warehousing, THC, etc., might be subject to local indirect taxes (VAT, etc.). If the seller has no place of business in the country he might not be able to apply for a refund or deduction of these taxes.

3. In order to avoid inclusion of these inland costs in the customs value, the seller will be advised to indicate these costs separately on the invoice.

4. The seller should be able to provide a freight-prepaid transport document, which in some countries is needed to establish the entered value.

5. The seller may be unable to deliver the goods at the agreed inland point of destination, should the buyer fail to timely handle import clearance. Articles B5 b) and B6 c) render the DAP buyer liable for the risks and costs resulting from any failure to timely handle import clearance.

6. Article A1 of the Incoterms® rule DAP only requires the seller to provide the buyer with documents (invoice and evidence of conformity) in support of the export and transit declaration up to the agreed place of destination (Article A2). The country of importation of the goods might submit these documents to different, specific formal requirements. The DAP seller's obligations to adapt the said documents or to obtain additional documents in view of the import procedures are limited to assistance at the buyer's request, risk and expense.

Transport

- Documents:

1. As Article A3a) requires the seller to contract for carriage and the goods are delivered ready for unloading from the arriving means of transport, a freight paid transport document will usually be presented by the seller to the buyer (if an independent carrier is used).

2. Article A7 requires the seller to notify the buyer in order to prepare receipt of the goods from the carrier. If the buyer is entitled to determine the exact time and place of reception of the goods, he must give the seller sufficient notice thereof (Article B7).

- Issues:

1. The seller is the shipper on the freight prepaid transport document (if an independent carrier is used).

2. The seller is not required to unload the goods from the arriving means of transportation. This may present problems when the named place of delivery/destination is not the buyer's premises. In such situations the Incoterms® rule DAT might be more appropriate.

Financing

- Documents: Freight prepaid transport document (see 'Proof of Delivery' and 'Transport'), export and transit documents (see 'Customs') and (export/transit) invoice (Article A1).

- Issues:

1. As the risk passes at destination, the DAP Incoterms® rule is not suitable if payment is made with a letter of credit. In a DAP sale the conclusive document should indeed be issued only after the goods have arrived and are ready to be unloaded. This is hardly conceivable in a documentary credit.

2. Documentary collections would also be complicated, especially if the named place is the buyer's premises as opposed to an arrival point on the buyer's side such as a port terminal.

Insurance

- Documents: None required (Article A3 b)/B3 b)).

- Issues: Sellers should consider obtaining adequate insurance cover as they are at risk up to arrival at the agreed point of destination (often the buyer's premises). The seller will be the applicant as well as the beneficiary of the policy. A global transport insurance policy might be an appropriate solution.

DELIVERED DUTY PAID

DDP (insert named place of destination) Incoterms® 2010

Proof of Delivery

- Documents: Article A8 requires the seller to provide the buyer with a document enabling the buyer to take delivery of the goods at the agreed point in the agreed place of destination, not unloaded from the arriving means of transportation.

- Issues: As the goods are to be delivered 'ready for unloading' the delivery document will usually be the transport document (freight prepaid), signed by the consignee upon arrival.

Customs

- Documents: Article A2 contractually obliges the seller to carry out all customs formalities and to obtain all documents, licences and authorizations, not only upon transit and export from its own country, but also for the import of the goods into the buyer's country. The buyer is only required to give assistance to the seller at the latter's request, risk and expense.

- Issues: DDP is the only Incoterms® rule tasking sellers with import clearance and with preshipment inspection, imposed by the government of the country of destination.

1. Under most customs laws, only companies with a place of business in the customs territory can act as importer, apply for import licences, etc. Also, in the EU, art. 64, 2, b of the Community Customs Code requires the declarant (i.e. the person making the customs declaration in his own name or the person in whose name a customs declaration is made) to be established in the Community.

2. As the 'importation' in itself is a taxable transaction (and as most countries do not accept a split up clearance for customs and VAT purposes), the seller would not only have to be registered for customs purposes, but also for VAT in the country of destination, and should invoice the sale with local VAT subsequent to the importation. Unless the seller can appoint a freight forwarder acting as a commission agent / tax representative, this registration might require a business licence, local address, permanent establishment, invoicing in local currency, etc.

3. As the seller has contractually agreed to be the 'importer of record', he is under a contractual obligation to obtain any import licence or other official authorization necessary for the import of the goods. Customs formalities upon importation do not only relate to tax issues but also to measures of economic policy (safety requirements, labelling, certification, etc.).

4. It may be impossible for the seller to comply with these obligations if the seller has no place of business in the country of destination. Thus the transaction may be qualified as a 'domestic sale' for administrative purposes (currency exchange, applicable law, competence of courts, etc.).

5. As mandatory PSI upon importation is usually a condition for obtaining an authorization to purchase hard currency and transfer it abroad, the Incoterms rules are not entirely in line with art. 54 of CISG, which always charges the buyer with all 'steps' and formalities to execute payment.

Transport

- Documents:

1. As Article A3 a) requires the seller to contract for carriage and the goods are delivered ready for unloading from the arriving means of transport, a freight paid transport document will usually be presented by the seller to the buyer (if an independent carrier is used).

2. Article A7 requires the seller to notify the buyer in order to prepare receipt of the goods from the carrier. If the buyer is entitled to determine the exact time and place of reception of the goods, it must give the seller sufficient notice thereof (Article B7).

- Issues:

1. The seller is the shipper on the freight prepaid transport document (if an independent carrier is used).

2. The seller is not required to unload the goods from the arriving means of transportation. This may present problems when the named place of delivery/destination is not the buyer's premises.

Financing

- Documents: Freight prepaid transport document (see 'Proof of Delivery' and 'Transport'), export, transit and import documents (see 'Customs') and import invoice (Article A1).

- Issues:

1. As the risk passes at destination, customs cleared, the DDP Incoterms® rule is not suitable if payment is made with a letter of credit. In a DDP sale the conclusive document should indeed be issued only after the goods have arrived, are customs cleared and ready to be unloaded. This is hardly conceivable in a documentary credit.

2. Documentary collections would also be complicated, especially if the named place is the buyer's premises as opposed to an arrival point on the buyer's side such as a port terminal.

Insurance

- Documents: None required (Article A3 b)/B3 b)).

- Issues: Sellers should consider obtaining adequate insurance cover as they are at risk up to arrival at the agreed point of destination (often the buyer's premises). The seller will be the applicant as well as the beneficiary of the policy. A global transport insurance policy might be an appropriate solution.

FREE ALONGSIDE SHIP
FAS (insert named port of shipment) Incoterms® 2010

Proof of Delivery
- Documents: Article A8 requires the seller to provide the buyer with the usual proof that the goods have been delivered.
- Issues: The seller must deliver the goods by placing them alongside the ship nominated by the buyer at the agreed loading point. In practice, FAS shipments are often delivered, not unloaded from the train, barge, truck … arriving alongside the ocean going vessel, and are directly transshipped from the means of pre-carriage to the ship. If an independent carrier is used for pre-carriage, the freight prepaid pre-carriage transport document, signed off by the buyer's appointed carrier or anyone acting on the buyer's behalf upon arrival, might be used. In certain ports, a receipt document alongside ship (quay receipt, dock receipt, etc.) is not commonly available.

Customs
- Documents: Article A2 requires the seller to carry out all customs formalities and to obtain all documents, licences and authorizations upon export (including export preshipment inspection – Article A9). Article B2 charges the buyer with transit and the import into its own country (including import preshipment inspection – Article B9). Parties must give each other assistance.
- Issues:

1. Article A2 contractually requires the seller to carry out all customs formalities upon export at the named place, even though delivery is prior to the material passing of the customs border.
2. Article 788(1) of the implementing provisions of the Community Customs Code (CCIP) imposes the export formalities upon the EU-company '*who is the owner of the goods or has a similar right of disposal at the time when the declaration is accepted*'. If the goods are to be shipped to a destination outside the EU, the FAS buyer, when established in the EU, may thus well have to be the exporter of record (and assume the liabilities), regardless of the contractual Incoterms provisions. This may complicate string sales.
3. When selling to countries requiring advance export customs reporting (EU), the FAS buyer might in a better position than the FAS seller to communicate the required information in good time, as he appoints the forwarder and/or carrier.

4. The Incoterms® rule FAS only requires the seller to provide the buyer with documents (invoice and evidence of conformity) to support the export declaration. The country of destination of the shipment (that the seller is not supposed to know) might submit these documents to different requirements. The FAS seller's obligations to adapt the said documents or to obtain other documents are limited to assistance at the buyer's request, risk and expense.

5. As delivery may well be inland, prior to passing the customs border, national VAT regulations may prohibit exemption of the seller's invoice of VAT. Moreover, the seller depends on the buyer's willingness to return a proof of physical exportation, justifying the VAT exemption for export (if allowed).

Transport

■ Documents:

1. Article A8 only requires the seller to provide the buyer with a transport document if this document is the usual proof that the goods have been delivered alongside the ship. If this is not the case, the seller's obligation is limited to the provision of assistance in obtaining a transport document.

2. Article B7 requires the buyer to give the seller sufficient notice of the vessel's name, loading point and, where necessary, the selected delivery time. Under Article A7, the seller must, at the buyer's risk and expense, give the buyer sufficient notice either that the goods have been delivered or that the vessel has failed to take the goods.

■ Issues:

1. The buyer should be both the 'loader' and 'sender' (= shipper) on the main transport document ('freight collect'/'freight payable at destination'). It is normally up to the buyer to provide a Dangerous Goods Declaration, ISPS, Cargo Tracking Notes, etc.

2. Article A3 a) imposes no obligation on the FAS seller to contract for carriage but allows the seller to do so '*if requested by the buyer or if it is commercial practice [...] on usual terms at the buyer's risk and expense*'. In such situations, the seller will become the 'shipper' and be the contracting party with the carrier under the contract of carriage. The seller will then control the transport documents.

Financing

- Documents: Apart from the documents mentioned under 'Proof of Delivery', 'Customs' and 'Transport', Article A1 requires the seller to provide the buyer with an (export) invoice. As the seller, in accordance with A9, also has to package the goods in the manner appropriate for their transport, the provision of a packing list will usually also be understood.

- Issues:

1. As the delivery document is '*the usual proof that the goods have been delivered in accordance with A4*', this document may not be a transport document, but a receipt document. If this is the case:
   - the liability of the person receiving the goods (on behalf of the buyer) may not be of a mandatory nature (Hague/Visby, Hamburg, CMR, COTIF, Montreal, etc.) and might be contractually excluded;
   - the presentation of the document is not settled by UCP 600 and ISBP (regarding signing, presentation, emission, cleanliness, etc.);
   - the document is not a title document, and therefore not very appropriate for structuring the financing of the operation.

2. As the FAS buyer is in principle supposed to book the freight, he will control the transport documentation process. This might make it difficult for sellers to find protection in document-driven payment terms. In general not suitable if payment is to be executed under a documentary credit or documentary collection.

Insurance

- Documents: None required (Articles A3 b)/B3 b)).

- Issues:

1. Buyer has the risk from arrival alongside the vessel at the named port of departure and should examine the need for insurance.

2. As the seller is at risk of not being paid, should the buyer not have sufficient insurance to cover possible transport damage to the goods, and as in such situations a credit insurance will normally not intervene, the seller might want to consider an insurance 'seller's contingency'.

COMMONLY-USED DOCUMENTS IN INCOTERMS® 2010 SALES

FREE ON BOARD

FOB (insert named port of shipment) Incoterms® 2010

Proof of Delivery

- Documents: Article A8 requires the seller to provide the buyer with the usual proof that the goods have been delivered, specifying that unless such proof is a transport document, the seller must only provide assistance to the buyer, at the buyer's request, risk and expense, in obtaining a transport document.

- Issues: The seller must deliver the goods by handing them over to the ship according to the port customs. If there is no port custom, the default position is that the seller must place the goods on board. In some ports, goods are considered 'on board' for delivery purposes when they are under ship's tackle. Thus a 'received for shipment B/L' or a mate's receipt might in certain situations be sufficient as a proof of delivery.

Customs

- Documents: Article A2 requires the seller to carry out all customs formalities and to obtain all documents, licences and authorizations upon export (including export preshipment inspection – Article A9). Article B2 charges the buyer with transit and the import after departure (including import preshipment inspection – Article B9). Parties must give each other assistance.

- Issues:

1. Customs legislation usually assimilates a delivery FOB with a delivery 'beyond the customs border' and thus, as a general rule, does not object to the seller acting as the exporter on the customs clearance form.

2. As delivery is supposed to be 'outside of the customs territory', national VAT-regulations will usually authorize exemption of the seller's invoice of VAT, and allow the seller to control the proof of physical exportation, justifying the VAT-exemption for export.

3. The Incoterms® rule FOB only requires the seller to provide the buyer with documents (invoice and evidence of conformity) to support the export declaration. The country of destination of the shipment (that the seller is not supposed to know) might subject these documents to different requirements. The FOB seller's obligations to adapt the said documents or to obtain other documents are limited to assistance at the buyer's request, risk and expense.

4. When selling to countries requiring pre-loading import reporting (i.e. US, EU), FOB buyers might be in a better position to obtain the required information in good time, as they appoint the forwarder or carrier.

Transport

- Documents:

1. Article A8 only requires the seller to provide the buyer with a transport document if this document is the usual proof that the goods have been delivered alongside the ship. If this is not the case, the seller's obligation is limited to the provision of assistance in obtaining a transport document.

2. Article B7 requires the buyer to give the seller sufficient notice of the vessel's name, loading point and, where necessary, the selected delivery time. Under Article A7, the seller must, at the buyer's risk and expense, give the buyer sufficient notice either that the goods have been delivered or that the vessel has failed to take the goods.

- Issues:

1. In practice, contracting parties will usually presume the seller to provide the buyer with an on-board B/L ('freight collect' or 'freight payable at destination').

2. This B/L need not be 'clean'.

3. The seller should be the 'loader' and thus be in charge of the Dangerous Goods Declaration.

4. The buyer should book the freight and thus be the 'sender'. In this quality, the seller would be in charge of ISPS, Cargo Tracking Notes, etc.

5. As the term 'shipper' on the B/L may cover both qualities of 'loader' and 'sender', a seller mentioned as the 'shipper' on the B/L might be advised to formally notify the carrier that he is not the contracting party to the contract of carriage.

6. Article A3 a) imposes no obligation on the FOB seller to contract for carriage but allows the seller to do so '*if requested by the buyer or if it is commercial practice [...] on usual terms at the buyer's risk and expense*'. In such situations, the seller will become the 'shipper' and be the contracting party with the carrier under the contract of carriage. The seller will then control the transport documents.

Financing

- Documents: Apart from the documents mentioned under 'Proof of Delivery', 'Customs' and 'Transport', Article A1 requires the seller to provide the buyer with an (export) invoice. As the seller, in accordance with A9, also has to package the goods in the manner appropriate for their transport, the provision of a packing list will usually also be understood.
- Issues:

1. As the delivery document is '*the usual proof that the goods have been delivered in accordance with A4*', this document might technically not be a transport document. In practice however the FOB delivery will usually be supposed to be evidenced by a B/L, and delivery will be presumed to coincide with the date on the B/L.

2. As the FOB buyer is in principle supposed to book the freight, he will control the transport documentation process. This might make it difficult for sellers to find protection in document-driven payment terms.

3. In general not suitable if payment is to be executed under a documentary collection as delivery and passing of the risk will normally occur prior to presentation of the document and collection.

Insurance

- Documents: None required (Article A3 b)/B3 b)).
- Issues:

1. Buyer has the risk from arrival on board the vessel at the named port of departure and should examine the need for insurance.

2. As the seller is at risk of not being paid, should the buyer not have sufficient insurance to cover possible transport damage to the goods, and as in such situations a credit insurance will normally not intervene, the seller might want to consider an insurance 'seller's contingency'.

COST AND FREIGHT
CFR (insert named port of destination) Incoterms® 2010

Proof of Delivery

- Documents: Article A8 requires the seller to provide the buyer with the usual transport document to the agreed point at the agreed port of destination, freight prepaid (or freight for shipper's account). This transport document must cover the contract goods, be dated within the period agreed for shipment, enable the buyer to claim the goods from the carrier at the port of destination and, unless otherwise agreed, enable the buyer to sell the goods in transit by the transfer of the document to a subsequent buyer or by notification to the carrier. When such a transport document is issued in negotiable form and in several originals, a full set of originals must be presented to the buyer (= B/L).

- Issues: As the Incoterms® rule CFR only refers to the 'ship to' port, the parties are well advised to also identify as precisely as possible in the contract the 'ship-from' port where the risk passes to the buyer and delivery takes place.

Customs

- Documents: Article A2 requires the seller to carry out all customs formalities and to obtain all documents, licences and authorizations upon export (including export preshipment inspection – Article A9). Article B2 charges the buyer with transit and import (including import preshipment inspection – Article B9). Parties must give each other assistance.

- Issues:

1. Article A1 of the Incoterms® rule CFR only requires the seller to provide the buyer with documents (invoice and evidence of conformity) in support of the export declaration (Article A2). The country of destination of the shipment might submit these documents to specific, different formal requirements. The CFR seller's obligations to adapt the said documents or to obtain additional documents are limited to assistance at the buyer's request, risk and expense.

2. Even though Article B2 requires the buyer to obtain, at its own risk and expense, any import licence or other official authorization and to carry out all customs formalities for the import of the goods (and for their transit), the seller will normally be better placed to obtain and deliver required information when exporting to countries requiring pre-loading import reporting, as he organizes carriage.

3. The seller is required to provide the buyer with a freight-paid transport document. In some countries this document is required to establish the customs value or to establish 'direct transportation' for tariff preference purposes.

Transport

- Documents:

1. Article A8 requires the seller to provide the buyer with the usual transport document to the agreed port, freight prepaid (or freight for shipper's account).

2. Article A7 moreover requires the seller to notify the buyer when the goods have been shipped so that the buyer can take reception of the goods upon arrival.

- Issues:

1. The default transport document required from the seller is a freight prepaid (or 'freight for shipper's account') port-to-port Bill of Lading on usual terms for carriage by the usual route in a vessel of the type normally used for the transport of the type of goods sold with the seller being the shipper (loader + sender).

2. The Incoterms rules do not require the transport document (unless otherwise agreed a port-to-port B/L) to be clean.

3. As the 'shipper', the seller will have to take care of the Dangerous Goods Declaration, ISPS at departure, Cargo Tracking Notes, etc.

4. Buyers bear the transport risk for carriers that they have not selected and with which they have not contracted. However, they inherit sellers' contractual rights against carriers.

Financing

- Documents: Freight prepaid port-to-port Bill of Lading (see 'Proof of Delivery' and 'Transport'), export documents (see 'Customs') and (export) invoice (Article A1).
- Issues:

1. Sellers control the documentation process, and can obtain real protection when financing the operation with a documentary credit. Therefore this Incoterms® rule is commonly used with documentary letter of credit terms.

2. In general not that suitable if payment is to be executed under a documentary collection, as delivery and passing of the risk will normally occur prior to presentation of the document and collection.

Insurance

- Documents: None required (Article A3 b)/B3 b)).
- Issues:

1. Buyers are at risk from the port of departure and should examine the need for adequate insurance.

2. As the seller is at risk of not being paid, should the buyer not have sufficient insurance to cover possible transport damage to the goods, and as in such situations a credit insurance will normally not intervene, the seller might want to consider an insurance 'seller's contingency'.

: COMMONLY-USED DOCUMENTS IN INCOTERMS® 2010 SALES

COST INSURANCE AND FREIGHT
CIF (insert named port of destination) Incoterms® 2010

Proof of Delivery

- Documents: Article A8 requires the seller to provide the buyer with the usual transport document to the agreed point at the agreed port of destination, freight prepaid (or freight for shipper's account). This transport document must cover the contract goods, be dated within the period agreed for shipment, enable the buyer to claim the goods from the carrier at the port of destination and, unless otherwise agreed, enable the buyer to sell the goods in transit by the transfer of the document to a subsequent buyer or by notification to the carrier. When such a transport document is issued in negotiable form and in several originals, a full set of originals must be presented to the buyer (= B/L).

- Issues: As the Incoterms® rule CIF only refers to the 'ship to'-port, the parties are well advised to also identify as precisely as possible in the contract the 'ship-from'-port where the risk passes to the buyer and delivery takes place.

Customs

- Documents: Article A2 requires the seller to carry out all customs formalities and to obtain all documents, licences and authorizations upon export (including export preshipment inspection – Article A9). Article B2 charges the buyer with transit and the import (including import preshipment inspection – Article B9). Parties must give each other assistance.

- Issues:

1. Article A1 of the Incoterms® rule CIF only requires the seller to provide the buyer with documents (invoice and evidence of conformity) in support of the export declaration (Article A2). The country of destination of the shipment might submit these documents to specific, different formal requirements. The CIF seller's obligations to adapt the said documents or to obtain additional documents are limited to assistance at the buyer's request, risk and expense.

2. Even though Article B2 requires the buyer to obtain, at its own risk and expense, any import licence or other official authorization and to carry out all customs formalities for the import of the goods (and for their transit), the seller will normally be better placed to obtain and deliver required information when exporting to countries requiring pre-loading import reporting, as he organizes carriage.

COMMONLY-USED DOCUMENTS IN INCOTERMS® 2010 SALES

3. The seller is required to provide the buyer with a freight-paid transport document and an insurance certificate. In some countries these documents are required to establish the customs value or to establish 'direct transportation' for tariff preference purposes.

Transport

- Documents:

1. Article A8 requires the seller to provide the buyer with the usual transport document to the agreed port, freight prepaid (or freight for shipper's account).

2. Article A7 moreover requires the seller to notify the buyer when the goods have been shipped so that the buyer can take reception of the goods upon arrival.

- Issues:

1. The default transport document required from the seller is a freight prepaid (or 'freight for shipper's account') port-to-port Bill of Lading on usual terms for carriage by the usual route in a vessel of the type normally used for the transport of the type of goods sold with the seller being the shipper (loader + sender).

2. The Incoterms rules do not require the transport document (unless otherwise agreed a port-to-port B/L) to be clean.

3. As the 'shipper', the seller will have to take care of the Dangerous Goods Declaration, ISPS at departure, Cargo Tracking Notes, etc.

4. Buyers bear the transport risk for carriers that they have not selected and with which they have not contracted. However, they inherit sellers' contractual rights against carriers.

Financing

- Documents: Freight prepaid port-to-port Bill of Lading (see 'Proof of Delivery' and 'Transport'), export documents (see 'Customs'), Insurance certificate and (export) invoice (Article A1).

- Issues:

1. Sellers control the documentation process, and can obtain real protection when financing the operation with a documentary credit. Therefore this Incoterms® rule is commonly used with documentary letter of credit terms.

2. In general not that suitable if payment is to be executed under a documentary collection as delivery and passing of the risk will normally occur prior to presentation of the document and collection.

3. The seller-provided insurance cover should be of interest for structuring the financing of the operation.

Insurance

- Documents: Article A3 b) requires the seller to provide for evidence of insurance for at least 110% of the value of the goods in the currency of the contract with Institute Cargo Clauses C cover, enabling the buyer or anyone else with an insurable interest to claim directly from the insurer.

- Issues:

1. The seller is the applicant of the insurance policy, the buyer is the beneficiary.

2. In some countries the insurance certificate is required to establish the customs value.

3. C Clauses cover is seldom adequate. Parties should consider additional cover (A or B plus war, strike (SRCC), and possibly warehouse-to-warehouse.

4. Some countries require exporters to contract for insurance with a national insurance company. If the buyer doubts the quality of this insurance, he might consider an umbrella insurance policy.

ANNEX 4
INCOTERMS® 2010 RULES

CONTENTS

Foreword	4
Introduction	5

INCOTERMS® 2010

Rules for any mode or modes of transport

EXW	15
FCA	23
CPT	33
CIP	41
DAT	53
DAP	61
DDP	69

Rules for sea and inland waterway transport

FAS	79
FOB	87
CFR	95
CIF	105

Incoterms® 2010 Drafting Group	119
ICC Dispute Resolution	124
Copyright notice and synopsis of trademark usage rules	125
ICC at a glance	126
Other Incoterms® 2010 products	127
ICC publications for global business	128

FOREWORD

By Rajat Gupta, ICC Chairman

The global economy has given businesses broader access than ever before to markets all over the world. Goods are sold in more countries, in larger quantities, and in greater variety. But as the volume and complexity of global sales increase, so do possibilities for misunderstandings and costly disputes when sale contracts are not adequately drafted.

The Incoterms® rules, the ICC rules on the use of domestic and international trade terms, facilitate the conduct of global trade. Reference to an Incoterms® 2010 rule in a sale contract clearly defines the parties' respective obligations and reduces the risk of legal complications.

Since the creation of the Incoterms rules by ICC in 1936, this globally accepted contractual standard has been regularly updated to keep pace with the development of international trade. The Incoterms® 2010 rules take account of the continued spread of customs-free zones, the increased use of electronic communications in business transactions, heightened concern about security in the movement of goods and changes in transport practices. *Incoterms® 2010* updates and consolidates the 'delivered' rules, reducing the total number of rules from 13 to 11, and offers a simpler and clearer presentation of all the rules. *Incoterms® 2010* is also the first version of the Incoterms rules to make all references to buyers and sellers gender-neutral.

The broad expertise of ICC's Commission on Commercial Law and Practice, whose membership is drawn from all parts of the world and all trade sectors, ensures that the Incoterms® 2010 rules respond to business needs everywhere.

ICC would like to express its gratitude to the members of the Commission, chaired by Fabio Bortolotti (Italy), to the Drafting Group, which comprised Charles Debattista (Co-Chair, UK), Christoph Martin Radtke (Co-Chair, France), Jens Bredow (Germany), Johnny Herre (Sweden), David Lowe (UK), Lauri Railas (Finland), Frank Reynolds (US), and Miroslav Subert (Czech Republic), and to Asko Raty (Finland) for assistance with the images depicting the 11 rules.

INTRODUCTION

The Incoterms®[1] rules explain a set of three-letter trade terms reflecting business-to-business practice in contracts for the sale of goods. The Incoterms rules describe mainly the tasks, costs and risks involved in the delivery of goods from sellers to buyers.

How to use the Incoterms® 2010 rules

1. Incorporate the Incoterms® 2010 rules into your contract of sale

If you want the Incoterms® 2010 rules to apply to your contract, you should make this clear in the contract, through such words as, "[*the chosen Incoterms rule including the named place, followed by*] Incoterms® 2010".

2. Choose the appropriate Incoterms rule

The chosen Incoterms rule needs to be appropriate to the goods, to the means of their transport, and above all to whether the parties intend to put additional obligations, for example such as the obligation to organize carriage or insurance, on the seller or on the buyer. The Guidance Note to each Incoterms rule contains information that is particularly helpful when making this choice. Whichever Incoterms rule is chosen, the parties should be aware that the interpretation of their contract may well be influenced by customs particular to the port or place being used.

3. Specify your place or port as precisely as possible

The chosen Incoterms rule can work only if the parties name a place or port, and will work best if the parties specify the place or port as precisely as possible.

A good example of such precision would be:

"FCA 38 Cours Albert 1er, Paris, France Incoterms® 2010".

Under the Incoterms rules Ex Works (EXW), Free Carrier (FCA), Delivered at Terminal (DAT), Delivered at Place (DAP), Delivered Duty Paid (DDP), Free Alongside Ship (FAS), and Free on Board (FOB), the named place is the place where delivery takes place and where risk passes from the seller to the buyer. Under the Incoterms rules Carriage Paid to (CPT), Carriage and Insurance Paid to (CIP), Cost and Freight (CFR) and Cost, Insurance and Freight (CIF), the named place differs from the place of delivery. Under these four Incoterms rules, the named

---

1. "Incoterms" is a registered trademark of the International Chamber of Commerce.

place is the place of destination to which carriage is paid. Indications as to place or destination can helpfully be further specified by stating a precise point in that place or destination in order to avoid doubt or argument.

4. Remember that Incoterms rules do not give you a complete contract of sale

Incoterms rules *do* say which party to the sale contract has the obligation to make carriage or insurance arrangements, when the seller delivers the goods to the buyer, and which costs each party is responsible for. Incoterms rules, however, say nothing about the price to be paid or the method of its payment. Neither do they deal with the transfer of ownership of the goods, or the consequences of a breach of contract. These matters are normally dealt with through express terms in the contract of sale or in the law governing that contract. The parties should be aware that mandatory local law may override any aspect of the sale contract, including the chosen Incoterms rule.

Main features of the Incoterms® 2010 rules

1. Two new Incoterms rules – DAT and DAP – have replaced the Incoterms 2000 rules DAF, DES, DEQ and DDU

The number of Incoterms rules has been reduced from 13 to 11. This has been achieved by substituting two new rules that may be used irrespective of the agreed mode of transport – DAT, Delivered at Terminal, and DAP, Delivered at Place – for the Incoterms 2000 rules DAF, DES, DEQ and DDU.

Under both new rules, delivery occurs at a named destination: in DAT, at the buyer's disposal unloaded from the arriving vehicle (as under the former DEQ rule); in DAP, likewise at the buyer's disposal, but ready for unloading (as under the former DAF, DES and DDU rules).

The new rules make the Incoterms 2000 rules DES and DEQ superfluous. The named terminal in DAT may well be in a port, and DAT can therefore safely be used in cases where the Incoterms 2000 rule DEQ once was. Likewise, the arriving "vehicle" under DAP may well be a ship and the named place of destination may well be a port: consequently, DAP can safely be used in cases where the Incoterms 2000 rule DES once was. These new rules, like their predecessors, are "delivered", with the seller bearing all the costs (other than those related to import clearance, where applicable) and risks involved in bringing the goods to the named place of destination.

Incoterms® 2010

2. Classification of the 11 Incoterms® 2010 rules

The 11 Incoterms® 2010 rules are presented in two distinct classes:

RULES FOR ANY MODE OR MODES OF TRANSPORT

EXW	EX WORKS
FCA	FREE CARRIER
CPT	CARRIAGE PAID TO
CIP	CARRIAGE AND INSURANCE PAID TO
DAT	DELIVERED AT TERMINAL
DAP	DELIVERED AT PLACE
DDP	DELIVERED DUTY PAID

RULES FOR SEA AND INLAND WATERWAY TRANSPORT

FAS	FREE ALONGSIDE SHIP
FOB	FREE ON BOARD
CFR	COST AND FREIGHT
CIF	COST INSURANCE AND FREIGHT

The first class includes the seven Incoterms® 2010 rules that can be used irrespective of the mode of transport selected and irrespective of whether one or more than one mode of transport is employed. EXW, FCA, CPT, CIP, DAT, DAP and DDP belong to this class. They can be used even when there is no maritime transport at all. It is important to remember, however, that these rules *can* be used in cases where a ship *is* used for part of the carriage.

In the second class of Incoterms® 2010 rules, the point of delivery and the place to which the goods are carried to the buyer are *both* ports, hence the label "sea and inland waterway" rules. FAS, FOB, CFR and CIF belong to this class. Under the last three Incoterms rules, all mention of the ship's rail as the point of delivery has been omitted in preference for the goods being delivered when they are "on board" the vessel. This more closely reflects modern commercial reality and avoids the rather dated image of the risk swinging to and fro across an imaginary perpendicular line.

3. Rules for domestic and international trade

Incoterms rules have traditionally been used in *international* sale contracts where goods pass across national borders. In various areas of the world, however, trade blocs, like the European Union, have made border formalities between different countries less significant. Consequently, the subtitle of the Incoterms® 2010 rules formally recognizes that they are available for application to both international and domestic sale contracts. As a result, the Incoterms® 2010 rules clearly state in a number of places that the obligation to comply with export/import formalities exists only where applicable.

Two developments have persuaded ICC that a movement in this direction is timely. Firstly, traders commonly use Incoterms rules for purely domestic sale contracts. The second reason is the greater willingness in the United States to use Incoterms rules in domestic trade rather than the former Uniform Commercial Code shipment and delivery terms.

4. Guidance Notes

Before each Incoterms® 2010 rule you will find a Guidance Note. The Guidance Notes explain the fundamentals of each Incoterms rule, such as when it should be used, when risk passes, and how costs are allocated between seller and buyer. The Guidance Notes are not part of the actual Incoterms® 2010 rules, but are intended to help the user accurately and efficiently steer towards the appropriate Incoterms rule for a particular transaction.

5. Electronic communication

Previous versions of Incoterms rules have specified those documents that could be replaced by EDI messages. Articles A1/B1 of the Incoterms® 2010 rules, however, now give electronic means of communication the same effect as paper communication, as long as the parties so agree or where customary. This formulation facilitates the evolution of new electronic procedures throughout the lifetime of the Incoterms® 2010 rules.

6. Insurance cover

The Incoterms® 2010 rules are the first version of the Incoterms rules since the revision of the Institute Cargo Clauses and take account of alterations made to those clauses. The Incoterms® 2010 rules place information duties relating to insurance in articles A3/B3, which deal with contracts of carriage and insurance. These provisions have been moved from the more generic articles found in articles A10/B10 of the

Incoterms 2000 rules. The language in articles A3/B3 relating to insurance has also been altered with a view to clarifying the parties' obligations in this regard.

7. Security-related clearances and information required for such clearances

There is heightened concern nowadays about security in the movement of goods, requiring verification that the goods do not pose a threat to life or property for reasons other than their inherent nature. Therefore, the Incoterms® 2010 rules have allocated obligations between the buyer and seller to obtain or to render assistance in obtaining security-related clearances, such as chain-of-custody information, in articles A2/B2 and A10/B10 of various Incoterms rules.

8. Terminal handling charges

Under Incoterms rules CPT, CIP, CFR, CIF, DAT, DAP, and DDP, the seller must make arrangements for the carriage of the goods to the agreed destination. While the freight is paid by the seller, it is actually paid *for* by the buyer as freight costs are normally included by the seller in the total selling price. The carriage costs will sometimes include the costs of handling and moving the goods within port or container terminal facilities and the carrier or terminal operator may well charge these costs to the buyer who receives the goods. In these circumstances, the buyer will want to avoid paying for the same service twice: once to the seller as part of the total selling price and once independently to the carrier or the terminal operator. The Incoterms® 2010 rules seek to avoid this happening by clearly allocating such costs in articles A6/B6 of the relevant Incoterms rules.

9. String sales

In the sale of commodities, as opposed to the sale of manufactured goods, cargo is frequently sold several times during transit "down a string". When this happens, a seller in the middle of the string does not "ship" the goods because these have already been shipped by the first seller in the string. The seller in the middle of the string therefore performs its obligations towards its buyer not by shipping the goods, but by "procuring" goods that have been shipped. For clarification purposes, Incoterms® 2010 rules include the obligation to "procure goods shipped" as an alternative to the obligation to ship goods in the relevant Incoterms rules.

Variants of Incoterms rules

Sometimes the parties want to alter an Incoterms rule. The Incoterms® 2010 rules do not prohibit such alteration, but there are dangers in so doing. In order to avoid any unwelcome surprises, the parties would need to make the intended effect of such alterations extremely clear in their contract. Thus, for example, if the allocation of costs in the Incoterms® 2010 rules is altered in the contract, the parties should also clearly state whether they intend to vary the point at which the risk passes from seller to buyer.

Status of this introduction

This introduction gives general information on the use and interpretation of the Incoterms® 2010 rules, but does not form part of those rules.

Explanation of terms used in the Incoterms® 2010 rules

As in the Incoterms 2000 rules, the seller's and buyer's obligations are presented in mirror fashion, reflecting under column A the seller's obligations and under column B the buyer's obligations. These obligations can be carried out personally by the seller or the buyer or sometimes, subject to terms in the contract or the applicable law, through intermediaries such as carriers, freight forwarders or other persons nominated by the seller or the buyer for a specific purpose.

The text of the Incoterms® 2010 rules is meant to be self-explanatory. However, in order to assist users the following text sets out guidance as to the sense in which selected terms are used throughout the document.

Carrier: For the purposes of the Incoterms® 2010 rules, the carrier is the party with whom carriage is contracted.

Customs formalities: These are requirements to be met in order to comply with any applicable customs regulations and may include documentary, security, information or physical inspection obligations.

Delivery: This concept has multiple meanings in trade law and practice, but in the Incoterms® 2010 rules, it is used to indicate where the risk of loss of or damage to the goods passes from the seller to the buyer.

Delivery document: This phrase is now used as the heading to article A8. It means a document used to prove that delivery has occurred. For many of the Incoterms® 2010 rules, the delivery document is a transport document or corresponding electronic record. However, with EXW, FCA, FAS and FOB, the delivery document may simply be a receipt. A delivery document may also have other functions, for example as part of the mechanism for payment.

Electronic record or procedure: A set of information constituted of one or more electronic messages and, where applicable, being functionally equivalent with the corresponding paper document.

Packaging: This word is used for different purposes:

1. The packaging of the goods to comply with any requirements under the contract of sale.

2. The packaging of the goods so that they are fit for transportation.

3. The stowage of the packaged goods within a container or other means of transport.

In the Incoterms® 2010 rules, packaging means both the first and second of the above. The Incoterms® 2010 rules do not deal with the parties' obligations for stowage within a container and therefore, where relevant, the parties should deal with this in the sale contract.

RULES FOR ANY MODE OR MODES OF TRANSPORT

EXW
EX WORKS

EXW (insert named place of delivery) Incoterms® 2010

GUIDANCE NOTE

This rule may be used irrespective of the mode of transport selected and may also be used where more than one mode of transport is employed. It is suitable for domestic trade, while FCA is usually more appropriate for international trade.

"Ex Works" means that the seller delivers when it places the goods at the disposal of the buyer at the seller's premises or at another named place (i.e., works, factory, warehouse, etc.). The seller does not need to load the goods on any collecting vehicle, nor does it need to clear the goods for export, where such clearance is applicable.

The parties are well advised to specify as clearly as possible the point within the named place of delivery, as the costs and risks to that point are for the account of the seller. The buyer bears all costs and risks involved in taking the goods from the agreed point, if any, at the named place of delivery.

EXW represents the minimum obligation for the seller. The rule should be used with care as:

a) The seller has no obligation to the buyer to load the goods, even though in practice the seller may be in a better position to do so. If the seller does load the goods, it does so at the buyer's risk and expense. In cases where the seller is in a better position to load the goods, FCA, which obliges the seller to do so at its own risk and expense, is usually more appropriate.

b) A buyer who buys from a seller on an EXW basis for export needs to be aware that the seller has an obligation to provide only such assistance as the buyer may require to effect that export: the seller is not bound to organize the export clearance. Buyers are therefore well advised not to use EXW if they cannot directly or indirectly obtain export clearance.

c) The buyer has limited obligations to provide to the seller any information regarding the export of the goods. However, the seller may need this information for, e.g., taxation or reporting purposes.

A THE SELLER'S OBLIGATIONS

A1 General obligations of the seller

The seller must provide the goods and the commercial invoice in conformity with the contract of sale and any other evidence of conformity that may be required by the contract.

Any document referred to in A1-A10 may be an equivalent electronic record or procedure if agreed between the parties or customary.

A2 Licences, authorizations, security clearances and other formalities

Where applicable, the seller must provide the buyer, at the buyer's request, risk and expense, assistance in obtaining any export licence, or other official authorization necessary for the export of the goods.

Where applicable, the seller must provide, at the buyer's request, risk and expense, any information in the possession of the seller that is required for the security clearance of the goods.

A3 Contracts of carriage and insurance

a) Contract of carriage
The seller has no obligation to the buyer to make a contract of carriage.

b) Contract of insurance
The seller has no obligation to the buyer to make a contract of insurance. However, the seller must provide the buyer, at the buyer's request, risk and expense (if any), with information that the buyer needs for obtaining insurance.

A4 Delivery

The seller must deliver the goods by placing them at the disposal of the buyer at the agreed point, if any, at the named place of delivery, not loaded on any collecting vehicle. If no specific point has been agreed within the named place of delivery, and if there are several points available, the seller may select the point that best suits its purpose. The seller must deliver the goods on the agreed date or within the agreed period.

Incoterms® 2010

B THE BUYER'S OBLIGATIONS

B1 General obligations of the buyer
The buyer must pay the price of the goods as provided in the contract of sale.

Any document referred to in B1-B10 may be an equivalent electronic record or procedure if agreed between the parties or customary.

B2 Licences, authorizations, security clearances and other formalities
Where applicable, it is up to the buyer to obtain, at its own risk and expense, any export and import licence or other official authorization and carry out all customs formalities for the export of the goods.

B3 Contracts of carriage and insurance
a) Contract of carriage
The buyer has no obligation to the seller to make a contract of carriage.

b) Contract of insurance
The buyer has no obligation to the seller to make a contract of insurance.

B4 Taking delivery
The buyer must take delivery of the goods when A4 and A7 have been complied with.

A5 Transfer of risks

The seller bears all risks of loss of or damage to the goods until they have been delivered in accordance with A4 with the exception of loss or damage in the circumstances described in B5.

A6 Allocation of costs

The seller must pay all costs relating to the goods until they have been delivered in accordance with A4, other than those payable by the buyer as envisaged in B6.

A7 Notices to the buyer

The seller must give the buyer any notice needed to enable the buyer to take delivery of the goods.

A8 Delivery document

The seller has no obligation to the buyer.

B5 Transfer of risks

The buyer bears all risks of loss of or damage to the goods from the time they have been delivered as envisaged in A4.

If the buyer fails to give notice in accordance with B7, then the buyer bears all risks of loss of or damage to the goods from the agreed date or the expiry date of the agreed period for delivery, provided that the goods have been clearly identified as the contract goods.

B6 Allocation of costs

The buyer must:

a) pay all costs relating to the goods from the time they have been delivered as envisaged in A4;

b) pay any additional costs incurred by failing either to take delivery of the goods when they have been placed at its disposal or to give appropriate notice in accordance with B7, provided that the goods have been clearly identified as the contract goods;

c) pay, where applicable, all duties, taxes and other charges, as well as the costs of carrying out customs formalities payable upon export; and

d) reimburse all costs and charges incurred by the seller in providing assistance as envisaged in A2.

B7 Notices to the seller

The buyer must, whenever it is entitled to determine the time within an agreed period and/or the point of taking delivery within the named place, give the seller sufficient notice thereof.

B8 Proof of delivery

The buyer must provide the seller with appropriate evidence of having taken delivery.

A9 Checking – packaging – marking

The seller must pay the costs of those checking operations (such as checking quality, measuring, weighing, counting) that are necessary for the purpose of delivering the goods in accordance with A4.

The seller must, at its own expense, package the goods, unless it is usual for the particular trade to transport the type of goods sold unpackaged. The seller may package the goods in the manner appropriate for their transport, unless the buyer has notified the seller of specific packaging requirements before the contract of sale is concluded. Packaging is to be marked appropriately.

A10 Assistance with information and related costs

The seller must, where applicable, in a timely manner, provide to or render assistance in obtaining for the buyer, at the buyer's request, risk and expense, any documents and information, including security-related information, that the buyer needs for the export and/or import of the goods and/or for their transport to the final destination.

B9 Inspection of goods

The buyer must pay the costs of any mandatory pre-shipment inspection, including inspection mandated by the authorities of the country of export.

B10 Assistance with information and related costs

The buyer must, in a timely manner, advise the seller of any security information requirements so that the seller may comply with A10.

The buyer must reimburse the seller for all costs and charges incurred by the seller in providing or rendering assistance in obtaining documents and information as envisaged in A10.

FCA
Free Carrier
FCA (insert named place of delivery) Incoterms® 2010

GUIDANCE NOTE

This rule may be used irrespective of the mode of transport selected and may also be used where more than one mode of transport is employed.

"Free Carrier" means that the seller delivers the goods to the carrier or another person nominated by the buyer at the seller's premises or another named place. The parties are well advised to specify as clearly as possible the point within the named place of delivery, as the risk passes to the buyer at that point.

If the parties intend to deliver the goods at the seller's premises, they should identify the address of those premises as the named place of delivery. If, on the other hand, the parties intend the goods to be delivered at another place, they must identify a different specific place of delivery.

FCA requires the seller to clear the goods for export, where applicable. However, the seller has no obligation to clear the goods for import, pay any import duty or carry out any import customs formalities.

A THE SELLER'S OBLIGATIONS

A1 General obligations of the seller

The seller must provide the goods and the commercial invoice in conformity with the contract of sale and any other evidence of conformity that may be required by the contract.

Any document referred to in A1-A10 may be an equivalent electronic record or procedure if agreed between the parties or customary.

A2 Licences, authorizations, security clearances and other formalities

Where applicable, the seller must obtain, at its own risk and expense, any export licence or other official authorization and carry out all customs formalities necessary for the export of the goods.

A3 Contracts of carriage and insurance

a) Contract of carriage
The seller has no obligation to the buyer to make a contract of carriage. However, if requested by the buyer or if it is commercial practice and the buyer does not give an instruction to the contrary in due time, the seller may contract for carriage on usual terms at the buyer's risk and expense. In either case, the seller may decline to make the contract of carriage and, if it does, shall promptly notify the buyer.

b) Contract of insurance
The seller has no obligation to the buyer to make a contract of insurance. However, the seller must provide the buyer, at the buyer's request, risk, and expense (if any), with information that the buyer needs for obtaining insurance.

A4 Delivery

The seller must deliver the goods to the carrier or another person nominated by the buyer at the agreed point, if any, at the named place on the agreed date or within the agreed period.

Delivery is completed:
a) If the named place is the seller's premises, when the goods have been loaded on the means of transport provided by the buyer.

b) In any other case, when the goods are placed at the disposal of the carrier or another person nominated by the buyer on the seller's means of transport ready for unloading.

B THE BUYER'S OBLIGATIONS

B1 General obligations of the buyer

The buyer must pay the price of the goods as provided in the contract of sale.

Any document referred to in B1-B10 may be an equivalent electronic record or procedure if agreed between the parties or customary.

B2 Licences, authorizations, security clearances and other formalities

Where applicable, it is up to the buyer to obtain, at its own risk and expense, any import licence or other official authorization and carry out all customs formalities for the import of the goods and for their transport through any country.

B3 Contracts of carriage and insurance

a) Contract of carriage

The buyer must contract at its own expense for the carriage of the goods from the named place of delivery, except when the contract of carriage is made by the seller as provided for in A3 a).

b) Contract of insurance

The buyer has no obligation to the seller to make a contract of insurance.

B4 Taking delivery

The buyer must take delivery of the goods when they have been delivered as envisaged in A4.

If no specific point has been notified by the buyer under B7 d) within the named place of delivery, and if there are several points available, the seller may select the point that best suits its purpose.

Unless the buyer notifies the seller otherwise, the seller may deliver the goods for carriage in such a manner as the quantity and/or nature of the goods may require.

A5   **Transfer of risks**
The seller bears all risks of loss of or damage to the goods until they have been delivered in accordance with A4, with the exception of loss or damage in the circumstances described in B5.

A6   **Allocation of costs**
The seller must pay
a) all costs relating to the goods until they have been delivered in accordance with A4, other than those payable by the buyer as envisaged in B6; and

b) where applicable, the costs of customs formalities necessary for export, as well as all duties, taxes, and other charges payable upon export.

B5 Transfer of risks

The buyer bears all risks of loss of or damage to the goods from the time they have been delivered as envisaged in A4.

If

a) the buyer fails in accordance with B7 to notify the nomination of a carrier or another person as envisaged in A4 or to give notice; or

b) the carrier or person nominated by the buyer as envisaged in A4 fails to take the goods into its charge,

then, the buyer bears all risks of loss of or damage to the goods:
(i) from the agreed date, or in the absence of an agreed date,
(ii) from the date notified by the seller under A7 within the agreed period; or, if no such date has been notified,
(iii) from the expiry date of any agreed period for delivery,

provided that the goods have been clearly identified as the contract goods.

B6 Allocation of costs

The buyer must pay

a) all costs relating to the goods from the time they have been delivered as envisaged in A4, except, where applicable, the costs of customs formalities necessary for export, as well as all duties, taxes, and other charges payable upon export as referred to in A6 b);

b) any additional costs incurred, either because:
(i) the buyer fails to nominate a carrier or another person as envisaged in A4, or
(ii) the carrier or person nominated by the buyer as envisaged in A4 fails to take the goods into its charge, or
(iii) the buyer has failed to give appropriate notice in accordance with B7,

provided that the goods have been clearly identified as the contract goods; and

FCA

A7 Notices to the buyer

The seller must, at the buyer's risk and expense, give the buyer sufficient notice either that the goods have been delivered in accordance with A4 or that the carrier or another person nominated by the buyer has failed to take the goods within the time agreed.

A8 Delivery document

The seller must provide the buyer, at the seller's expense, with the usual proof that the goods have been delivered in accordance with A4.

The seller must provide assistance to the buyer, at the buyer's request, risk and expense, in obtaining a transport document.

A9 Checking – packaging – marking

The seller must pay the costs of those checking operations (such as checking quality, measuring, weighing, counting) that are necessary for the purpose of delivering the goods in accordance with A4, as well as the costs of any pre-shipment inspection mandated by the authority of the country of export.

The seller must, at its own expense, package the goods, unless it is usual for the particular trade to transport the type of goods sold unpackaged. The seller may package the goods in the manner appropriate for their transport, unless the buyer has notified the seller of specific packaging requirements before the contract of sale is concluded. Packaging is to be marked appropriately.

c) where applicable, all duties, taxes and other charges as well as the costs of carrying out customs formalities payable upon import of the goods and the costs for their transport through any country.

B7 Notices to the seller

The buyer must notify the seller of

a) the name of the carrier or another person nominated as envisaged in A4 within sufficient time as to enable the seller to deliver the goods in accordance with that article;

b) where necessary, the selected time within the period agreed for delivery when the carrier or person nominated will take the goods;

c) the mode of transport to be used by the person nominated; and

d) the point of taking delivery within the named place.

B8 Proof of delivery

The buyer must accept the proof of delivery provided as envisaged in A8.

B9 Inspection of goods

The buyer must pay the costs of any mandatory pre-shipment inspection, except when such inspection is mandated by the authorities of the country of export.

FCA

A10   **Assistance with information and related costs**

The seller must, where applicable, in a timely manner, provide to or render assistance in obtaining for the buyer, at the buyer's request, risk and expense, any documents and information, including security-related information, that the buyer needs for the import of the goods and/or for their transport to the final destination.

The seller must reimburse the buyer for all costs and charges incurred by the buyer in providing or rendering assistance in obtaining documents and information as envisaged in B10.

B10 **Assistance with information and related costs**

The buyer must, in a timely manner, advise the seller of any security information requirements so that the seller may comply with A10.

The buyer must reimburse the seller for all costs and charges incurred by the seller in providing or rendering assistance in obtaining documents and information as envisaged in A10.

The buyer must, where applicable, in a timely manner, provide to or render assistance in obtaining for the seller, at the seller's request, risk and expense, any documents and information, including security-related information, that the seller needs for the transport and export of the goods and for their transport through any country.

CPT
CARRIAGE PAID TO

CPT (insert named place of destination) Incoterms® 2010

GUIDANCE NOTE

This rule may be used irrespective of the mode of transport selected and may also be used where more than one mode of transport is employed.

"Carriage Paid to" means that the seller delivers the goods to the carrier or another person nominated by the seller at an agreed place (if any such place is agreed between the parties) and that the seller must contract for and pay the costs of carriage necessary to bring the goods to the named place of destination.

When CPT, CIP, CFR or CIF are used, the seller fulfils its obligation to deliver when it hands the goods over to the carrier and not when the goods reach the place of destination.

This rule has two critical points, because risk passes and costs are transferred at different places. The parties are well advised to identify as precisely as possible in the contract both the place of delivery, where the risk passes to the buyer, and the named place of destination to which the seller must contract for the carriage. If several carriers are used for the carriage to the agreed destination and the parties do not agree on a specific point of delivery, the default position is that risk passes when the goods have been delivered to the first carrier at a point entirely of the seller's choosing and over which the buyer has no control. Should the parties wish the risk to pass at a later stage (e.g., at an ocean port or airport), they need to specify this in their contract of sale.

The parties are also well advised to identify as precisely as possible the point within the agreed place of destination, as the costs to that point are for the account of the seller. The seller is advised to procure contracts of carriage that match this choice precisely. If the seller incurs costs under its contract of carriage related to unloading at the named place of destination, the seller is not entitled to recover such costs from the buyer unless otherwise agreed between the parties.

CPT requires the seller to clear the goods for export, where applicable. However, the seller has no obligation to clear the goods for import, pay any import duty or carry out any import customs formalities.

A THE SELLER'S OBLIGATIONS

A1 General obligations of the seller

The seller must provide the goods and the commercial invoice in conformity with the contract of sale and any other evidence of conformity that may be required by the contract.

Any document referred to in A1-A10 may be an equivalent electronic record or procedure if agreed between the parties or customary.

A2 Licences, authorizations, security clearances and other formalities

Where applicable, the seller must obtain, at its own risk and expense, any export licence or other official authorization and carry out all customs formalities necessary for the export of the goods, and for their transport through any country prior to delivery.

A3 Contracts of carriage and insurance

a) Contract of carriage
The seller must contract or procure a contract for the carriage of the goods from the agreed point of delivery, if any, at the place of delivery to the named place of destination or, if agreed, any point at that place. The contract of carriage must be made on usual terms at the seller's expense and provide for carriage by the usual route and in a customary manner. If a specific point is not agreed or is not determined by practice, the seller may select the point of delivery and the point at the named place of destination that best suit its purpose.

b) Contract of insurance
The seller has no obligation to the buyer to make a contract of insurance. However, the seller must provide the buyer, at the buyer's request, risk, and expense (if any), with information that the buyer needs for obtaining insurance.

A4 Delivery

The seller must deliver the goods by handing them over to the carrier contracted in accordance with A3 on the agreed date or within the agreed period.

Incoterms® 2010

B THE BUYER'S OBLIGATIONS

B1 **General obligations of the buyer**
The buyer must pay the price of the goods as provided in the contract of sale.

Any document referred to in B1-B10 may be an equivalent electronic record or procedure if agreed between the parties or customary.

B2 **Licences, authorizations, security clearances and other formalities**
Where applicable, it is up to the buyer to obtain, at its own risk and expense, any import licence or other official authorization and carry out all customs formalities for the import of the goods and for their transport through any country.

B3 **Contracts of carriage and insurance**
a) Contract of carriage
The buyer has no obligation to the seller to make a contract of carriage.

b) Contract of insurance
The buyer has no obligation to the seller to make a contract of insurance. However, the buyer must provide the seller, upon request, with the necessary information for obtaining insurance.

B4 **Taking delivery**
The buyer must take delivery of the goods when they have been delivered as envisaged in A4 and receive them from the carrier at the named place of destination.

A5 Transfer of risks

The seller bears all risks of loss of or damage to the goods until they have been delivered in accordance with A4, with the exception of loss or damage in the circumstances described in B5.

A6 Allocation of costs

The seller must pay

a) all costs relating to the goods until they have been delivered in accordance with A4, other than those payable by the buyer as envisaged in B6;

b) the freight and all other costs resulting from A3 a), including the costs of loading the goods and any charges for unloading at the place of destination that were for the seller's account under the contract of carriage; and

c) where applicable, the costs of customs formalities necessary for export, as well as all duties, taxes and other charges payable upon export, and the costs for their transport through any country that were for the seller's account under the contract of carriage.

A7 Notices to the buyer

The seller must notify the buyer that the goods have been delivered in accordance with A4.

The seller must give the buyer any notice needed in order to allow the buyer to take measures that are normally necessary to enable the buyer to take the goods.

Incoterms® 2010

B5 **Transfer of risks**
The buyer bears all risks of loss of or damage to the goods from the time they have been delivered as envisaged in A4.

If the buyer fails to give notice in accordance with B7, it must bear all risks of loss of or damage to the goods from the agreed date or the expiry date of the agreed period for delivery, provided that the goods have been clearly identified as the contract goods.

B6 **Allocation of costs**
The buyer must, subject to the provisions of A3 a), pay
a) all costs relating to the goods from the time they have been delivered as envisaged in A4, except, where applicable, the costs of customs formalities necessary for export, as well as all duties, taxes, and other charges payable upon export as referred to in A6 c);

b) all costs and charges relating to the goods while in transit until their arrival at the agreed place of destination, unless such costs and charges were for the seller's account under the contract of carriage;

c) unloading costs, unless such costs were for the seller's account under the contract of carriage;

d) any additional costs incurred if the buyer fails to give notice in accordance with B7, from the agreed date or the expiry date of the agreed period for dispatch, provided that the goods have been clearly identified as the contract goods; and

e) where applicable, all duties, taxes and other charges, as well as the costs of carrying out customs formalities payable upon import of the goods and the costs for their transport through any country, unless included within the cost of the contract of carriage.

B7 **Notices to the seller**
The buyer must, whenever it is entitled to determine the time for dispatching the goods and/or the named place of destination or the point of receiving the goods within that place, give the seller sufficient notice thereof.

A8   **Delivery document**
If customary or at the buyer's request, the seller must provide the buyer, at the seller's expense, with the usual transport document[s] for the transport contracted in accordance with A3.

This transport document must cover the contract goods and be dated within the period agreed for shipment. If agreed or customary, the document must also enable the buyer to claim the goods from the carrier at the named place of destination and enable the buyer to sell the goods in transit by the transfer of the document to a subsequent buyer or by notification to the carrier.

When such a transport document is issued in negotiable form and in several originals, a full set of originals must be presented to the buyer.

A9   **Checking – packaging – marking**
The seller must pay the costs of those checking operations (such as checking quality, measuring, weighing, counting) that are necessary for the purpose of delivering the goods in accordance with A4, as well as the costs of any pre-shipment inspection mandated by the authority of the country of export.

The seller must, at its own expense, package the goods, unless it is usual for the particular trade to transport the type of goods sold unpackaged. The seller may package the goods in the manner appropriate for their transport, unless the buyer has notified the seller of specific packaging requirements before the contract of sale is concluded. Packaging is to be marked appropriately.

A10   **Assistance with information and related costs**
The seller must, where applicable, in a timely manner, provide to or render assistance in obtaining for the buyer, at the buyer's request, risk and expense, any documents and information, including security-related information, that the buyer needs for the import of the goods and/or for their transport to the final destination.

The seller must reimburse the buyer for all costs and charges incurred by the buyer in providing or rendering assistance in obtaining documents and information as envisaged in B10.

Incoterms® 2010

B8 **Proof of delivery**
The buyer must accept the transport document provided as envisaged in A8 if it is in conformity with the contract.

B9 **Inspection of goods**
The buyer must pay the costs of any mandatory pre-shipment inspection, except when such inspection is mandated by the authorities of the country of export.

B10 **Assistance with information and related costs**
The buyer must, in a timely manner, advise the seller of any security information requirements so that the seller may comply with A10.

The buyer must reimburse the seller for all costs and charges incurred by the seller in providing or rendering assistance in obtaining documents and information as envisaged in A10.

The buyer must, where applicable, in a timely manner, provide to or render assistance in obtaining for the seller, at the seller's request, risk and expense, any documents and information, including security-related information, that the seller needs for the transport and export of the goods and for their transport through any country.

CIP

CARRIAGE AND INSURANCE PAID TO

CIP (insert named place of destination) Incoterms® 2010

GUIDANCE NOTE

This rule may be used irrespective of the mode of transport selected and may also be used where more than one mode of transport is employed.

"Carriage and Insurance Paid to" means that the seller delivers the goods to the carrier or another person nominated by the seller at an agreed place (if any such place is agreed between the parties) and that the seller must contract for and pay the costs of carriage necessary to bring the goods to the named place of destination.

The seller also contracts for insurance cover against the buyer's risk of loss of or damage to the goods during the carriage. The buyer should note that under CIP the seller is required to obtain insurance only on minimum cover. Should the buyer wish to have more insurance protection, it will need either to agree as much expressly with the seller or to make its own extra insurance arrangements.

When CPT, CIP, CFR or CIF are used, the seller fulfils its obligation to deliver when it hands the goods over to the carrier and not when the goods reach the place of destination.

This rule has two critical points, because risk passes and costs are transferred at different places. The parties are well advised to identify as precisely as possible in the contract both the place of delivery, where the risk passes to the buyer, and the named place of destination to which the seller must contract for carriage. If several carriers are used for the carriage to the agreed destination and the parties do not agree on a specific point of delivery, the default position is that risk passes when the goods have been delivered to the first carrier at a point entirely of the seller's choosing and over which the buyer has no control. Should the parties wish the risk to pass at a later stage (e.g., at an ocean port or an airport), they need to specify this in their contract of sale.

The parties are also well advised to identify as precisely as possible the point within the agreed place of destination, as the costs to that point are for the account of the seller. The seller is advised to procure contracts of carriage that match this choice precisely. If the seller incurs costs under its contract of carriage related to unloading at the named place of destination, the seller is not entitled to recover such costs from the buyer unless otherwise agreed between the parties.

CIP requires the seller to clear the goods for export, where applicable. However, the seller has no obligation to clear the goods for import, pay any import duty or carry out any import customs formalities.

A THE SELLER'S OBLIGATIONS

A1 General obligations of the seller

The seller must provide the goods and the commercial invoice in conformity with the contract of sale and any other evidence of conformity that may be required by the contract.

Any document referred to in A1-A10 may be an equivalent electronic record or procedure if agreed between the parties or customary.

A2 Licences, authorizations, security clearances and other formalities

Where applicable, the seller must obtain, at its own risk and expense, any export licence or other official authorization and carry out all customs formalities necessary for the export of the goods and for their transport through any country prior to delivery.

B THE BUYER'S OBLIGATIONS

B1 General obligations of the buyer

The buyer must pay the price of the goods as provided in the contract of sale.

Any document referred to in B1-B10 may be an equivalent electronic record or procedure if agreed between the parties or customary.

B2 Licences, authorizations, security clearances and other formalities

Where applicable, it is up to the buyer to obtain, at its own risk and expense, any import licence or other official authorization and carry out all customs formalities for the import of the goods and for their transport through any country.

A3 Contracts of carriage and insurance

a) Contract of carriage

The seller must contract or procure a contract for the carriage of the goods from the agreed point of delivery, if any, at the place of delivery to the named place of destination or, if agreed, any point at that place. The contract of carriage must be made on usual terms at the seller's expense and provide for carriage by the usual route and in a customary manner. If a specific point is not agreed or is not determined by practice, the seller may select the point of delivery and the point at the named place of destination that best suit its purpose.

b) Contract of insurance

The seller must obtain at its own expense cargo insurance complying at least with the minimum cover as provided by Clauses (C) of the Institute Cargo Clauses (LMA/IUA) or any similar clauses. The insurance shall be contracted with underwriters or an insurance company of good repute and entitle the buyer, or any other person having an insurable interest in the goods, to claim directly from the insurer.

When required by the buyer, the seller shall, subject to the buyer providing any necessary information requested by the seller, provide at the buyer's expense any additional cover, if procurable, such as cover as provided by Clauses (A) or (B) of the Institute Cargo Clauses (LMA/IUA) or any similar clauses, and/or cover complying with the Institute War Clauses and/or Institute Strikes Clauses (LMA/IUA) or any similar clauses.

The insurance shall cover, at a minimum, the price provided in the contract plus 10% (i.e., 110%) and shall be in the currency of the contract.

The insurance shall cover the goods from the point of delivery set out in A4 and A5 to at least the named place of destination.

The seller must provide the buyer with the insurance policy or other evidence of insurance cover.

Moreover, the seller must provide the buyer, at the buyer's request, risk, and expense (if any), with information that the buyer needs to procure any additional insurance.

A4 Delivery

The seller must deliver the goods by handing them over to the carrier contracted in accordance with A3 on the agreed date or within the agreed period.

B3 Contracts of carriage and insurance

a) Contract of carriage

The buyer has no obligation to the seller to make a contract of carriage.

b) Contract of insurance

The buyer has no obligation to the seller to make a contract of insurance. However, the buyer must provide the seller, upon request, with any information necessary for the seller to procure any additional insurance requested by the buyer as envisaged in A3 b).

B4 Taking delivery

The buyer must take delivery of the goods when they have been delivered as envisaged in A4 and receive them from the carrier at the named place of destination.

A5 Transfer of risks

The seller bears all risks of loss of or damage to the goods until they have been delivered in accordance with A4, with the exception of loss or damage in the circumstances described in B5.

A6 Allocation of costs

The seller must pay

a) all costs relating to the goods until they have been delivered in accordance with A4, other than those payable by the buyer as envisaged in B6;

b) the freight and all other costs resulting from A3 a), including the costs of loading the goods and any charges for unloading at the place of destination that were for the seller's account under the contract of carriage;

c) the costs of insurance resulting from A3 b); and

d) where applicable, the costs of customs formalities necessary for export, as well as all duties, taxes and other charges payable upon export, and the costs for their transport through any country that were for the seller's account under the contract of carriage.

A7 Notices to the buyer

The seller must notify the buyer that the goods have been delivered in accordance with A4.

The seller must give the buyer any notice needed in order to allow the buyer to take measures that are normally necessary to enable the buyer to take the goods.

B5 Transfer of risks

The buyer bears all risks of loss of or damage to the goods from the time they have been delivered as envisaged in A4.

If the buyer fails to give notice in accordance with B7, it must bear all risks of loss of or damage to the goods from the agreed date or the expiry date of the agreed period for delivery, provided that the goods have been clearly identified as the contract goods.

B6 Allocation of costs

The buyer must, subject to the provisions of A3 a), pay
a) all costs relating to the goods from the time they have been delivered as envisaged in A4, except, where applicable, the costs of customs formalities necessary for export, as well as all duties, taxes and other charges payable upon export as referred to in A6 d);

b) all costs and charges relating to the goods while in transit until their arrival at the agreed place of destination, unless such costs and charges were for the seller's account under the contract of carriage;

c) unloading costs, unless such costs were for the seller's account under the contract of carriage;

d) any additional costs incurred if it fails to give notice in accordance with B7, from the agreed date or the expiry date of the agreed period for dispatch, provided that the goods have been clearly identified as the contract goods;

e) where applicable, all duties, taxes and other charges as well as the costs of carrying out customs formalities payable upon import of the goods and the costs for their transport through any country, unless included within the cost of the contract of carriage; and

f) the costs of any additional insurance procured at the buyer's request under A3 and B3.

B7 Notices to the seller

The buyer must, whenever it is entitled to determine the time for dispatching the goods and/or the named place of destination or the point of receiving the goods within that place, give the seller sufficient notice thereof.

A8 Delivery document

If customary or at the buyer's request, the seller must provide the buyer, at the seller's expense, with the usual transport document[s] for the transport contracted in accordance with A3.

This transport document must cover the contract goods and be dated within the period agreed for shipment. If agreed or customary, the document must also enable the buyer to claim the goods from the carrier at the named place of destination and enable the buyer to sell the goods in transit by the transfer of the document to a subsequent buyer or by notification to the carrier.

When such a transport document is issued in negotiable form and in several originals, a full set of originals must be presented to the buyer.

A9 Checking – packaging – marking

The seller must pay the costs of those checking operations (such as checking quality, measuring, weighing, counting) that are necessary for the purpose of delivering the goods in accordance with A4 as well as the costs of any pre-shipment inspection mandated by the authority of the country of export.

The seller must, at its own expense, package the goods, unless it is usual for the particular trade to transport the type of goods sold unpackaged. The seller may package the goods in the manner appropriate for their transport, unless the buyer has notified the seller of specific packaging requirements before the contract of sale is concluded. Packaging is to be marked appropriately.

A10 Assistance with information and related costs

The seller must, where applicable, in a timely manner, provide to or render assistance in obtaining for the buyer, at the buyer's request, risk and expense, any documents and information, including security-related information, that the buyer needs for the import of the goods and/or for their transport to the final destination.

The seller must reimburse the buyer for all costs and charges incurred by the buyer in providing or rendering assistance in obtaining documents and information as envisaged in B10.

Incoterms® 2010

B8 **Proof of delivery**
The buyer must accept the transport document provided as envisaged in A8 if it is in conformity with the contract.

B9 **Inspection of goods**
The buyer must pay the costs of any mandatory pre-shipment inspection, except when such inspection is mandated by the authorities of the country of export.

B10 **Assistance with information and related costs**
The buyer must, in a timely manner, advise the seller of any security information requirements so that the seller may comply with A10.

The buyer must reimburse the seller for all costs and charges incurred by the seller in providing or rendering assistance in obtaining documents and information as envisaged in A10.

The buyer must, where applicable, in a timely manner, provide to or render assistance in obtaining for the seller, at the seller's request, risk and expense, any documents and information, including security-related information, that the seller needs for the transport and export of the goods and for their transport through any country.

DAT
DELIVERED AT TERMINAL

DAT (insert named terminal at port or place of destination)
Incoterms® 2010

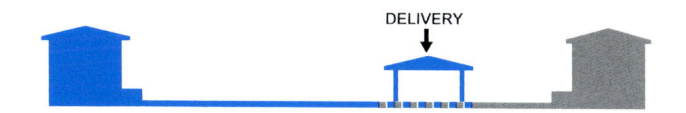

GUIDANCE NOTE

This rule may be used irrespective of the mode of transport selected and may also be used where more than one mode of transport is employed.

"Delivered at Terminal" means that the seller delivers when the goods, once unloaded from the arriving means of transport, are placed at the disposal of the buyer at a named terminal at the named port or place of destination. "Terminal" includes any place, whether covered or not, such as a quay, warehouse, container yard or road, rail or air cargo terminal. The seller bears all risks involved in bringing the goods to and unloading them at the terminal at the named port or place of destination.

The parties are well advised to specify as clearly as possible the terminal and, if possible, a specific point within the terminal at the agreed port or place of destination, as the risks to that point are for the account of the seller. The seller is advised to procure a contract of carriage that matches this choice precisely.

Moreover, if the parties intend the seller to bear the risks and costs involved in transporting and handling the goods from the terminal to another place, then the DAP or DDP rules should be used.

DAT requires the seller to clear the goods for export, where applicable. However, the seller has no obligation to clear the goods for import, pay any import duty or carry out any import customs formalities.

A THE SELLER'S OBLIGATIONS

A1 General obligations of the seller

The seller must provide the goods and the commercial invoice in conformity with the contract of sale and any other evidence of conformity that may be required by the contract.

Any document referred to in A1-A10 may be an equivalent electronic record or procedure if agreed between the parties or customary.

A2 Licences, authorizations, security clearances and other formalities

Where applicable, the seller must obtain, at its own risk and expense, any export licence and other official authorization and carry out all customs formalities necessary for the export of the goods and for their transport through any country prior to delivery.

A3 Contracts of carriage and insurance

a) Contract of carriage
The seller must contract at its own expense for the carriage of the goods to the named terminal at the agreed port or place of destination. If a specific terminal is not agreed or is not determined by practice, the seller may select the terminal at the agreed port or place of destination that best suits its purpose.

b) Contract of insurance
The seller has no obligation to the buyer to make a contract of insurance. However, the seller must provide the buyer, at the buyer's request, risk, and expense (if any), with information that the buyer needs for obtaining insurance.

A4 Delivery

The seller must unload the goods from the arriving means of transport and must then deliver them by placing them at the disposal of the buyer at the named terminal referred to in A3 a) at the port or place of destination on the agreed date or within the agreed period.

Incoterms® 2010

B THE BUYER'S OBLIGATIONS

B1 General obligations of the buyer

The buyer must pay the price of the goods as provided in the contract of sale.

Any document referred to in B1-B10 may be an equivalent electronic record or procedure if agreed between the parties or customary.

B2 Licences, authorizations, security clearances and other formalities

Where applicable, the buyer must obtain, at its own risk and expense, any import licence or other official authorization and carry out all customs formalities for the import of the goods.

B3 Contracts of carriage and insurance

a) Contract of carriage
The buyer has no obligation to the seller to make a contract of carriage.

b) Contract of insurance
The buyer has no obligation to the seller to make a contract of insurance. However, the buyer must provide the seller, upon request, with the necessary information for obtaining insurance.

B4 Taking delivery

The buyer must take delivery of the goods when they have been delivered as envisaged in A4.

A5 Transfer of risks
The seller bears all risks of loss of or damage to the goods until they have been delivered in accordance with A4 with the exception of loss or damage in the circumstances described in B5.

A6 Allocation of costs
The seller must pay
a) in addition to costs resulting from A3 a), all costs relating to the goods until they have been delivered in accordance with A4, other than those payable by the buyer as envisaged in B6; and

b) where applicable, the costs of customs formalities necessary for export as well as all duties, taxes and other charges payable upon export and the costs for their transport through any country, prior to delivery in accordance with A4.

A7 Notices to the buyer
The seller must give the buyer any notice needed in order to allow the buyer to take measures that are normally necessary to enable the buyer to take delivery of the goods.

A8 Delivery document
The seller must provide the buyer, at the seller's expense, with a document enabling the buyer to take delivery of the goods as envisaged in A4/B4.

B5 Transfer of risks

The buyer bears all risks of loss of or damage to the goods from the time they have been delivered as envisaged in A4.

If
a) the buyer fails to fulfil its obligations in accordance with B2, then it bears all resulting risks of loss of or damage to the goods; or

b) the buyer fails to give notice in accordance with B7, then it bears all risks of loss of or damage to the goods from the agreed date or the expiry date of the agreed period for delivery,

provided that the goods have been clearly identified as the contract goods.

B6 Allocation of costs

The buyer must pay
a) all costs relating to the goods from the time they have been delivered as envisaged in A4;

b) any additional costs incurred by the seller if the buyer fails to fulfil its obligations in accordance with B2, or to give notice in accordance with B7, provided that the goods have been clearly identified as the contract goods; and

c) where applicable, the costs of customs formalities as well as all duties, taxes and other charges payable upon import of the goods.

B7 Notices to the seller

The buyer must, whenever it is entitled to determine the time within an agreed period and/or the point of taking delivery at the named terminal, give the seller sufficient notice thereof.

B8 Proof of delivery

The buyer must accept the delivery document provided as envisaged in A8.

A9   **Checking – packaging – marking**
The seller must pay the costs of those checking operations (such as checking quality, measuring, weighing, counting) that are necessary for the purpose of delivering the goods in accordance with A4, as well as the costs of any pre-shipment inspection mandated by the authority of the country of export.

The seller must, at its own expense, package the goods, unless it is usual for the particular trade to transport the type of goods sold unpackaged. The seller may package the goods in the manner appropriate for their transport, unless the buyer has notified the seller of specific packaging requirements before the contract of sale is concluded. Packaging is to be marked appropriately.

A10   **Assistance with information and related costs**
The seller must, where applicable, in a timely manner, provide to or render assistance in obtaining for the buyer, at the buyer's request, risk and expense, any documents and information, including security-related information, that the buyer needs for the import of the goods and/or for their transport to the final destination.

The seller must reimburse the buyer for all costs and charges incurred by the buyer in providing or rendering assistance in obtaining documents and information as envisaged in B10.

Incoterms® 2010

B9 **Inspection of goods**
The buyer must pay the costs of any mandatory pre-shipment inspection, except when such inspection is mandated by the authorities of the country of export.

B10 **Assistance with information and related costs**
The buyer must, in a timely manner, advise the seller of any security information requirements so that the seller may comply with A10.

The buyer must reimburse the seller for all costs and charges incurred by the seller in providing or rendering assistance in obtaining documents and information as envisaged in A10.

The buyer must, where applicable, in a timely manner, provide to or render assistance in obtaining for the seller, at the seller's request, risk and expense, any documents and information, including security-related information, that the seller needs for the transport and export of the goods and for their transport through any country.

DAP
DELIVERED AT PLACE
DAP (insert named place of destination) Incoterms® 2010

GUIDANCE NOTE

This rule may be used irrespective of the mode of transport selected and may also be used where more than one mode of transport is employed.

"Delivered at Place" means that the seller delivers when the goods are placed at the disposal of the buyer on the arriving means of transport ready for unloading at the named place of destination. The seller bears all risks involved in bringing the goods to the named place.

The parties are well advised to specify as clearly as possible the point within the agreed place of destination, as the risks to that point are for the account of the seller. The seller is advised to procure contracts of carriage that match this choice precisely. If the seller incurs costs under its contract of carriage related to unloading at the place of destination, the seller is not entitled to recover such costs from the buyer unless otherwise agreed between the parties.

DAP requires the seller to clear the goods for export, where applicable. However, the seller has no obligation to clear the goods for import, pay any import duty or carry out any import customs formalities. If the parties wish the seller to clear the goods for import, pay any import duty and carry out any import customs formalities, the DDP term should be used.

A THE SELLER'S OBLIGATIONS

A1 General obligations of the seller

The seller must provide the goods and the commercial invoice in conformity with the contract of sale and any other evidence of conformity that may be required by the contract.

Any document referred to in A1-A10 may be an equivalent electronic record or procedure if agreed between the parties or customary.

A2 Licences, authorizations, security clearances and other formalities

Where applicable, the seller must obtain, at its own risk and expense, any export licence and other official authorization and carry out all customs formalities necessary for the export of the goods and for their transport through any country prior to delivery.

A3 Contracts of carriage and insurance

a) Contract of carriage
The seller must contract at its own expense for the carriage of the goods to the named place of destination or to the agreed point, if any, at the named place of destination. If a specific point is not agreed or is not determined by practice, the seller may select the point at the named place of destination that best suits its purpose.

b) Contract of insurance
The seller has no obligation to the buyer to make a contract of insurance. However, the seller must provide the buyer, at the buyer's request, risk, and expense (if any), with information that the buyer needs for obtaining insurance.

A4 Delivery

The seller must deliver the goods by placing them at the disposal of the buyer on the arriving means of transport ready for unloading at the agreed point, if any, at the named place of destination on the agreed date or within the agreed period.

Incoterms® 2010

B THE BUYER'S OBLIGATIONS

B1 **General obligations of the buyer**
The buyer must pay the price of the goods as provided in the contract of sale.

Any document referred to in B1-B10 may be an equivalent electronic record or procedure if agreed between the parties or customary.

B2 **Licences, authorizations, security clearances and other formalities**
Where applicable, the buyer must obtain, at its own risk and expense, any import licence or other official authorization and carry out all customs formalities for the import of the goods.

B3 **Contracts of carriage and insurance**
a) Contract of carriage
The buyer has no obligation to the seller to make a contract of carriage.

b) Contract of insurance
The buyer has no obligation to the seller to make a contract of insurance. However, the buyer must provide the seller, upon request, with the necessary information for obtaining insurance.

B4 **Taking delivery**
The buyer must take delivery of the goods when they have been delivered as envisaged in A4.

A5 Transfer of risks

The seller bears all risks of loss of or damage to the goods until they have been delivered in accordance with A4, with the exception of loss or damage in the circumstances described in B5.

A6 Allocation of costs

The seller must pay

a) in addition to costs resulting from A3 a), all costs relating to the goods until they have been delivered in accordance with A4, other than those payable by the buyer as envisaged in B6;

b) any charges for unloading at the place of destination that were for the seller's account under the contract of carriage; and

c) where applicable, the costs of customs formalities necessary for export as well as all duties, taxes and other charges payable upon export and the costs for their transport through any country, prior to delivery in accordance with A4.

A7 Notices to the buyer

The seller must give the buyer any notice needed in order to allow the buyer to take measures that are normally necessary to enable the buyer to take delivery of the goods.

Incoterms® 2010

B5 **Transfer of risks**
The buyer bears all risks of loss of or damage to the goods from the time they have been delivered as envisaged in A4.

If
a) the buyer fails to fulfil its obligations in accordance with B2, then it bears all resulting risks of loss of or damage to the goods; or

b) the buyer fails to give notice in accordance with B7, then it bears all risks of loss of or damage to the goods from the agreed date or the expiry date of the agreed period for delivery,

provided that the goods have been clearly identified as the contract goods.

B6 **Allocation of costs**
The buyer must pay
a) all costs relating to the goods from the time they have been delivered as envisaged in A4;

b) all costs of unloading necessary to take delivery of the goods from the arriving means of transport at the named place of destination, unless such costs were for the seller's account under the contract of carriage;

c) any additional costs incurred by the seller if the buyer fails to fulfil its obligations in accordance with B2 or to give notice in accordance with B7, provided that the goods have been clearly identified as the contract goods; and

d) where applicable, the costs of customs formalities, as well as all duties, taxes and other charges payable upon import of the goods.

B7 **Notices to the seller**
The buyer must, whenever it is entitled to determine the time within an agreed period and/or the point of taking delivery within the named place of destination, give the seller sufficient notice thereof.

A8   **Delivery document**
The seller must provide the buyer, at the seller's expense, with a document enabling the buyer to take delivery of the goods as envisaged in A4/B4.

A9   **Checking – packaging – marking**
The seller must pay the costs of those checking operations (such as checking quality, measuring, weighing, counting) that are necessary for the purpose of delivering the goods in accordance with A4, as well as the costs of any pre-shipment inspection mandated by the authority of the country of export.

The seller must, at its own expense, package the goods, unless it is usual for the particular trade to transport the type of goods sold unpackaged. The seller may package the goods in the manner appropriate for their transport, unless the buyer has notified the seller of specific packaging requirements before the contract of sale is concluded. Packaging is to be marked appropriately.

A10   **Assistance with information and related costs**
The seller must, where applicable, in a timely manner, provide to or render assistance in obtaining for the buyer, at the buyer's request, risk and expense, any documents and information, including security-related information, that the buyer needs for the import of the goods and/or for their transport to the final destination.

The seller must reimburse the buyer for all costs and charges incurred by the buyer in providing or rendering assistance in obtaining documents and information as envisaged in B10.

B8 **Proof of delivery**
The buyer must accept the delivery document provided as envisaged in A8.

B9 **Inspection of goods**
The buyer must pay the costs of any mandatory pre-shipment inspection, except when such inspection is mandated by the authorities of the country of export.

B10 **Assistance with information and related costs**
The buyer must, in a timely manner, advise the seller of any security information requirements so that the seller may comply with A10.

The buyer must reimburse the seller for all costs and charges incurred by the seller in providing or rendering assistance in obtaining documents and information as envisaged in A10.

The buyer must, where applicable, in a timely manner, provide to or render assistance in obtaining for the seller, at the seller's request, risk and expense, any documents and information, including security-related information, that the seller needs for the transport and export of the goods and for their transport through any country.

DDP

DELIVERED DUTY PAID

DDP (insert named place of destination) Incoterms® 2010

GUIDANCE NOTE

This rule may be used irrespective of the mode of transport selected and may also be used where more than one mode of transport is employed.

"Delivered Duty Paid" means that the seller delivers the goods when the goods are placed at the disposal of the buyer, cleared for import on the arriving means of transport ready for unloading at the named place of destination. The seller bears all the costs and risks involved in bringing the goods to the place of destination and has an obligation to clear the goods not only for export but also for import, to pay any duty for both export and import and to carry out all customs formalities.

DDP represents the maximum obligation for the seller.

The parties are well advised to specify as clearly as possible the point within the agreed place of destination, as the costs and risks to that point are for the account of the seller. The seller is advised to procure contracts of carriage that match this choice precisely. If the seller incurs costs under its contract of carriage related to unloading at the place of destination, the seller is not entitled to recover such costs from the buyer unless otherwise agreed between the parties.

The parties are well advised not to use DDP if the seller is unable directly or indirectly to obtain import clearance.

If the parties wish the buyer to bear all risks and costs of import clearance, the DAP rule should be used.

Any VAT or other taxes payable upon import are for the seller's account unless expressly agreed otherwise in the sale contract.

A THE SELLER'S OBLIGATIONS

A1 General obligations of the seller

The seller must provide the goods and the commercial invoice in conformity with the contract of sale and any other evidence of conformity that may be required by the contract.

Any document referred to in A1-A10 may be an equivalent electronic record or procedure if agreed between the parties or customary.

A2 Licences, authorizations, security clearances and other formalities

Where applicable, the seller must obtain, at its own risk and expense, any export and import licence and other official authorization and carry out all customs formalities necessary for the export of the goods, for their transport through any country and for their import.

A3 Contracts of carriage and insurance

a) Contract of carriage
The seller must contract at its own expense for the carriage of the goods to the named place of destination or to the agreed point, if any, at the named place of destination. If a specific point is not agreed or is not determined by practice, the seller may select the point at the named place of destination that best suits its purpose.

b) Contract of insurance
The seller has no obligation to the buyer to make a contract of insurance. However, the seller must provide the buyer, at the buyer's request, risk, and expense (if any), with information that the buyer needs for obtaining insurance.

A4 Delivery

The seller must deliver the goods by placing them at the disposal of the buyer on the arriving means of transport ready for unloading at the agreed point, if any, at the named place of destination on the agreed date or within the agreed period.

Incoterms® 2010

B   THE BUYER'S OBLIGATIONS

B1   **General obligations of the buyer**
The buyer must pay the price of the goods as provided in the contract of sale.

Any document referred to in B1-B10 may be an equivalent electronic record or procedure if agreed between the parties or customary.

B2   **Licences, authorizations, security clearances and other formalities**
Where applicable, the buyer must provide assistance to the seller, at the seller's request, risk and expense, in obtaining any import licence or other official authorization for the import of the goods.

B3   **Contracts of carriage and insurance**
a) Contract of carriage
The buyer has no obligation to the seller to make a contract of carriage.

b) Contract of insurance
The buyer has no obligation to the seller to make a contract of insurance. However, the buyer must provide the seller, upon request, with the necessary information for obtaining insurance.

B4   **Taking delivery**
The buyer must take delivery of the goods when they have been delivered as envisaged in A4.

A5 Transfer of risks
The seller bears all risks of loss of or damage to the goods until they have been delivered in accordance with A4, with the exception of loss or damage in the circumstances described in B5.

A6 Allocation of costs
The seller must pay
a) in addition to costs resulting from A3 a), all costs relating to the goods until they have been delivered in accordance with A4, other than those payable by the buyer as envisaged in B6;

b) any charges for unloading at the place of destination that were for the seller's account under the contract of carriage; and

c) where applicable, the costs of customs formalities necessary for export and import as well as all duties, taxes and other charges payable upon export and import of the goods, and the costs for their transport through any country prior to delivery in accordance with A4.

A7 Notices to the buyer
The seller must give the buyer any notice needed in order to allow the buyer to take measures that are normally necessary to enable the buyer to take delivery of the goods.

A8 Delivery document
The seller must provide the buyer, at the seller's expense, with a document enabling the buyer to take delivery of the goods as envisaged in A4/B4.

Incoterms® 2010

B5 **Transfer of risks**
The buyer bears all risks of loss of or damage to the goods from the time they have been delivered as envisaged in A4.

If
a) the buyer fails to fulfil its obligations in accordance with B2, then it bears all resulting risks of loss of or damage to the goods; or

b) the buyer fails to give notice in accordance with B7, then it bears all risks of loss of or damage to the goods from the agreed date or the expiry date of the agreed period for delivery,

provided that the goods have been clearly identified as the contract goods.

B6 **Allocation of costs**
The buyer must pay
a) all costs relating to the goods from the time they have been delivered as envisaged in A4;

b) all costs of unloading necessary to take delivery of the goods from the arriving means of transport at the named place of destination, unless such costs were for the seller's account under the contract of carriage; and

c) any additional costs incurred if it fails to fulfil its obligations in accordance with B2 or to give notice in accordance with B7, provided that the goods have been clearly identified as the contract goods.

B7 **Notices to the seller**
The buyer must, whenever it is entitled to determine the time within an agreed period and/or the point of taking delivery within the named place of destination, give the seller sufficient notice thereof.

B8 **Proof of delivery**
The buyer must accept the proof of delivery provided as envisaged in A8.

A9 Checking – packaging – marking

The seller must pay the costs of those checking operations (such as checking quality, measuring, weighing, counting) that are necessary for the purpose of delivering the goods in accordance with A4, as well as the costs of any pre-shipment inspection mandated by the authority of the country of export or of import.

The seller must, at its own expense, package the goods, unless it is usual for the particular trade to transport the type of goods sold unpackaged. The seller may package the goods in the manner appropriate for their transport, unless the buyer has notified the seller of specific packaging requirements before the contract of sale is concluded. Packaging is to be marked appropriately.

A10 Assistance with information and related costs

The seller must, where applicable, in a timely manner, provide to or render assistance in obtaining for the buyer, at the buyer's request, risk and expense, any documents and information, including security-related information, that the buyer needs for the transport of the goods to the final destination, where applicable, from the named place of destination.

The seller must reimburse the buyer for all costs and charges incurred by the buyer in providing or rendering assistance in obtaining documents and information as envisaged in B10.

B9　　**Inspection of goods**

The buyer has no obligation to the seller to pay the costs of any mandatory pre-shipment inspection mandated by the authority of the country of export or of import.

B10　　**Assistance with information and related costs**

The buyer must, in a timely manner, advise the seller of any security information requirements so that the seller may comply with A10.

The buyer must reimburse the seller for all costs and charges incurred by the seller in providing or rendering assistance in obtaining documents and information as envisaged in A10.

The buyer must, where applicable, in a timely manner, provide to or render assistance in obtaining for the seller, at the seller's request, risk and expense, any documents and information, including security-related information, that the seller needs for the transport, export and import of the goods and for their transport through any country.

RULES FOR SEA AND INLAND WATERWAY TRANSPORT

FAS
FREE ALONGSIDE SHIP
FAS (insert named port of shipment) Incoterms® 2010

GUIDANCE NOTE

This rule is to be used only for sea or inland waterway transport.

"Free Alongside Ship" means that the seller delivers when the goods are placed alongside the vessel (e.g., on a quay or a barge) nominated by the buyer at the named port of shipment. The risk of loss of or damage to the goods passes when the goods are alongside the ship, and the buyer bears all costs from that moment onwards.

The parties are well advised to specify as clearly as possible the loading point at the named port of shipment, as the costs and risks to that point are for the account of the seller and these costs and associated handling charges may vary according to the practice of the port.

The seller is required either to deliver the goods alongside the ship or to procure goods already so delivered for shipment. The reference to "procure" here caters for multiple sales down a chain ('string sales'), particularly common in the commodity trades.

Where the goods are in containers, it is typical for the seller to hand the goods over to the carrier at a terminal and not alongside the vessel. In such situations, the FAS rule would be inappropriate, and the FCA rule should be used.

FAS requires the seller to clear the goods for export, where applicable. However, the seller has no obligation to clear the goods for import, pay any import duty or carry out any import customs formalities.

A THE SELLER'S OBLIGATIONS

A1 General obligations of the seller

The seller must provide the goods and the commercial invoice in conformity with the contract of sale and any other evidence of conformity that may be required by the contract.

Any document referred to in A1-A10 may be an equivalent electronic record or procedure if agreed between the parties or customary.

A2 Licences, authorizations, security clearances and other formalities

Where applicable, the seller must obtain, at its own risk and expense, any export licence or other official authorization and carry out all customs formalities necessary for the export of the goods.

A3 Contracts of carriage and insurance

a) Contract of carriage
The seller has no obligation to the buyer to make a contract of carriage. However, if requested by the buyer or if it is commercial practice and the buyer does not give an instruction to the contrary in due time, the seller may contract for carriage on usual terms at the buyer's risk and expense. In either case, the seller may decline to make the contract of carriage and, if it does, shall promptly notify the buyer.

b) Contract of insurance
The seller has no obligation to the buyer to make a contract of insurance. However, the seller must provide the buyer, at the buyer's request, risk, and expense (if any), with information that the buyer needs for obtaining insurance.

A4 Delivery

The seller must deliver the goods either by placing them alongside the ship nominated by the buyer at the loading point, if any, indicated by the buyer at the named port of shipment or by procuring the goods so delivered. In either case, the seller must deliver the goods on the agreed date or within the agreed period and in the manner customary at the port.

If no specific loading point has been indicated by the buyer, the seller may select the point within the named port of shipment that best suits its purpose. If the parties have agreed that delivery should take place within a period, the buyer has the option to choose the date within that period.

Incoterms® 2010

B THE BUYER'S OBLIGATIONS

B1 General obligations of the buyer
The buyer must pay the price of the goods as provided in the contract of sale.

Any document referred to in B1-B10 may be an equivalent electronic record or procedure if agreed between the parties or customary.

B2 Licences, authorizations, security clearances and other formalities
Where applicable, it is up to the buyer to obtain, at its own risk and expense, any import licence or other official authorization and carry out all customs formalities for the import of the goods and for their transport through any country.

B3 Contracts of carriage and insurance
a) Contract of carriage
The buyer must contract, at its own expense for the carriage of the goods from the named port of shipment, except where the contract of carriage is made by the seller as provided for in A3 a).

b) Contract of insurance
The buyer has no obligation to the seller to make a contract of insurance.

B4 Taking delivery
The buyer must take delivery of the goods when they have been delivered as envisaged in A4.

81

A5 Transfer of risks
The seller bears all risks of loss of or damage to the goods until they have been delivered in accordance with A4 with the exception of loss or damage in the circumstances described in B5.

A6 Allocation of costs
The seller must pay
a) all costs relating to the goods until they have been delivered in accordance with A4, other than those payable by the buyer as envisaged in B6; and

b) where applicable, the costs of customs formalities necessary for export as well as all duties, taxes and other charges payable upon export.

A7 Notices to the buyer
The seller must, at the buyer's risk and expense, give the buyer sufficient notice either that the goods have been delivered in accordance with A4 or that the vessel has failed to take the goods within the time agreed.

Incoterms® 2010

B5 **Transfer of risks**
The buyer bears all risks of loss of or damage to the goods from the time they have been delivered as envisaged in A4.

If
a) the buyer fails to give notice in accordance with B7; or

b) the vessel nominated by the buyer fails to arrive on time, or fails to take the goods or closes for cargo earlier than the time notified in accordance with B7;

then the buyer bears all risks of loss of or damage to the goods from the agreed date or the expiry date of the agreed period for delivery, provided that the goods have been clearly identified as the contract goods.

B6 **Allocation of costs**
The buyer must pay
a) all costs relating to the goods from the time they have been delivered as envisaged in A4, except, where applicable, the costs of customs formalities necessary for export as well as all duties, taxes, and other charges payable upon export as referred to in A6 b);

b) any additional costs incurred, either because:
(i) the buyer has failed to give appropriate notice in accordance with B7, or
(ii) the vessel nominated by the buyer fails to arrive on time, is unable to take the goods, or closes for cargo earlier than the time notified in accordance with B7,

provided that the goods have been clearly identified as the contract goods; and

c) where applicable, all duties, taxes and other charges, as well as the costs of carrying out customs formalities payable upon import of the goods and the costs for their transport through any country.

B7 **Notices to the seller**
The buyer must give the seller sufficient notice of the vessel name, loading point and, where necessary, the selected delivery time within the agreed period.

A8 **Delivery document**

The seller must provide the buyer, at the seller's expense, with the usual proof that the goods have been delivered in accordance with A4.

Unless such proof is a transport document, the seller must provide assistance to the buyer, at the buyer's request, risk and expense, in obtaining a transport document.

A9 **Checking – packaging – marking**

The seller must pay the costs of those checking operations (such as checking quality, measuring, weighing, counting) that are necessary for the purpose of delivering the goods in accordance with A4, as well as the costs of any pre-shipment inspection mandated by the authority of the country of export.

The seller must, at its own expense, package the goods, unless it is usual for the particular trade to transport the type of goods sold unpackaged. The seller may package the goods in the manner appropriate for their transport, unless the buyer has notified the seller of specific packaging requirements before the contract of sale is concluded. Packaging is to be marked appropriately.

A10 **Assistance with information and related costs**

The seller must, where applicable, in a timely manner, provide to or render assistance in obtaining for the buyer, at the buyer's request, risk and expense, any documents and information, including security-related information, that the buyer needs for the import of the goods and/or for their transport to the final destination.

The seller must reimburse the buyer for all costs and charges incurred by the buyer in providing or rendering assistance in obtaining documents and information as envisaged in B10.

B8 Proof of delivery
The buyer must accept the proof of delivery provided as envisaged in A8.

B9 Inspection of goods
The buyer must pay the costs of any mandatory pre-shipment inspection, except when such inspection is mandated by the authorities of the country of export.

B10 Assistance with information and related costs
The buyer must, in a timely manner, advise the seller of any security information requirements so that the seller may comply with A10.

The buyer must reimburse the seller for all costs and charges incurred by the seller in providing or rendering assistance in obtaining documents and information as envisaged in A10.

The buyer must, where applicable, in a timely manner, provide to or render assistance in obtaining for the seller, at the seller's request, risk and expense, any documents and information, including security-related information, that the seller needs for the transport and export of the goods and for their transport through any country.

FOB
FREE ON BOARD
FOB (insert named port of shipment) Incoterms® 2010

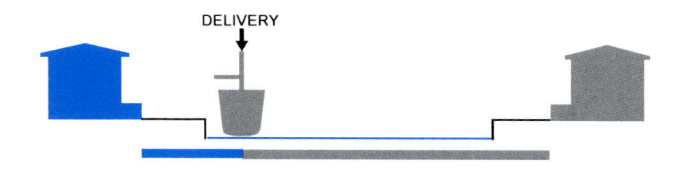

GUIDANCE NOTE

This rule is to be used only for sea or inland waterway transport.

"Free on Board" means that the seller delivers the goods on board the vessel nominated by the buyer at the named port of shipment or procures the goods already so delivered. The risk of loss of or damage to the goods passes when the goods are on board the vessel, and the buyer bears all costs from that moment onwards.

The seller is required either to deliver the goods on board the vessel or to procure goods already so delivered for shipment. The reference to "procure" here caters for multiple sales down a chain ('string sales'), particularly common in the commodity trades.

FOB may not be appropriate where goods are handed over to the carrier before they are on board the vessel, for example goods in containers, which are typically delivered at a terminal. In such situations, the FCA rule should be used.

FOB requires the seller to clear the goods for export, where applicable. However, the seller has no obligation to clear the goods for import, pay any import duty or carry out any import customs formalities.

A THE SELLER'S OBLIGATIONS

A1 General obligations of the seller

The seller must provide the goods and the commercial invoice in conformity with the contract of sale and any other evidence of conformity that may be required by the contract.

Any document referred to in A1-A10 may be an equivalent electronic record or procedure if agreed between the parties or customary.

A2 Licences, authorizations, security clearances and other formalities

Where applicable, the seller must obtain, at its own risk and expense, any export licence or other official authorization and carry out all customs formalities necessary for the export of the goods.

A3 Contracts of carriage and insurance

a) Contract of carriage
The seller has no obligation to the buyer to make a contract of carriage. However, if requested by the buyer or if it is commercial practice and the buyer does not give an instruction to the contrary in due time, the seller may contract for carriage on usual terms at the buyer's risk and expense. In either case, the seller may decline to make the contract of carriage and, if it does, shall promptly notify the buyer.

b) Contract of insurance
The seller has no obligation to the buyer to make a contract of insurance. However, the seller must provide the buyer, at the buyer's request, risk, and expense (if any), with information that the buyer needs for obtaining insurance.

A4 Delivery

The seller must deliver the goods either by placing them on board the vessel nominated by the buyer at the loading point, if any, indicated by the buyer at the named port of shipment or by procuring the goods so delivered. In either case, the seller must deliver the goods on the agreed date or within the agreed period and in the manner customary at the port.

If no specific loading point has been indicated by the buyer, the seller may select the point within the named port of shipment that best suits its purpose.

Incoterms® 2010

B THE BUYER'S OBLIGATIONS

B1 General obligations of the buyer

The buyer must pay the price of the goods as provided in the contract of sale.

Any document referred to in B1-B10 may be an equivalent electronic record or procedure if agreed between the parties or customary.

B2 Licences, authorizations, security clearances and other formalities

Where applicable, it is up to the buyer to obtain, at its own risk and expense, any import licence or other official authorization and carry out all customs formalities for the import of the goods and for their transport through any country.

B3 Contracts of carriage and insurance

a) Contract of carriage

The buyer must contract, at its own expense for the carriage of the goods from the named port of shipment, except where the contract of carriage is made by the seller as provided for in A3 a).

b) Contract of insurance

The buyer has no obligation to the seller to make a contract of insurance.

B4 Taking delivery

The buyer must take delivery of the goods when they have been delivered as envisaged in A4.

A5 Transfer of risks

The seller bears all risks of loss of or damage to the goods until they have been delivered in accordance with A4 with the exception of loss or damage in the circumstances described in B5.

A6 Allocation of costs

The seller must pay

a) all costs relating to the goods until they have been delivered in accordance with A4, other than those payable by the buyer as envisaged in B6; and

b) where applicable, the costs of customs formalities necessary for export, as well as all duties, taxes and other charges payable upon export.

Incoterms® 2010

B5 **Transfer of risks**

The buyer bears all risks of loss of or damage to the goods from the time they have been delivered as envisaged in A4.

If
a) the buyer fails to notify the nomination of a vessel in accordance with B7; or

b) the vessel nominated by the buyer fails to arrive on time to enable the seller to comply with A4, is unable to take the goods, or closes for cargo earlier than the time notified in accordance with B7;

then, the buyer bears all risks of loss of or damage to the goods:
(i) from the agreed date, or in the absence of an agreed date,
(ii) from the date notified by the seller under A7 within the agreed period, or, if no such date has been notified,
(iii) from the expiry date of any agreed period for delivery,

provided that the goods have been clearly identified as the contract goods.

B6 **Allocation of costs**

The buyer must pay
a) all costs relating to the goods from the time they have been delivered as envisaged in A4, except, where applicable, the costs of customs formalities necessary for export, as well as all duties, taxes and other charges payable upon export as referred to in A6 b);

b) any additional costs incurred, either because:
(i) the buyer has failed to give appropriate notice in accordance with B7, or
(ii) the vessel nominated by the buyer fails to arrive on time, is unable to take the goods, or closes for cargo earlier than the time notified in accordance with B7,

provided that the goods have been clearly identified as the contract goods; and

c) where applicable, all duties, taxes and other charges, as well as the costs of carrying out customs formalities payable upon import of the goods and the costs for their transport through any country.

91

A7 Notices to the buyer

The seller must, at the buyer's risk and expense, give the buyer sufficient notice either that the goods have been delivered in accordance with A4 or that the vessel has failed to take the goods within the time agreed.

A8 Delivery document

The seller must provide the buyer, at the seller's expense, with the usual proof that the goods have been delivered in accordance with A4.

Unless such proof is a transport document, the seller must provide assistance to the buyer, at the buyer's request, risk and expense, in obtaining a transport document.

A9 Checking – packaging – marking

The seller must pay the costs of those checking operations (such as checking quality, measuring, weighing, counting) that are necessary for the purpose of delivering the goods in accordance with A4, as well as the costs of any pre-shipment inspection mandated by the authority of the country of export.

The seller must, at its own expense, package the goods, unless it is usual for the particular trade to transport the type of goods sold unpackaged. The seller may package the goods in the manner appropriate for their transport, unless the buyer has notified the seller of specific packaging requirements before the contract of sale is concluded. Packaging is to be marked appropriately.

A10 Assistance with information and related costs

The seller must, where applicable, in a timely manner, provide to or render assistance in obtaining for the buyer, at the buyer's request, risk and expense, any documents and information, including security-related information, that the buyer needs for the import of the goods and/or for their transport to the final destination.

The seller must reimburse the buyer for all costs and charges incurred by the buyer in providing or rendering assistance in obtaining documents and information as envisaged in B10.

B7   **Notices to the seller**
       The buyer must give the seller sufficient notice of the vessel name, loading point and, where necessary, the selected delivery time within the agreed period.

B8   **Proof of delivery**
       The buyer must accept the proof of delivery provided as envisaged in A8.

B9   **Inspection of goods**
       The buyer must pay the costs of any mandatory pre-shipment inspection, except when such inspection is mandated by the authorities of the country of export.

B10   **Assistance with information and related costs**
       The buyer must, in a timely manner, advise the seller of any security information requirements so that the seller may comply with A10.

       The buyer must reimburse the seller for all costs and charges incurred by the seller in providing or rendering assistance in obtaining documents and information as envisaged in A10.

       The buyer must, where applicable, in a timely manner, provide to or render assistance in obtaining for the seller, at the seller's request, risk and expense, any documents and information, including security-related information, that the seller needs for the transport and export of the goods and for their transport through any country.

CFR
COST AND FREIGHT
CFR (insert named port of destination) Incoterms® 2010

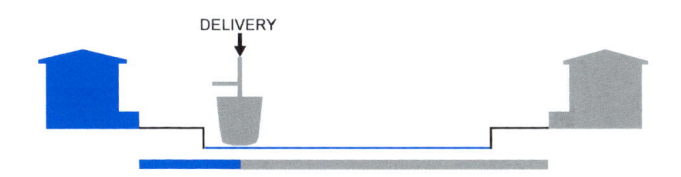

GUIDANCE NOTE

This rule is to be used only for sea or inland waterway transport.

"Cost and Freight" means that the seller delivers the goods on board the vessel or procures the goods already so delivered. The risk of loss of or damage to the goods passes when the goods are on board the vessel. The seller must contract for and pay the costs and freight necessary to bring the goods to the named port of destination.

When CPT, CIP, CFR or CIF are used, the seller fulfils its obligation to deliver when it hands the goods over to the carrier in the manner specified in the chosen rule and not when the goods reach the place of destination.

This rule has two critical points, because risk passes and costs are transferred at different places. While the contract will always specify a destination port, it might not specify the port of shipment, which is where risk passes to the buyer. If the shipment port is of particular interest to the buyer, the parties are well advised to identify it as precisely as possible in the contract.

The parties are well advised to identify as precisely as possible the point at the agreed port of destination, as the costs to that point are for the account of the seller. The seller is advised to procure contracts of carriage that match this choice precisely. If the seller incurs costs under its contract of carriage related to unloading at the specified point at the port of destination, the seller is not entitled to recover such costs from the buyer unless otherwise agreed between the parties.

The seller is required either to deliver the goods on board the vessel or to procure goods already so delivered for shipment to the destination. In addition, the seller is required either to make a contract of carriage or to procure such a contract. The reference to "procure" here caters for multiple sales down a chain ('string sales'), particularly common in the commodity trades.

CFR may not be appropriate where goods are handed over to the carrier before they are on board the vessel, for example goods in containers, which are typically delivered at a terminal. In such circumstances, the CPT rule should be used.

CFR requires the seller to clear the goods for export, where applicable. However, the seller has no obligation to clear the goods for import, pay any import duty or carry out any import customs formalities.

A THE SELLER'S OBLIGATIONS

A1 General obligations of the seller

The seller must provide the goods and the commercial invoice in conformity with the contract of sale and any other evidence of conformity that may be required by the contract.

Any document referred to in A1-A10 may be an equivalent electronic record or procedure if agreed between the parties or customary.

A2 Licences, authorizations, security clearances and other formalities

Where applicable, the seller must obtain, at its own risk and expense, any export licence or other official authorization and carry out all customs formalities necessary for the export of the goods.

A3 Contracts of carriage and insurance

a) Contract of carriage
The seller must contract or procure a contract for the carriage of the goods from the agreed point of delivery, if any, at the place of delivery to the named port of destination or, if agreed, any point at that port. The contract of carriage must be made on usual terms at the seller's expense and provide for carriage by the usual route in a vessel of the type normally used for the transport of the type of goods sold.

b) Contract of insurance
The seller has no obligation to the buyer to make a contract of insurance. However, the seller must provide the buyer, at the buyer's request, risk, and expense (if any), with information that the buyer needs for obtaining insurance.

A4 Delivery

The seller must deliver the goods either by placing them on board the vessel or by procuring the goods so delivered. In either case, the seller must deliver the goods on the agreed date or within the agreed period and in the manner customary at the port.

Incoterms® 2010

B THE BUYER'S OBLIGATIONS

B1 General obligations of the buyer
The buyer must pay the price of the goods as provided in the contract of sale.

Any document referred to in B1-B10 may be an equivalent electronic record or procedure if agreed between the parties or customary.

B2 Licences, authorizations, security clearances and other formalities
Where applicable, it is up to the buyer to obtain, at its own risk and expense, any import licence or other official authorization and carry out all customs formalities for the import of the goods and for their transport through any country.

B3 Contracts of carriage and insurance
a) Contract of carriage
The buyer has no obligation to the seller to make a contract of carriage.

b) Contract of insurance
The buyer has no obligation to the seller to make a contract of insurance. However, the buyer must provide the seller, upon request, with the necessary information for obtaining insurance.

B4 Taking delivery
The buyer must take delivery of the goods when they have been delivered as envisaged in A4 and receive them from the carrier at the named port of destination.

A5 **Transfer of risks**

The seller bears all risks of loss of or damage to the goods until they have been delivered in accordance with A4, with the exception of loss or damage in the circumstances described in B5.

A6 **Allocation of costs**

The seller must pay
a) all costs relating to the goods until they have been delivered in accordance with A4, other than those payable by the buyer as envisaged in B6;

b) the freight and all other costs resulting from A3 a), including the costs of loading the goods on board and any charges for unloading at the agreed port of discharge that were for the seller's account under the contract of carriage; and

c) where applicable, the costs of customs formalities necessary for export as well as all duties, taxes and other charges payable upon export, and the costs for their transport through any country that were for the seller's account under the contract of carriage.

A7 **Notices to the buyer**

The seller must give the buyer any notice needed in order to allow the buyer to take measures that are normally necessary to enable the buyer to take the goods.

B5 Transfer of risks

The buyer bears all risks of loss of or damage to the goods from the time they have been delivered as envisaged in A4.

If the buyer fails to give notice in accordance with B7, then it bears all risks of loss of or damage to the goods from the agreed date or the expiry date of the agreed period for shipment, provided that the goods have been clearly identified as the contract goods.

B6 Allocation of costs

The buyer must, subject to the provisions of A3 a), pay
a) all costs relating to the goods from the time they have been delivered as envisaged in A4, except, where applicable, the costs of customs formalities necessary for export as well as all duties, taxes, and other charges payable upon export as referred to in A6 c);

b) all costs and charges relating to the goods while in transit until their arrival at the port of destination, unless such costs and charges were for the seller's account under the contract of carriage;

c) unloading costs including lighterage and wharfage charges, unless such costs and charges were for the seller's account under the contract of carriage;

d) any additional costs incurred if it fails to give notice in accordance with B7, from the agreed date or the expiry date of the agreed period for shipment, provided that the goods have been clearly identified as the contract goods; and

e) where applicable, all duties, taxes and other charges, as well as the costs of carrying out customs formalities payable upon import of the goods and the costs for their transport through any country unless included within the cost of the contract of carriage.

B7 Notices to the seller

The buyer must, whenever it is entitled to determine the time for shipping the goods and/or the point of receiving the goods within the named port of destination, give the seller sufficient notice thereof.

A8 Delivery document

The seller must, at its own expense, provide the buyer without delay with the usual transport document for the agreed port of destination.

This transport document must cover the contract goods, be dated within the period agreed for shipment, enable the buyer to claim the goods from the carrier at the port of destination and, unless otherwise agreed, enable the buyer to sell the goods in transit by the transfer of the document to a subsequent buyer or by notification to the carrier.

When such a transport document is issued in negotiable form and in several originals, a full set of originals must be presented to the buyer.

A9 Checking – packaging – marking

The seller must pay the costs of those checking operations (such as checking quality, measuring, weighing, counting) that are necessary for the purpose of delivering the goods in accordance with A4, as well as the costs of any pre-shipment inspection mandated by the authority of the country of export.

The seller must, at its own expense, package the goods, unless it is usual for the particular trade to transport the type of goods sold unpackaged. The seller may package the goods in the manner appropriate for their transport, unless the buyer has notified the seller of specific packaging requirements before the contract of sale is concluded. Packaging is to be marked appropriately.

A10 Assistance with information and related costs

The seller must, where applicable, in a timely manner, provide to or render assistance in obtaining for the buyer, at the buyer's request, risk and expense, any documents and information, including security-related information, that the buyer needs for the import of the goods and/or for their transport to the final destination.

The seller must reimburse the buyer for all costs and charges incurred by the buyer in providing or rendering assistance in obtaining documents and information as envisaged in B10.

B8 Proof of delivery

The buyer must accept the transport document provided as envisaged in A8 if it is in conformity with the contract.

B9 Inspection of goods

The buyer must pay the costs of any mandatory pre-shipment inspection, except when such inspection is mandated by the authorities of the country of export.

B10 Assistance with information and related costs

The buyer must, in a timely manner, advise the seller of any security information requirements so that the seller may comply with A10.

The buyer must reimburse the seller for all costs and charges incurred by the seller in providing or rendering assistance in obtaining documents and information as envisaged in A10.

The buyer must, where applicable, in a timely manner, provide to or render assistance in obtaining for the seller, at the seller's request, risk and expense, any documents and information, including security-related information, that the seller needs for the transport and export of the goods and for their transport through any country.

CIF
COST INSURANCE AND FREIGHT
CIF (insert named port of destination) Incoterms® 2010

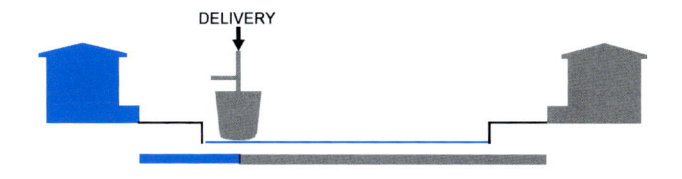

GUIDANCE NOTE

This rule is to be used only for sea or inland waterway transport.

"Cost, Insurance and Freight" means that the seller delivers the goods on board the vessel or procures the goods already so delivered. The risk of loss of or damage to the goods passes when the goods are on board the vessel. The seller must contract for and pay the costs and freight necessary to bring the goods to the named port of destination.

The seller also contracts for insurance cover against the buyer's risk of loss of or damage to the goods during the carriage. The buyer should note that under CIF the seller is required to obtain insurance only on minimum cover. Should the buyer wish to have more insurance protection, it will need either to agree as much expressly with the seller or to make its own extra insurance arrangements.

When CPT, CIP, CFR, or CIF are used, the seller fulfils its obligation to deliver when it hands the goods over to the carrier in the manner specified in the chosen rule and not when the goods reach the place of destination.

This rule has two critical points, because risk passes and costs are transferred at different places. While the contract will always specify a destination port, it might not specify the port of shipment, which is where risk passes to the buyer. If the shipment port is of particular interest to the buyer, the parties are well advised to identify it as precisely as possible in the contract.

The parties are well advised to identify as precisely as possible the point at the agreed port of destination, as the costs to that point are for the account of the seller. The seller is advised to procure contracts of carriage that match this choice precisely. If the seller incurs costs under its contract of carriage related to unloading at the specified point at the port of destination, the seller is not entitled to recover such costs from the buyer unless otherwise agreed between the parties.

The seller is required either to deliver the goods on board the vessel or to procure goods already so delivered for shipment to the destination. In addition the seller is required either to make a contract of carriage or to procure such a contract. The reference to "procure" here caters for multiple sales down a chain ('string sales'), particularly common in the commodity trades.

CIF may not be appropriate where goods are handed over to the carrier before they are on board the vessel, for example goods in containers, which are typically delivered at a terminal. In such circumstances, the CIP rule should be used.

CIF requires the seller to clear the goods for export, where applicable. However, the seller has no obligation to clear the goods for import, pay any import duty or carry out any import customs formalities.

A THE SELLER'S OBLIGATIONS

A1 General obligations of the seller

The seller must provide the goods and the commercial invoice in conformity with the contract of sale and any other evidence of conformity that may be required by the contract.

Any document referred to in A1-A10 may be an equivalent electronic record or procedure if agreed between the parties or customary.

A2 Licences, authorizations, security clearances and other formalities

Where applicable, the seller must obtain, at its own risk and expense, any export licence or other official authorization and carry out all customs formalities necessary for the export of the goods.

B THE BUYER'S OBLIGATIONS

B1 General obligations of the buyer

The buyer must pay the price of the goods as provided in the contract of sale.

Any document referred to in B1-B10 may be an equivalent electronic record or procedure if agreed between the parties or customary.

B2 Licences, authorizations, security clearances and formalities

Where applicable, it is up to the buyer to obtain, at its own risk and expense, any import licence or other official authorization and carry out all customs formalities for the import of the goods and for their transport through any country.

A3 **Contracts of carriage and insurance**

a) Contract of carriage
The seller must contract or procure a contract for the carriage of the goods from the agreed point of delivery, if any, at the place of delivery to the named port of destination or, if agreed, any point at that port. The contract of carriage must be made on usual terms at the seller's expense and provide for carriage by the usual route in a vessel of the type normally used for the transport of the type of goods sold.

b) Contract of insurance
The seller must obtain, at its own expense, cargo insurance complying at least with the minimum cover provided by Clauses (C) of the Institute Cargo Clauses (LMA/IUA) or any similar clauses. The insurance shall be contracted with underwriters or an insurance company of good repute and entitle the buyer, or any other person having an insurable interest in the goods, to claim directly from the insurer.

When required by the buyer, the seller shall, subject to the buyer providing any necessary information requested by the seller, provide at the buyer's expense any additional cover, if procurable, such as cover as provided by Clauses (A) or (B) of the Institute Cargo Clauses (LMA/IUA) or any similar clauses and/or cover complying with the Institute War Clauses and/or Institute Strikes Clauses (LMA/IUA) or any similar clauses.

The insurance shall cover, at a minimum, the price provided in the contract plus 10% (i.e., 110%) and shall be in the currency of the contract.

The insurance shall cover the goods from the point of delivery set out in A4 and A5 to at least the named port of destination.

The seller must provide the buyer with the insurance policy or other evidence of insurance cover.

Moreover, the seller must provide the buyer, at the buyer's request, risk, and expense (if any), with information that the buyer needs to procure any additional insurance.

A4 **Delivery**
The seller must deliver the goods either by placing them on board the vessel or by procuring the goods so delivered. In either case, the seller must deliver the goods on the agreed date or within the agreed period and in the manner customary at the port.

B3 Contracts of carriage and insurance

a) Contract of carriage
The buyer has no obligation to the seller to make a contract of carriage.

b) Contract of insurance
The buyer has no obligation to the seller to make a contract of insurance. However, the buyer must provide the seller, upon request, with any information necessary for the seller to procure any additional insurance requested by the buyer as envisaged in A3 b).

B4 Taking delivery

The buyer must take delivery of the goods when they have been delivered as envisaged in A4 and receive them from the carrier at the named port of destination.

A5 **Transfer of risks**

The seller bears all risks of loss of or damage to the goods until they have been delivered in accordance with A4, with the exception of loss or damage in the circumstances described in B5.

A6 **Allocation of costs**

The seller must pay
a) all costs relating to the goods until they have been delivered in accordance with A4, other than those payable by the buyer as envisaged in B6;

b) the freight and all other costs resulting from A3 a), including the costs of loading the goods on board and any charges for unloading at the agreed port of discharge that were for the seller's account under the contract of carriage;

c) the costs of insurance resulting from A3 b); and

d) where applicable, the costs of customs formalities necessary for export, as well as all duties, taxes and other charges payable upon export, and the costs for their transport through any country that were for the seller's account under the contract of carriage.

B5 Transfer of risks

The buyer bears all risks of loss of or damage to the goods from the time they have been delivered as envisaged in A4.

If the buyer fails to give notice in accordance with B7, then it bears all risks of loss of or damage to the goods from the agreed date or the expiry date of the agreed period for shipment, provided that the goods have been clearly identified as the contract goods.

B6 Allocation of costs

The buyer must, subject to the provisions of A3 a), pay
a) all costs relating to the goods from the time they have been delivered as envisaged in A4, except, where applicable, the costs of customs formalities necessary for export, as well as all duties, taxes and other charges payable upon export as referred to in A6 d);

b) all costs and charges relating to the goods while in transit until their arrival at the port of destination, unless such costs and charges were for the seller's account under the contract of carriage;

c) unloading costs including lighterage and wharfage charges, unless such costs and charges were for the seller's account under the contract of carriage;

d) any additional costs incurred if it fails to give notice in accordance with B7, from the agreed date or the expiry date of the agreed period for shipment, provided that the goods have been clearly identified as the contract goods;

e) where applicable, all duties, taxes and other charges, as well as the costs of carrying out customs formalities payable upon import of the goods and the costs for their transport through any country, unless included within the cost of the contract of carriage; and

f) the costs of any additional insurance procured at the buyer's request under A3 b) and B3 b).

A7   **Notices to the buyer**
The seller must give the buyer any notice needed in order to allow the buyer to take measures that are normally necessary to enable the buyer to take the goods.

A8   **Delivery document**
The seller must, at its own expense provide the buyer without delay with the usual transport document for the agreed port of destination.

This transport document must cover the contract goods, be dated within the period agreed for shipment, enable the buyer to claim the goods from the carrier at the port of destination and, unless otherwise agreed, enable the buyer to sell the goods in transit by the transfer of the document to a subsequent buyer or by notification to the carrier.

When such a transport document is issued in negotiable form and in several originals, a full set of originals must be presented to the buyer.

A9   **Checking – packaging – marking**
The seller must pay the costs of those checking operations (such as checking quality, measuring, weighing, counting) that are necessary for the purpose of delivering the goods in accordance with A4, as well as the costs of any pre-shipment inspection mandated by the authority of the country of export.

The seller must, at its own expense, package the goods, unless it is usual for the particular trade to transport the type of goods sold unpackaged. The seller may package the goods in the manner appropriate for their transport, unless the buyer has notified the seller of specific packaging requirements before the contract of sale is concluded. Packaging is to be marked appropriately.

B7 Notices to the seller
The buyer must, whenever it is entitled to determine the time for shipping the goods and/or the point of receiving the goods within the named port of destination, give the seller sufficient notice thereof.

B8 Proof of delivery
The buyer must accept the transport document provided as envisaged in A8 if it is in conformity with the contract.

B9 Inspection of goods
The buyer must pay the costs of any mandatory pre-shipment inspection, except when such inspection is mandated by the authorities of the country of export.

A10 **Assistance with information and related costs**

The seller must, where applicable, in a timely manner, provide to or render assistance in obtaining for the buyer, at the buyer's request, risk and expense, any documents and information, including security-related information, that the buyer needs for the import of the goods and/or for their transport to the final destination.

The seller must reimburse the buyer for all costs and charges incurred by the buyer in providing or rendering assistance in obtaining documents and information as envisaged in B10.

B10 **Assistance with information and related costs**

The buyer must, in a timely manner, advise the seller of any security information requirements so that the seller may comply with A10.

The buyer must reimburse the seller for all costs and charges incurred by the seller in providing or rendering assistance in obtaining documents and information as envisaged in A10.

The buyer must, where applicable, in a timely manner, provide to or render assistance in obtaining for the seller, at the seller's request, risk and expense, any documents and information, including security-related information, that the seller needs for the transport and export of the goods and for their transport through any country.

INCOTERMS® 2010 DRAFTING GROUP

The Incoterms® 2010 rules were drafted by a select international group of ICC member experts, in consultation with the broader global ICC membership through the network of ICC national committees. The wide geographical and sectoral scope of the consultative process ensures that the Incoterms® 2010 rules reflect the current realities of international trade and respond to business needs everywhere.

CO-CHAIRS

CHARLES DEBATTISTA

Charles Debattista is an active arbitrator in international trade disputes and takes appointments under ICC and other institutional rules. He is also a Registered European Lawyer with the Bar of England and Wales and accepts instructions as counsel before international arbitral tribunals.

Mr Debattista is also a professor of Commercial Law at the University of Southampton in the UK. He has written many books and articles on international sale contracts, the carriage of goods by sea and letters of credit. He is a member of ICC's Commercial Law and Practice Commission, of the Banking Commission and of the Transport Commission. He was Chair of the Incoterms 2000 Drafting Group and Co-Chair of the Incoterms® 2010 Drafting Group.

CHRISTOPH MARTIN RADTKE

Christoph Martin Radtke is a partner of the French law firm Lamy & Associés. He leads the firm's international team and specializes in international trade law, agency and distribution, EC law, French and German business law, international arbitration, and international litigation. Admitted at the French and the German Bar, Mr Radtke has published articles on international contract law and arbitration and has taught at the Paris-based Institut de Droit Comparé.

In addition to his role on the Incoterms® 2010 Drafting Group, Mr Radtke is Chair of the Commercial Law and Practice Commission of ICC France, and Vice-Chair of the French-German Lawyers' Association.

He lectures widely on the Incoterms rules and has contributed to ICC model contracts including the ICC Model Distributorship Contract and the Commercial Agency Contract, as well as to the ICC Legal Handbook on Global Sourcing Contracts.

DRAFTING GROUP MEMBERS

JENS BREDOW

Jens Bredow is the Secretary General of the German Institution of Arbitration in Cologne and an attorney in private practice, specializing in international trade law and arbitration. In addition, he serves as an adviser to the German Ministry of Justice as a participant in UNCITRAL's Working Party on Arbitration and Conciliation, and is also a lecturer at Bonn University. He is also an experienced arbitrator, serving frequently as chair or sole arbitrator in a range of international proceedings.

Mr Bredow, the former Director of ICC Germany, was also a member of the Drafting Groups that revised the Incoterms® rules in 1990 and 2000. He currently sits on the Incoterms rules Panel of Experts.

JOHNNY HERRE

Johnny Herre is a Supreme Court Justice at the Supreme Court of Sweden. Prior to joining the court, he spent many years as a Professor at the Stockholm School of Economics, where he served a term as Head of the Department of Law and from which he earned a Master of Science in Economics and Business and a PhD in Law, with a focus on damages in sale of goods law.

In addition to publishing widely on issues related to the sale of goods, contracts, the law of obligations and consumer law, Professor Herre has extensive experience in arbitration, including as arbitrator and chair of tribunals in international arbitral proceedings. A member of the Study Group on a European Civil Code for many years, he is currently Chair of ICC Sweden's group on Commercial Law and Practice.

DAVID LOWE

A partner at the London office of international law firm Wragge & Co LLP, David Lowe leads the firm's commercial contracts team. His expertise is in advising supply chain clients on the international supply of goods. In this capacity, he has advised:

- international retailers on sourcing products in the Far East;
- manufacturers of industrial products on international distribution networks;
- European distributors on import arrangements with international manufacturers;
- international commodity traders ranging from bulk cement to coal;
- European manufacturers and retailers on entering new international markets; and
- international suppliers entering the European market.

Mr Lowe's experience of advising buyers and sellers of manufactured goods (which are typically transported in containers) has shaped his contribution to Incoterms® 2010. Mr Lowe also chairs the ICC UK Commercial Law and Practice Committee.

LAURI RAILAS

Lauri Railas, LL.M. (Helsinki and London), LL.D. (Helsinki), is an attorney-at-law at Krogerus Attorneys in Finland. He is a member of the Finnish Bar.

Dr Railas is the former Secretary General of ICC Finland and the former Secretary of the Arbitration Institute of the Central Chamber of Commerce of Finland. His experience and practice include international trade and transport law, marine insurance and electronic commerce. Dr Railas has been involved in trade facilitation work under the auspices of the United Nations and has written books and articles on international trade law. In addition to Incoterms® 2010, Dr Railas has contributed to various ICC model contracts, including the ICC Model International Sale Contract. He is also the Co-Chair of the ICC Task Force on Public Procurement.

FRANK REYNOLDS

Frank Reynolds is the President of International Projects Inc., a US-based international trading and consulting firm. Besides representing the US for the Incoterms® 2000 and Incoterms® 2010 revisions, he has written or co-authored 16 books on various international trade topics including ICC's *A to Z of International Trade* dictionary. He also has written over 300 columns for such international publications as the *Journal of Commerce*, *The Exporter* and ICC's *Documentary Credit Insight*.

Mr Reynolds has lectured throughout the US on such trade-related topics as the Incoterms® rules, documentary credits, US free-trade agreements, export and import procedures and the Harmonized System for over 25 years. He served on the US Commerce Department's District Export Council for 22 years, and his international projects received an *E Award for Export Excellence*. He also holds a customs broker licence from the US Department of Homeland Security, Customs and Border Protection.

MIROSLAV SUBERT

Miroslav Subert holds a *juris doctor* degree from Charles University in Prague. A long-time expert on the Incoterms® rules, he worked for many years at senior management level in companies dealing with foreign trade, shipping and forwarding in the United Kingdom, Croatia, Belgium and the Czech Republic.

Dr Subert currently serves as a lecturer at a number of institutions in Prague, including the University of Economics, the Institute for Foreign Trade, Transport and Forwarding and the Perner Institute. He is the Vice-Chair of the Czech Society for Transport Law and a professional and legal adviser on foreign trade, transport and insurance to ICC Czech Republic. He has written widely on international trade issues, including books on international transport, sales and documentary credits, and is a regular contributor to professional publications and newspapers. Dr Subert wrote a guide to Incoterms rules in 2000 and has spearheaded the translation of recent versions of the Incoterms rules into Czech.

ICC SECRETARIAT

EMILY O'CONNOR

Emily O'Connor is the Senior Policy Manager of the ICC Commission on Commercial Law and Practice and oversaw the development of *Incoterms® 2010*. She joined the ICC International Secretariat in Paris in 2006, after several years at the US Council for International Business in New York, where she managed intellectual property and competition law issues.

Ms O'Connor graduated from Columbia Law School in New York, first practising in the US State Department's Office of the Legal Adviser, focusing on International Court of Justice cases on the US application of the death penalty to foreign nationals. She then practised international corporate law at Debevoise & Plimpton, working on future flow equity issuances, mergers and acquisitions and a range of media deals, before moving to the international policy arena.

SHANE DALY

Shane Daly is a graduate of the National University of Ireland, Galway and University College London, specializing in International Commercial Law with Dispute Resolution and International Public Law. He also holds a diploma from the Université de Poitiers. In addition to his work as an assistant to the Incoterms® 2010 Drafting Group, Mr Daly has contributed to other projects of the ICC Commission on Commercial Law and Practice, including model contracts on mergers and acquisitions and on subcontracting. He is to commence as a trainee solicitor in Dublin in 2011.

ICC Dispute Resolution

Incorporating one or more of the Incoterms® rules into a contract does not in itself constitute an agreement to use ICC dispute resolution services. Contracting parties that wish to resort to one or more or these services in the event of a dispute should reach a specific and clear agreement to that effect. For this purpose, ICC offers suggested and standard clauses that parties may incorporate into their contracts. Failing this, parties should agree on the use of ICC rules in an exchange of correspondence.

ICC offers an array of services to help parties overcome disputes arising from international trade. These services respond to different needs and different situations. Each is governed by a set of rules defining a neutral procedure capable of accommodating cultural, linguistic and legal diversity, as well as the specificities of given sectors and activities.

Arbitration, administered by the ICC International Court of Arbitration, generally leads to a binding decision issued by a tribunal of one or three arbitrators. The decision is widely enforceable because of the legal recognition arbitration enjoys in almost all the world's trading nations.

Amicable dispute resolution embraces various methods of dispute resolution that seek a settlement by consensual means. The neutral third party and the parties to the dispute decide on the settlement technique to be used, which may be mediation, neutral evaluation, a mini-trial or a combination of different techniques.

Dispute boards are ongoing bodies set up for the duration of a contract to resolve disputes as and when they arise during the life of the contract. Different types of dispute boards are available, depending on the powers the parties wish to grant to the members of the board and the force of their determinations.

Expertise consists of engaging a specialist to give an opinion on a matter requiring specialist knowledge and skills, such as technical, financial or legal know-how. The services offered range from the search for a suitable expert to the complete administration of the expert's mission. A specific service called DOCDEX is offered for disputes relating to documentary credits, bank-to-bank reimbursements, collections and guarantees.

For further information, including all rules and clauses, visit our dispute resolution pages at **www.iccwbo.org**

Synopsis of trademark usage rules for *Incoterms® 2010*

"Incoterms" is a registered trademark of the International Chamber of Commerce.

Although ICC encourages and promotes the use of the Incoterms® rules by third parties in sales contracts in compliance with ICC's copyright policy, "Incoterms" is not a generic term that may be used to designate any trade terms, but is a trademark used to designate only the terms devised by ICC and products and services from ICC.

Below are some rules on the correct usage of the "Incoterms" trademark:

- Use the trademark "Incoterms" to refer only to ICC's Incoterms® rules and other Incoterms® products and services from ICC.

- In text, use "Incoterms" as an adjective, not a noun.

- Do not use "Incoterms" without the initial letter as a capital letter.

- Do not use "Incoterm" (without the final "s"). An individual term from the Incoterms® rules should be referred to as an Incoterms® rule, and never as an "Incoterm".

- Use the registered trademark symbol ® next to the trademark "Incoterms".

- Any use of the trademark "Incoterms" in association with products and services not from ICC requires a licence from ICC.

More information on the correct usage of ICC's "Incoterms" trademark can be found on ICC's website on the Incoterms® rules at **www.incoterms.org**

ICC AT A GLANCE

ICC is the world business organization, a representative body that speaks with authority on behalf of enterprises from all sectors in every part of the world.

The fundamental mission of ICC is to promote open international trade and investment and help business meet the challenges and opportunities of globalization. Its conviction that trade is a powerful force for peace and prosperity dates from the organization's origins early in the 20th century. The small group of far-sighted business leaders who founded ICC called themselves "the merchants of peace".

ICC has three main activities: rule setting, dispute resolution, and policy advocacy. Because its member companies and associations are themselves engaged in international business, ICC has unrivalled authority in making rules that govern the conduct of business across borders. Although these rules are voluntary, they are observed in countless thousands of transactions every day and have become part of the fabric of international trade.

ICC also provides essential services, foremost among them the ICC International Court of Arbitration, the world's leading arbitral institution. Another service is the World Chambers Federation, ICC's worldwide network of chambers of commerce, fostering interaction and exchange of chamber best practice. ICC also offers specialized training and seminars and is an industry-leading publisher of practical and educational reference tools for international business, banking and arbitration.

Business leaders and experts drawn from the ICC membership establish the business stance on broad issues of trade and investment policy as well as on relevant technical subjects. These include anti-corruption, banking, the digital economy, marketing ethics, environment and energy, competition policy and intellectual property, among others.

ICC works closely with the United Nations, the World Trade Organization and intergovernmental forums including the G20.

ICC was founded in 1919. Today its global network comprises over 6 million companies, chambers of commerce and business associations in more than 130 countries. National committees work with ICC members in their countries to address their concerns and convey to their governments the business views formulated by ICC.

International Chamber of Commerce
The world business organization

SELECTED ICC PUBLICATIONS

ICC Model International Sale Contract
ICC Pub. No. 738E, €75

This updated version of ICC's most successful Model Contract takes into account recent developments in international business and trade finance and incorporates the latest trade rules, ICC's Incoterms® 2010, as well as the new Bank Payment Obligation (BPO) rules developed jointly by the ICC Banking Commission and SWIFT. PLUS: The CD-Rom containing the text of the contract is now even easier to use with check and choose boxes, and alerts when important fields were not filled in.

ICC Guide to Export/Import
Global Standards for International Trade
by Prof. Guillermo C. Jimenez
ICC Pub. No. 686E, €65 (2012 Edition)

The 4th edition of this much acclaimed Guide is written by renowned international trade expert Guillermo C. Jimenez and will help exporters, importers, logistics experts, lawyers and students to more effectively do their jobs. This essential resource covers everything you need to know about international business: from IP issues and dispute resolution to electronic documentation,

ICC Guide to Incoterms® 2010
by Prof. Jan Ramberg
ICC Pub. No. 720E, €65

ICC's official guide to the world's standard trade terms! This invaluable companion to the rules book will help you use the Incoterms® 2010 rules in the most efficient way.

**Order now at www.iccbooks.com –
ICC Publications, your key to international business**